SYNCHROSERVICE!

SYNCHROSERVICE!
The Innovative Way to Build a Dynasty of Customers

Richard J. Schonberger

Edward M. Knod, Jr.

IRWIN
Professional Publishing
Burr Ridge, Illinois
New York, New York

IRWIN
Concerned About Our Environment

In recognition of the fact that our company is a large end-user of fragile yet replenishable resources, we at IRWIN can assure you that every effort is made to meet or exceed Environmental Protection Agency (EPA) recommendations and requirements for a "greener" workplace.

To preserve these natural assets, a number of environmental policies, both companywide and department-specific, have been implemented. From the use of 50% recycled paper in our textbooks to the printing of promotional materials with recycled stock and soy inks to our office paper recycling program, we are committed to reducing waste and replacing environmentally unsafe products with safer alternatives.

Sponsoring editor:	Carol Rogala
Project editor:	Stephanie M. Britt
Production manager:	Irene H. Sotiroff
Interior designer:	Larry J. Cope
Art coordinator:	Mark Malloy
Compositor:	Carlisle Communications, Ltd.
Typeface:	11/13 Times Roman
Printer:	Book Press, Inc.

Library of Congress Cataloging-in-Publication Data

Schonberger, Richard.
    Synchroservice! : the innovative way to build a dynasty of customers / Richard J. Schonberger and Edward M. Knod, Jr.
      p.   cm.
    Includes index.
    ISBN 0-7863-0245-3
    1. Customer service. 2. Total quality management.
HF5415.5.S35 1994
650'.0285'5369—dc20   94–2259

Printed in the United States of America
1 2 3 4 5 6 7 8 9 0   BP   1 0 9 8 7 6 5 4

Preface

Your consciousness has been raised: Now you believe in total quality service and quick response.

But the question is, how do you do it? What does it mean for each of the functions of the service enterprise? How will old practices be modified? And how is my own role in the service organization affected?

Synchroservice! is a how-to-do-it book. It deals with gaining allegiance and retention of customers, which requires smoothly synchronized actions involving every service associate. We earn our pay, and much of our job satisfaction as well, from serving internal and final customers well—which means with high and ever-improving quality. Synchroservice aims squarely at this customer-serving objective.

Doing it includes engaging, blending, and continually upgrading operating resources: data, equipment, tools, space, for-sale items, supplies, and, especially, people. Synchroservice harnesses the talents of frontline employees, technicians, experts, supervisors, and upper-level managers. Their skills—as salespeople, designers, accountants, trainers, and so on—are important but not enough. Individuals too easily get fixated on their own narrow role. Their view of the service itself and of the customers receiving it can get blurry.

Therefore, this how-to treatment emphasizes ways in which people operate in teams that cross functional and company boundaries. It relies heavily on process data, data analysis, and local ownership of results.

These themes—customer-focused, team-driven, data-based continuous improvement—are centerpieces of the worldwide total quality management (TQM) movement. While some companies are well along the TQM path, others aren't. Therefore, we present and compare both conventional approaches and TQM-enhanced concepts.

Part of continuous improvement is not letting things go wrong. Prevention greatly simplifies planning and service delivery. It avoids unexpected service delays and slowdowns, which cuts out corrections that ripple back through the processes disruptively. The simplification theme, found throughout the book, cuts both ways: Simplify to reduce mistakes. Reduce mistakes to make work life simpler.

This does not mean that synchroservice is itself simple and easy to master. Service management, even in small firms, is complex because it involves coordination of diverse resources, processes, suppliers, and customer demands. Company policies and procedures may help, but common principles are what is vitally needed.

We believe that the dramatic changes now occurring in service management are based primarily on just that: management by principles. Furthermore, those principles must, for superior performance, be customer-focused. In the introductory chapter we present a 16-point set of principles of synchroservice. Often throughout the remaining chapters, we note the principle that applies to the point under discussion.

Some busy readers read selectively. If you are one of those who seeks out certain topics or chapters, our advice is to spend most of your time on Chapter 1 (the principles), Chapters 2 and 4 (basics and details of service quality management), Chapter 7 (serving with *speed*), Chapter 12 (performance management issues), and Chapter 14 (a message for you, personally). These chapters are important for everybody. Other parts of the book are more specialized. For example, if you are in retailing, wholesaling, or especially concerned about business supplies and materials, you'll want to spend time on Chapter 8 (purchasing) and Chapter 9 (waste-free management of materials). All other chapters will have some relevance to everyone, and special relevance to some.

If you are a service employee, whether on the front lines or in an off-line support role, *Synchroservice!* should give you a wealth of ideas on how to improve your own service activities. More than that, you will learn how to influence your service colleagues to adopt change and improvement as a superior, more rewarding work life.

To our many associates who have already begun their implementation of the principles of synchroservice and have shared their stories and data, we thank you for helping us continue to grow. We are also indebted to Richard S. Johnson, Johnson Quality Consulting, and Steve Clyburn, Coopers and Lybrand, who reviewed this manuscript and whose astute advice was mostly incorporated. Finally, we are grateful to Irwin Professional Publishing's acquisition editors Jean Geracie and Carol Rogala for their support, and to project editor Stephanie Britt, who tended the helm superbly, we extend another sincere and well-deserved thank you.

Richard J. Schonberger
Edward M. Knod, Jr.

Contents in Brief

Contents

I

INTRODUCTION TO SYNCHROSERVICE

CHAPTER 1 CUSTOMERS, COMPETITIVE STRATEGIES,
AND PRINCIPLES

In most organizations, failure-prone frontline services are backed up by a jumble of failure-prone support services. Quick-fix service recovery on the front lines ripples unevenly throughout the organization.

Synchroservice aims at permanent recovery. It requires grounding all service elements in the same customer-centered concepts so they will interlock synchronously. The introductory chapter provides an overview and sets forth the book's theme: teaming up for continually improving service to next and final customers. This is the strategic, overriding goal of synchroservice. Chapter 1 provides a set of principles to guide service associates in this journey.

Chapter One

Customers, Competitive Strategies, and Principles

Service Operations and Their Management
Teaming Up with Customers
  Disconnections Spell Trouble
  Connecting with the Customer
  A Short List of Basic Customer Wants
Service Strategy
  Integrated Business Strategy
  Distinctive Competency
  Continuous Improvement
Principles of Synchroservice—As Strategy
Service Managers

The moment of truth (eye-to-eye with the customer) is just one element of service excellence. Backing it up are chains of support operations. Usually, however, they don't act like chains—just loose links. *Synchroservice* is seamless connectivity. It extends from the glimmer of an idea for a new or revised service through all support steps to final service delivery—plus follow-through.

Synchroservice is not static. It interweaves (again seamlessly) with customer-centered, employee-driven continuous improvement, nourished by fresh ideas and methods. Synchronized, continuous, rapid improvement builds a service dynasty. A less-ambitious strategy brings on customer defection, employee insecurity, and new competition. Standards of service quality are not standing still but are continually rising. Service performance must rise to match.

This chapter offers a broad view of service operations and what it takes to closely connect them.

SERVICE OPERATIONS AND THEIR MANAGEMENT

A service consists of resource inputs transformed into service outputs. Frontline service transformations take place with final customers present—in hospital admitting offices and surgical suites, at restaurant tables and take-out windows, on public roads and in air corridors, and at bank teller windows and satellite cash machines. These services rely on plenty of support services. Supporting transformations occur in back offices, laboratories, kitchens, back docks, warehouses, theater wings, and boiler rooms. These inputs—the knowledge and skills of people, capital, natural resources, materials, and technology—interact in complex patterns at all the transaction points. It takes good management to cope with the complexity.

Management of service operations includes the usual cycle of planning, implementing, and monitoring/controlling. Today's more effective approach, however, places special emphasis on *people* dedicated to repeating the plan-implement-monitor cycle rapidly, with the aim of fast-paced *continuous improvement.*

Fresh ideas about service operations began to emerge during the 1980s and include the following:

- The driving force for service operations must be an overriding goal of continually improving service to customers, where *customer* means the next process, as well as the final, external user.
- Broad principles have been developed to guide service associates along the path of continual improvement.
- The critical mechanism for translating the goals and principles into action is total involvement of the workforce, ideally in action teams and other partnership arrangements.
- Because service excellence requires the entire workforce to be involved in continual improvement, the term *service manager* includes everybody, not just those with *manager* in their title.
- Quality is the standard, and it applies to both service outputs and transformation processes.

We will expand on these ideas in the remainder of Chapter 1.

TEAMING UP WITH CUSTOMERS

We've all been customers, with needs and expectations about how those needs should be met. We convey our feelings in the form of requirements (or gripes when our needs are poorly met). In a bank, hardware store, or optometrist's office, face-to-face meetings and real-time discussions generally result in a more satisfying relationship. The oft-heard question "May I help you?" is a comforting reminder that the supplier–customer connection is a close one.

Maintaining a close supplier–customer connection is basic to effective frontline service delivery. However, the value of close connections applies equally to every operation leading to the final customer.

Disconnections Spell Trouble

What happens when supplier and customer are disconnected? Consider design work, for example. Not only is the final customer not around during the design stage, but designing takes place weeks or months before it's ready for the customer. In addition, design may have taken place across a continent or an ocean. Such time-and-distance separation between supplier and customer invites trouble.

Further, there seems to be a human tendency to react to these kinds of problems by pulling back from, instead of reaching out to, the customer. Even grocery store clerks, almost eyeball to eyeball with customers, are susceptible:

Question: "What's your job?"

Answer: "I run the cash register and sack groceries."

Question: "But isn't your job to serve the customer?"

Answer: "I suppose so, but my job description doesn't say that."

In grocery stores, where the supplier–customer relationship is immediate, the service management system is hard-pressed to maintain a customer focus. In government service or any kind of back-office operation, where time and distance make it much easier to stay in the background, the management challenge is enlarged. The almost certain consequences of inadequate contact with customers are obvious: lost customers, declining revenue, closed businesses, loss of jobs, and economic decline.

CONTRAST

Classifying People

Them versus Us	*We*
Common *people* terminology:	Uncommon alternative: Some firms
Managers and professionals versus workers.	call all employees associates; they banish words implying that a man-
Salaried versus wage earners.	ager class has charge of improve-
Skilled versus unskilled.	ments and a worker class carries
Exempts (from US Wage and Hour Law) versus nonexempts.	them out.

Connecting with the Customer

Against that bleak backdrop, there nevertheless is cause for cheer. For one thing, we have a potent new concept of the *customer:* The customer is the next process—where the work goes next.[1]

The next-process concept has its roots in the worldwide quality movement, and it has caught the attention not only of managers but also of frontline and indirect associates in many organizations. A buyer's customer is the associate in the department to whom the purchased item goes; and a cost accountant's customer is the manager who uses the accounting information to make a decision. Thus, the next-process concept makes it clear that every employee, not just the caseworker or salesperson, has a customer. It is also clear that throughout the organization, people not only have customers, they are customers. Let's turn our attention to what customers want.

A Short List of Basic Customer Wants

What do customers want? As consumers, our personal requirements are constantly changing, and the same is true for businesses. Although these requirements can be stated in great detail, the number of persistent general requirements appears to be small and they seem to apply universally, regardless of person or organization.

Customers have six requirements of their providers (see Exhibit 1–1):

1. High levels of quality.

EXHIBIT 1–1
General Customer Requirements

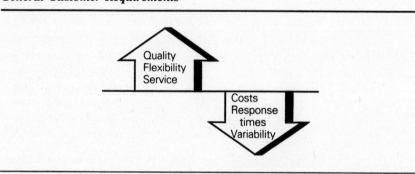

2. A high degree of flexibility (to adjust to changes in volume or type of service demanded).
3. High levels of service.
4. Low costs.
5. Short response times, including time to market for new services.
6. Little or no variability (deviation from target).

The six customer requirements dictate, to some extent, the topics and concepts presented in this book, for a well-conceived service delivery system must attempt to meet all six of these attributes.

Be careful not to view these six as potential trade-offs. Customers don't. For example, as customers, we don't want to settle for either high quality or low costs, or for increased flexibility or shorter response times; we require that all of these needs be met. Nevertheless, until recently, the trade-off viewpoint prevailed.

In general, updated thinking regarding trade-offs may be summed up as follows: (1) weak companies suffer from trade-offs that appear to be clear opposites, (2) improving companies develop immunities to some of the trade-offs that once plagued them, and (3) world-class companies have largely eliminated trade-off obstacles and are recognized for excellence in providing all six customer wants.

Equally important, customer requirements are not static. Customers want—and expect—improvement along all six dimensions.

An organizational commitment with wide-ranging effects, such as continuing improvement in meeting customer needs, is called a strategy. Next, we consider service strategies and their relationship to business strategies.

SERVICE STRATEGY

Organizational strategy entails three key elements: the organization itself, the customers, and the competitors.[2] These strategic elements apply to any organization—including churches, charities, and government agencies. Such nonbusiness entities have their own kinds of customers and competitors. They compete with one another (and sometimes with profit-making businesses as well) for funding, client allegiance, volunteers, and so forth. (*Competitor:* Another organization vying with yours for sales and customers as well as for employees, permits, funding, supplier loyalty, and so on.)

Managers should strive for balance among the three elements. Strategy itself is necessary because of competition, and successful strategy ensures that company strengths match customer requirements. In short, getting well acquainted with the customer and the competition has strategic implications for the company.

Integrated Business Strategy

Whether private or public, service organizations have four basic functions that must be managed: money, design, demand, and operations. These are known as line functions. As organizations begin to grow, line functions tend to become the first departments, such as the departments of finance, research and development, marketing, and operations, or maybe accounting, design, sales, and production.

To meet its aims, the business team must plan strategy in all four line functions. A comprehensive strategic plan deals with issues affecting the whole organization: employees, markets, location, line of services, customers, capital and financing, profitability, competition, public image, and so forth.

If formulated correctly, the four functional strategies of the overall plan are mutually reinforcing and compatible. All too often, however, that has not been the case. Planners have tended to develop careful and thorough strategies for marketing and finance but have paid scant attention to service design and operations. A firm lacking proper strategy is like an anchored ship. Finance and marketing may set the rudder and expect the ship to steam off, but with anchor set, the ship won't move, or moves reluctantly, dragging its burden.

Service design and operating strategies should be consistent with the business plan or organizational mission, but with a narrower focus:

- *Capacity* (operating resources): frontline and support people, information, equipment and tools, supplies, location (space). Capacity strategies deal with such matters as when and where to add or remove a unit of capacity, skills and flexibility of the workforce, and whether or not to contract for certain services.
- *Services, processes, methods, and systems:* Strategies might include level of investment in service and process development, standardization, and manual versus automated information processes.
- *Outputs:* Quality, cost, response time, flexibility, variation, and service.

In integrating all of these elements into a potent strategy, organizational leaders must keep in mind the importance of distinctive competency.

Distinctive Competency

After a series of biological experiments in 1934, Professor G. F. Gause, of Moscow University, postulated his principle of competitive exclusion: No two species that make their living the same way can coexist.[3] Thus, a key element of business strategy will be the firm's efforts to distinguish itself from its competitors.

Consider a town with three hospitals. The average citizen may see little difference among them. But an administrator or board member at one of the hospitals might explain, "We are the only hospital in the city with a fully certified burn center," or perhaps, "We have the only neonatal care unit in the entire region." What they are highlighting is the hospital's distinctive competency.

Distinctive competencies might be obvious to customers; fast service, very clean premises, and superior quality are examples. Less-obvious factors also qualify—things like expert maintenance, low operating costs, and effective design and development of new services. All of these might help a firm satisfy one or more of the six customer requirements in some special or unique way. This ability allows the firm, as Professor Gause put it, to make its living a little differently from its competitors to achieve success and survival.

It is usually easier to develop and maintain distinctive competencies when strategy focuses on doing a few things well, thus avoiding the ills of too much diversity. Shouldice Hospital near Toronto, which treats only hernia patients, is an example. Facility layout, medical staff, cafeteria, surgery and recovery rooms, and lounges all cater to that type of patient. By doing numerous hernia repairs each year, and no other surgeries, Shouldice doctors have become proficient. The narrow focus allows nurses to give better care to a greater number of patients, avoids the need for expensive equipment that diversified hospitals must have, and, most important, results in higher-quality care. As measured by number of patients needing repeat hernia treatment, Shouldice is 10 times more effective than other hospitals.[4]

When a company is unable to sustain any distinctive competencies, it goes under. But when a company can be distinctively competent in several ways, it wows the world. Walt Disney Co., McDonald's, and United Parcel Service, are examples. All have dependably high quality. UPS has very low operating costs. Disney offers unparalleled customer service. McDonald's and UPS have very efficient process control, which leads to service uniformity. McDonald's provides very fast response to customer orders.

The challenge for these companies is to press on, striving for superiority in meeting all six basic customer needs. Developing *more* distinctive competencies helps retain existing customers and invites new business. Thus, continuous improvement is essential even in superior firms and agencies.

It should be understood that some paths to wealth, such as buying companies and milking them dry, that were exploited in recent decades and that have been criticized on ethical grounds, are riskier today.

CONTRAST

Takeover versus Investment

We Win, You Lose	Win–Win
Strategy: Take over a weak business (with other people's money) and make it strong (and us rich) by mass shutdowns and layoffs of its weakest elements.	Strategy: For a weak business, invest not just (or mainly) money but also training and help in implementing customer-centered quality, efficiency, and continuous improvement.

Moreover, a tired, run-down state-owned hotel chain in Hungary or Lithuania needs more than Western money. It needs to learn customer- and quality-centered improvement methods. This kind of help cures basic weaknesses, thereby protecting the investor, and it helps preserve and strengthen the business and the jobs and skills of its associates. When a management action yields a good result for each party, business people call it a win–win situation.

Continuous Improvement

Much that is in this book was absent from service management lore just a few years ago. Vigorous international competition has generated a lot of the newer concepts and methods and the impetus for *continuous improvement*.

However, if continuous improvement is confined to the ranks of management and technical experts, it is a weak strategy. It must be woven into the fabric of the everyday work of all employees. Moreover, to be strategically effective, continuous improvement must encompass the requirements of customers, the attributes of competitors, and the organization's internal capacities and capabilities.

Continuous improvement got its start in operations, first in leading Japanese export companies, then in competing companies elsewhere in the world. The idea has not varied—continually and incrementally change and improve *everything:* equipment, procedures, employee skills, throughput time, quality, supplier relations, and so on. When functioning everywhere, continual improvement is a breakthrough strategy.

This approach, often called *total quality management (TQM),* is so powerful that it has become the strategic leading edge in many companies. This occurred first within Japan's manufacturing sector, where furious competition reduced the number of motorcycle makers from over 1,000 to a handful. Similar outcomes occurred in many other industries, which resulted in a few very strong companies that turned their sights to the United States, the world's largest market.

Competition has caused the pattern to repeat in other countries. Widespread transfer of knowledge has carried continuous improvement further, first to back offices of manufacturers and then to the entire service sector. The movement is by no means restricted to the economically developed countries. For example, Eicher Tractor Ltd., of India, has honed continuous improvement to a fine edge, and not only in its

factories. In personal transportation, Eicher drivers are assuming ownership of vehicle maintenance and have teamed up on a parking lot
improvement project. In the finance department, an improvement team
has cut the time to issue stock certificates (to investors) from three
months to one week.

Eicher Tractor's application of continuous improvement in the back
office is a natural extension of doing it in the plant. The same thing has
been taking place in the offices of leading manufacturers globally.
Manufacturers have several names for this strategy (e.g., lean, world-
class, or Toyota system), but the service sector tends to favor the single
term total quality management. While TQM can take on a narrow
definition, it is also used broadly, encompassing organization-wide
continuous improvement in meeting customers' requirements.

PRINCIPLES OF SYNCHROSERVICE— AS STRATEGY

It is remarkable that so many diverse organizations are adopting similar
operations management strategies. This fact suggests, not only that
attitudes have changed fundamentally, but also that certain basic principles may serve as guides for implementing service strategies.

Listed below is a 16-point set of principles of synchroservice, that is,
the principles of employee- and team-driven, customer-centered continuous improvement in service operations.

Principles of synchroservice

Service strategy—formulation:
Customers:
1. Get to know and team up with the next and final customer.
2. Become dedicated to continual, rapid improvement in
   quality, cost, response time, flexibility, variability,
   and service.
Company:
3. Achieve unified purpose via shared information and
   rewards, and team involvement in planning and implementation of change.
Competitors:
4. Get to know the competition and the world-class leaders.

Service strategy—implementation:
Design and organization:
5. Cut the number of service operations and the number of suppliers to a few good ones.
6. Organize resources into multiple "chains of customers," each focused on a service or customer family; create multi-functional service centers.

Capacity:
7. Continually invest in human resources through cross-training (for mastery of multiple skills), education, job and career-path rotation, and improved health, safety, and security.
8. Automate incrementally when process variability cannot otherwise be reduced.
9. Look for simple, flexible, movable, low cost equipment that can be acquired in multiple copies each assignable to multifunctional service centers.

Processing:
10. Make it easier to provide services without error or process variation.
11. Cut flow time (wait time) and distance all along the chain of customers.
12. Cut setup, get-ready, and startup times.
13. Operate at the customer's rate; provide services just in time.

Problem solving and control:
14. Record and *own* quality, process, and problem data at the workplace.
15. Ensure that frontline improvement teams get first chance at problem solving—before staff experts.
16. Cut transactions and reporting; control causes, not symptoms.

These principles serve as a strategic foundation for any service organization, just as running and blocking are fundamentals for any team in a variety of sports. Synchroservice strategy in the firm is comparable to a sports team's game plan. In each case, execution of the plan depends on strength in the fundamentals.

The 16 principles are in two broad groups and seven categories. The first group, formulation of service strategy, must account for customers, the company, and competitors if the strategy is to be complete. The second group, implementation, includes the other four categories, which are the building blocks of strategic support for the first group.

The principles have a commonsense ring. Nevertheless, numerous companies take a different path—sometimes an opposite one—as we discuss below.

CONTRAST

Strategy

Conventional Wisdom	New Thinking
Strategy is something done by senior executives, often with advice from highly paid consultants.	Much of strategic management can be reduced to basic principles.
Strategy permeates the organization through level-by-level, top-down planning.	Widely shared information and involvement in strategic planning fosters unified purpose and eases implementation of strategies.

---

1. Get to know and team up with the next and final customer. The customer, whether final consumer or next process, is the object of the first and most important principle. The remaining principles, which follow from this one, concern *how* to serve the customer better.

Getting to know and teaming up with the customer often requires breaking barriers—especially departmental walls. Teaming up can mean moving associates out of functional departments and into teams and cells, that is, organizing associates by how the work flows. If that isn't practical, then organize cross-functional improvement teams. Although these teams do not "live" together, they meet periodically to solve problems.

Geography is often a barrier (e.g., a customer is located miles away). But responses to such barriers can be creative. A good example is Intuit, the largest provider of easy-to-use financial software for small users. Intuit people at all levels—development programmers, project leaders, marketers, order processors—go out on week-long nationwide trips. They meet customers and bring back ideas for improving next versions or products.[5]

2. Become dedicated to continual, rapid improvement in quality, cost, response time, flexibility, variability, and service. A decade ago the slow pace of economic improvement (or lack of it) prompted journalists to declare a productivity crisis. The situation could

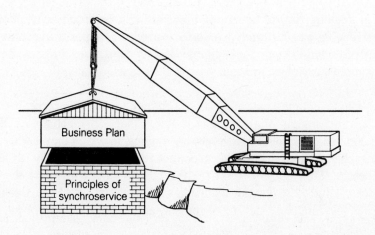

just as well have been called a quality crisis—where *quality* is broadly defined as improved delivery of all of the customers' requirements. This principle aims squarely at resolving that crisis by prescribing a customer-oriented agenda suitable for any business. Still, each business is unique, and the next two principles aim at tailoring service strategy to the particular organization and its competitive environment.

3. Achieve unified purpose via shared information and rewards, and team involvement in planning and implementation of change. Information and rewards must be shared throughout the organization if employee-driven continuous improvement is to occur. For instance, at Starbucks, a fast-growing espresso coffee-bar company, all 3,500 employees get stock options. This includes the 60 percent who work part-time. Starbucks won't franchise. CEO Howard Shultz says, "They wouldn't treat our employees as well as we do."[6]

And few companies apply the team-involvement idea as well as Zytec Corp., a Malcolm Baldrige National Quality Award winner. Zytec involves a broad mix of 20 percent of its 750 people in its five-year strategic planning; a few key suppliers and customers comment on the plan, too. Then every employee and team helps translate the plan into action elements and monthly goals.[7]

4. Get to know the competition and the world-class leaders. In many firms, getting to know the competition has been viewed as a sales and marketing function, useful for competitive pricing, positioning, and promotion. But for superior companies, that approach is insufficient. Operations associates cannot be effective without competitive information. They need to learn about competitors' designs, capacities, skill base, and supplier/customer linkages—as well as costs, quality, flexibility, and response times.

Old-style competitive analysis is limited to sampling competitors' services; continuous improvement requires that and much more. Blue-chip companies conduct benchmarking studies, in which they gather data and exchange visits with other companies, often in totally different businesses. They seek to discover the best practices, not just the best services. Among the popular companies to benchmark are L. L. Bean (for order processing and stock management) and Disney World (for keeping facilities in tip-top condition).

Failure to learn about the strengths of the competition or about the best performance in any industry (e.g., the ability to deliver better quality or offer quicker response) leads to complacency and decline. But obtaining and using such information helps motivate a company's people to make necessary improvements, which are stated as principles 5 through 16.

5. Cut the number of service operations and number of suppliers to a few good ones. Having too many service operations or too many suppliers makes it difficult to do justice to any of them. Limiting the number of operations (simplified service design) makes the service easier to do correctly every time; it is a hallmark of successful service firms, from H & R Block to ServiceMaster to Taco Bell. Cutting down on the number of suppliers (of component parts or services) is closely related, and it is becoming common practice in both manufacturing and service organizations.

This principle, the first of two in the design and organization category, pertains to things; the next deals with people.

6. Organize resources into multiple chains of customers, each focused on a service or customer family; create multifunctional service centers. This principle addresses problems implicit in familiar bureaucratic statements like "This office is responsible for issuing the permit" or "Our department processes those forms." Department-to-department work flows can be impersonal and invite finger pointing—at the other department—when things go wrong.

To ensure good coordination, error prevention, and continuous improvement, the customer at the next process should be known and familiar, a real partner or team member. A related need is for a dependable work flow path. These are among the reasons why some insurance companies (e.g., Aetna and AAL) are breaking up underwriting and claims-processing departments and reorganizing into multifunctional teams, and why factory support offices are organizing focused cells by the way the paperwork flows.

7. Continually invest in human resources through cross-training (for mastery of multiple skills), education, job and career-path rotation, and improved health, safety, and security. Capacity is high in cost and has long-term impact. That goes not only for physical capacity, treated in principles 8 and 9, but also for human resource capacity.

The human resource department is not responsible for human resource management; it is just the overseer. Since human resources are involved in formulating service strategy and are the driving force for carrying it out, it is necessary to put increased emphasis on development of human resources.

Old practices: Divide work into jobs so small and simple that any unskilled person, paid minimum wage, could master it the first day. Assign managers, experts, and professionals to a single career track and keep them there for life so they can really learn their specialty.

Continuous improvement: Each associate masters multiple jobs, job support skills, problem-solving techniques, and self (team) management. Through job switching, associates learn the impact of job A on job B; they discover their collective impact on the whole service, as well as their effect on customer satisfaction; and they understand their contribution to employee health, safety, and security. Managers and professionals require occasional career-path switching. The purpose is to gain a broader outlook, to increase their value to the company, and to achieve greater personal career security.

8. Automate incrementally when process variability cannot otherwise be reduced. People are variable, and variability stands in the way of serving the customer. Progress will therefore require new equipment and service automation. The easy, cheap way to achieve progress is for associates to tighten up their slack habits and bad practices. This defers the cost and complexity of automation. It also avoids succumbing to the glamour of automation and the tendency to automate for the wrong reasons. For example:

- "Replace run-down, poorly maintained present equipment, and cope with quality variation." Automation actually requires a higher degree of attention to equipment care and maintenance and better process controls on quality.
- "Become more flexible." But the most flexible resource is the human resource, not flexible automation.
- "Invest retained earnings." Investing retained earnings in automation sometimes makes sense, but investing in the company's existing human and physical infrastructure is always a good choice.
- "Eliminate the 'labor problem.'" Automation causes major work force changes and potentially even greater labor problems. Labor problems (which often are management problems) are best solved before piling on other major changes.

9. Look for simple, flexible, movable, low-cost equipment that can be acquired in multiple copies—each assignable to multifunctional service centers. How is growing demand to be served? The common tendency is to speed up the existing process: to add more people or to replace a small computer with a bigger, faster, costlier one.

Companies that have followed such practices for several generations of growth may find themselves with serious capacity obstacles. Their single, fast process is not divisible into focused units; it can process only one service order or customer at a time, which usually will be out of phase with actual customer demand patterns; it may be in the wrong location and too costly to move.

This plurality principle is the antidote to these problems. Successful examples are everywhere, from bank cash machines to community-based satellite police facilities. Planning in multiple-capacity units allows growth to occur at the same time as the organization becomes customer focused. Moreover, focusing equipment and operating teams on narrow families of services/customers helps large and growing companies act like small, customer-service-minded ones.

10. Make it easier to provide services without error or process variation. This and the next three principles involve the processing itself—the transformation of resources into services. This broad principle might be abbreviated: Do it right the first time. It enlists concepts and practices stretching from designing for quality, to partnering up with suppliers and customers for quality, to controlling processes for quality, to collecting and analyzing data for removal of the sources of poor quality.

This approach replaces poor but conventional practices in which causes of good and bad quality were not treated. Instead, organizations relied on checkers, inspectors, and monitors (e.g., listening in on telemarketing clerks). Usually, plenty of bad results still slipped through, which were dealt with in the complaint department.

11. Cut flow time (wait time) and distance all along the chain of customers. This and the next two principles are closely associated with just-in-time operations, which cut out process delays and improve responsiveness to customers.

The chain of customers from (and within) factories to distribution warehouses to retail storerooms and display counters is typically choked with inventories. It's a long, loose chain full of waste and delay. Human customers are similarly shunted from waiting line to waiting line, and documents pile up in in-baskets that impede their journey from desk to desk.

The customer often will not wait. Discovery of mistakes is also slow, and the mistakes can pile up before they are noted. By the time they are discovered, their causes may be unclear because the trail is cold.

One way to speed up the flow and take out wastes is simply to limit the queues in front of each process. For example, strive to keep in-baskets and waiting lines empty. This allows each job or customer to be processed without delay. Often it is possible to get the desired results by moving process stages closer together—shortening the flow path—which at the same time reduces response time.

12. Cut setup, get-ready, and startup times. This principle deals with preparation-to-serve delays of all kinds. For example, if you want to run a program on your personal computer, you must first get set up. You have to boot the disk, which, on your older model, takes 39 seconds. Then you make a menu selection (29 seconds), instruct the computer to read disk drive A (10 seconds), and call the desired program into memory (22 seconds). After a total of 1 minute and 40 seconds of setup, you are ready to perform useful work. Not so long, perhaps, but what if you need to switch from a word processing program to a spreadsheet? Would you have to go through another setup? And then perhaps another, to use a database program?

Excess setup time on a computer can be a mild annoyance, or it can seriously detract from someone's productivity. Or, if a client is waiting for the computer to process something, it's a serious problem of poor service.

Similarly, a customer may fume while a clerk hunts for an order book or a nurse opens cabinets looking for a roll of tape. Such examples of unpreparedness are commonplace and usually easy to fix. Systematic procedures for attacking these problems have migrated from the manufacturing sector to a growing number of service organizations.

13. Operate at the customer's rate; provide services just in time. That is: Don't go as fast as you can go, only to see documents or clients pile up in front of the next process. Don't invest in equipment that runs many times faster than the work can be processed downstream. And don't save up large piles of work before sending it on to the next process. Although those practices are common in typically disconnected companies, they are wasteful and stretch out the response time. Customers may not be willing to wait.

14. Record and own quality, process, and problem data at the workplace. Problem solving and control, the topic of the last three principles, are ineffective if problem-solving *data* ends up in the wrong place. A common mistake is sending quality, process, and problem data from the front lines to experts in back offices. That leaves frontline associates (the majority of company employees) out of the problem-solving, control, and process ownership loop. Data are what gets them back in.

15. Ensure that frontline improvement teams get first chance at problem solving—before staff experts. This principle follows from the previous one: Front-liners can do little about quality and problems without process data, but they can do plenty when they have the data, especially in teams in which knowledge, skills, and ideas are readily shared. Staff experts may have more problem-solving skills, but they have less understanding of the processes where problems occur. Also, staff people are not only expensive and relatively scarce, they are often tied up in other projects. This leaves little time for solving ongoing process problems and on-the-spot emergencies, which are the natural responsibility of frontline associates.

16. Cut transactions and reporting: Control causes, not symptoms. Transactions and reports often deal with symptoms (e.g., too many complaints, too much overtime last month). But effective quality control and flow control replace transactions and reports (as much as possible) with process data—categorized and detailed as to causes. Those data fuel the continuous improvement effort and need not end up in a report. In fact, in the improvement mode, by the time a report of a problem comes out, a team of associates would probably already be working on it—or may already have solved it.

The 16 principles may serve *as* strategy, but they do not cover the whole strategic waterfront. For example, they cannot directly guide a decision on where to locate a warehouse or set up a branch office, or if or when to do this. Complex issues like these simply involve too many variables, and executive-level strategic planning will still be required. But it should follow principle number 3, enlisting the broadest possible involvement in the effort.

SERVICE MANAGERS

The 16 principles of synchroservice tell what to strive for and how to manage services effectively. They provide guidance for the entire workforce, who, taken collectively, are the actual service managers. They include:

1. *The associates who provide the service.* In any enterprise, every employee is a manager of the immediate workplace, which consists of supplies, equipment, space, and information.[8] In the best companies, every employee is teamed up with others in a workflow relationship and periodically joins a special project team. Their role—meeting current demand exactly and managing and improving processes and products— involves data collection, problem solving, process control, and ever better service to the customer.

Principle 15: Associates get first chance at problem solving.

2. *First-line supervisors.* Their proper role involves little traditional supervising; rather, they are coordinating mixtures of human and physical resources in the cause of customer satisfaction and continuing improvement.

3. *Upper-level managers, such as department heads and general managers.* One of their more important tasks is to manage the training, reward, and recognition system to bring out the potential of line associates to become involved in improvement. Good managers are teachers. Another role is to serve as focal points for coordinating the support staff of experts, whose skills back up the direct efforts of line employees to solve problems and make improvements.

4. *Staff experts.* These include designers, buyers, hirers, trainers, schedulers, maintenance technicians, management accountants, inspectors, programmers, and analysts. Most organizations over-rely on staff experts, because line associates' capacities have not been solidly tapped. Still, staff expertise will always be needed. The role of staff people is to plan for change, respond expertly to problems, and serve on improvement teams.

Alarms have sounded for these managers. Service productivity and effectiveness are under the microscope. The need is for seamless connections that put services in sync with customers' needs, expectations, and demands. Foremost is the worldwide demand for quality.

II

QUALITY-DRIVEN CONNECTIONS

The global demand for quality has ushered in a rash of new ways to improve service operations and provides a home for a few older, tried-and-true tools. More than that, it has crystallized our thinking. The three chapters in Part II delve into the roots, concepts, and details of service quality management and improvement.

Customer requirements are the driving force. Chapter 2 focuses on infusing continuous improvement of quality—customers' first concern—into the fabric of service operations.

Seldom fully satisfied with what's available, customers keep shifting, usually elevating, their expectations. The response of superior organizations, explained in Chapter 3, is to design innovative services and continually improve the service design processes themselves.

Chapter 4 looks at quality management from a planning and competitive standpoint and describes an assortment of techniques useful throughout the sequence of service operations.

Chapter Two

The Quality Imperative

 Members of the 217-person student body of Mt. Edgecumbe High School in Sitka, Alaska, have been on the speaking circuit. At the invitation of blue-chip companies, they have traveled the continent telling their story of continuous quality improvement at company management meetings.

Mt. Edgecumbe is a state-run public boarding school mostly for native Alaskan students. The high school is the world's first to embrace the tools of total quality—or as they call it, the continuous improvement process.

Students spend 90 minutes weekly in quality improvement training and problem solving, track their own performance, study each other's learning methods, and team up with faculty and staff on improvement projects.

    Principle 15:   Involve associates in problem solving.

It has taken a while, but quality is no longer an intangible I-know-it-when-I-see-it concept. It is a set of teachable practices that serve as the centerpiece of good management (even in high schools). It is an imperative for global competitiveness.

Quality is no longer treated as a specialty ("Quality? Third door on your left, Complaint Department."). Instead, it is everybody's business—collectively as a competitive requirement; jointly, in improvement teams, for continual improvement; and singly in the performance of one's job. Besides involving everybody, today's quality emphasis includes the quality of every process, because intermediate process quality determines the output quality of the end service.

In this chapter, we discuss the breadth and roots of quality—the quality pioneers and the progression from artisanship to total quality management (TQM). Remaining chapter topics include the competitive importance of quality, the role of benchmarking and quality certifications and awards, and TQM's grounding in human commitment, teamwork, training, and local "ownership."

QUALITY: A BROAD VIEW

Quality is a complex concept. Brief, focused definitions (e.g., fitness for use and conformance to requirements) have remained popular. Our interest is in *service* quality, the dimensions of which are itemized below.

10 dimensions of service quality[1]

Reliability—consistency of performance and dependability.

Responsiveness—willingness or readiness to provide service; timeliness.

Competence—possession of the skills and knowledge required to perform the service.

Access—approachability and ease of contact.

Courtesy—politeness, respect, consideration for property, clean and neat appearance.

Communication—educating and informing customers in language they can understand; listening to customers.

Credibility—trustworthiness, believability; having customer's best interest at heart.

Security—freedom from danger, risk, or doubt.

Understanding—making an effort to understand the customer's needs; learning the specific requirements; providing individualized attention; recognizing the regular customer.

Tangibles—the physical evidence of service (facilities, tools, equipment).

This list is intended to reflect how *customers* think about quality. The list's breadth suggests the following:

1. Since quality is complex, it requires diverse implementation measures.
2. The implementation measures should be targeted to the specific customer's current concerns, which may shift over time. A customer's top concern may be reliability; later, that customer may want, *in addition to reliability,* improved timeliness.

CONTRAST

Quality and Speed

Old View	*New View**
Good quality takes time. Speed (e.g., quicker response) makes poor quality.	"It may sound absurd, but perhaps the surest way to improve quality is speed—by cutting the cycle time from inception to delivery, be the product a car, a piece of research, or an insurance claim."
	James F. Swallow, vice president, A. T. Kearney (consultants)

*Source: Otis Port and John Carey, "Questing for the Best," *Business Week,* October 25, 1991, pp. 8–16.

---

3. Quality requires continuing improvement. If a service has excellent reliability and timeliness, next comes another dimension—perhaps easier access. Continually adding to the dimensions of quality broadens a service's appeal to existing customers and gains the interest of new kinds of customers as well.

4. Quality is whatever the customer wants.

The fourth point is gospel in the community of quality experts. It easily admits the six general requirements of all customers: continual improvement of quality per se, cost, response time, flexibility, variability, and service.

QUALITY HERITAGE

The quality imperative is rooted in the experiences, research, writings, and teachings of several pioneers and leaders of the quality movement. As the concept of total quality continues to evolve, the contributions of others will certainly come to the forefront, but for now, the work of five pioneers stands out: W. Edwards Deming, Joseph M. Juran, Armand V. Feigenbaum, Kaoru Ishikawa, and Philip B. Crosby. Their thinking and influence are not limited to the management of quality alone. They all speak of companywide integration of purpose and high regard for the human element, as individuals and in teams dedicated to continuing improvement.

W. Edwards Deming

Although relatively unknown in his native country, the late W. Edwards Deming has been a Japanese hero for some 40 years. He began to gain recognition in the United States for his contributions to quality management on June 24, 1980, when NBC broadcast "If Japan Can . . . Why Can't We?" That documentary highlights Deming's role in Japan's industrial ascendancy.

Japan named its top national prize for contributions to quality after Deming and first awarded the Deming Prize in 1951. Deming continued to travel to Japan over the next three decades, sharing his concepts on data-based quality, developing a competitive edge, and management's role in these areas in general.[2]

EXHIBIT 2–1
The Plan-Do-Check-Act Cycle for Continuing Improvement

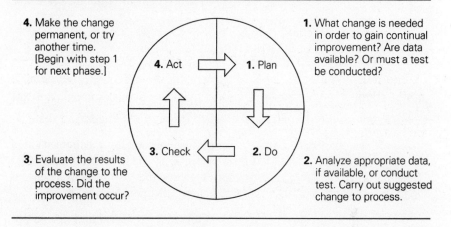

4. Make the change permanent, or try another time. [Begin with step 1 for next phase.]

4. Act

1. Plan

1. What change is needed in order to gain continual improvement? Are data available? Or must a test be conducted?

3. Check

2. Do

3. Evaluate the results of the change to the process. Did the improvement occur?

2. Analyze appropriate data, if available, or conduct test. Carry out suggested change to process.

In recent years, Deming traveled extensively, advocating his 14 points for management. He believed that while quality is everyone's job, management must lead the effort.

As a statistician, Deming was an ardent proponent of the use of process data to make decisions and solve problems: Use analysis if the data exist; if not, use experimentation and data collection. He followed an orderly approach to continual improvement known as the *Plan-Do-Check-Act (PDCA) cycle,* which is among the best-known tools in the TQM arsenal. One form is shown in Exhibit 2–1.

Joseph M. Juran

Like Deming, Joseph M. Juran was a pioneer of quality education in Japan. He has been known in the Western world for his textbooks and as editor-in-chief of *The Quality Control Handbook.* Like Deming, however, Juran was largely ignored by American management until the 1980s.

Juran's research has shown that over 80 percent of quality defects are *management controllable* and it is therefore management that most needs change. Juran's now-classic definition of quality is *fitness for use.* He intends those words to apply broadly, to include such properties as service response time, service availability, and price.

Juran defines quality management in terms of the *quality trilogy,* which consists of quality planning, quality control, and quality improvement.[3]

Armand V. Feigenbaum

Armand V. Feigenbaum is best known for originating the concept of *total quality control (TQC)*. In his book *Total Quality Control,* Feigenbaum explains that quality must be attended to through all stages and that

control must start with identification of customer quality requirements and end only when the product has been placed in the hands of a customer who remains satisfied. Total quality control guides the coordinated actions of people, machines, and information to achieve this goal.[4]

To Feigenbaum, responsibility for TQC must be shared and should not rest with the quality assurance function alone. Feigenbaum also clarified the idea of *quality costs*—costs associated with poor quality. He was among the first to argue that better quality is, in the long run, cheaper.

Kaoru Ishikawa

Kaoru Ishikawa, the late Japanese quality authority, acknowledged Deming's and Juran's influence on his thinking. However, Ishikawa must be recognized for his own contributions. He developed *quality control circles*—small groups of employees that meet regularly to plan and (often) carry out process changes to improve quality, productivity, or the work environment.

He also originated Ishikawa cause-effect charts, or "fishbone diagrams," so named because of their structural resemblance to the skeleton of a fish (discussed in Chapter 4). Like Deming, Juran, and Feigenbaum, Ishikawa also emphasized quality as a way of management.

Philip B. Crosby

Philip B. Crosby is the author of the popular book *Quality Is Free: The Art of Making Quality Certain.* Crosby explains that what costs money is all the things that prevent jobs from being done right the first time. When quality is made certain, an organization avoids these expenses.

Crosby proposes *zero defects* as the goal for quality. To any who find that too ambitious, he simply asks, "If not zero defects, then what goal would you propose?" One often-used figure is the acceptable quality level (AQL). Briefly, AQL allows a certain proportion of defective items. Crosby explains that an AQL is a commitment to a certain amount of defects—before we start! The AQL idea is certainly out of step with continuous improvement. Taking the consumer's view, Crosby makes his point bluntly:

> Consider the AQL you would establish on the product you buy. Would you accept an automobile that you knew in advance was 15 percent defective? 5 percent? 1 percent? one-half of 1 percent? How about the nurses that care for newborn babies? Would an AQL of 3 percent on mishandling be too rigid?[5]

Crosby also has popularized Feigenbaum's cost-of-quality idea.

COST OF QUALITY

Conventional managers want to see everything in monetary numbers. So, in the transition to the broader TQM mode, managers may ask, "What does it cost?" Quality costs fall into four categories:

Internal failure costs. Costs the provider incurs directly—prior to final customer service—as a result of defective work. Examples are scrap, rework, retest, downtime, materials disposition and searches for something misplaced.

External failure costs. Costs to the provider when defects are discovered after final service delivery. Included are returns, warranty expenses, allowances, complaint processing, and service recovery. In extreme cases, liability settlements and legal fees would be included.

Appraisal costs. Costs of determining the degree of quality. They include monitoring and inspection and related equipment and supplies.

Prevention costs. Costs of efforts to minimize appraisal and failure costs. They include quality planning, training, new-service review, reporting, and improvement projects.

Quality advocates in a number of well-known firms used the cost-of-quality argument for shock value in the formative stages of their TQM efforts. Cost-minded senior managers were often startled to learn that "costs of *un*-quality" in their companies were 10 percent to 20 percent of annual revenue. When other arguments for managerial commitment to quality improvement programs failed, the cost-of-quality speech often got results. (Note: Leading Japanese companies, having launched TQM by other means, had little use for cost-of-quality accounts or logic.)

Should firms that already have a thriving TQM effort continue doing annual cost-of-quality audits? Probably not. Consider, for example, a process improvement that prevents defective output. In a TQM company, it's a better-than-even bet that that change has other benefits; perhaps it results in faster or better new-service introduction, reduces response times, or improves after-sale service. Is the expense of the change a cost of quality? or of design, frontline operations, or marketing? Under TQM, quality is everybody's business; it's woven into the fabric of every job. So, the amount spent to achieve quality is difficult to state precisely. But even if we could find it, it isn't a cost we want to eliminate anyway.

The phase of raising quality awareness may be nearly behind us, as evidenced by the growth of quality awards, certifications, and registrations. We shall briefly consider these topics, along with benchmarking, which details top quality practices among outside firms.

BENCHMARKING AND QUALITY AWARDS

Benchmarking, developed at Xerox Corporation in the late 1970s, is the systematic search for best practices, from whatever source, to be used in improving a company's own practices.

At first, Xerox people called it competitive benchmarking. As the words suggest, it was limited to finding their direct competitors' best practices. Xerox benchmarking teams boldly contacted competing manufacturers of copiers, computers, and other Xerox products. They said, "How about we visit you and you visit us? We'll exchange information about each other's practices and put the information to use."

Why would rivals go for such a brazen proposal? Because the two companies would each benefit relative to other rivals not involved. Besides, with cross-hiring of people from one company to the other, plenty of information leaks out anyway. So why not be more systematic about this search for information?

CONTRAST

Toward Benchmarking

Keep It a Secret	*Trade It*
Our results, practices, and process knowledge are for our eyes only. Lock the doors, frown on outside visitors.	Our results, practices, and knowledge are valuable assets; so are those of other good companies. Let's trade.

Best Practices—Anywhere

But why restrict benchmarking to competitors? Why not *non*competitive benchmarking? Xerox teams began to fan out in search of best practices in *any* organization.

Principle 4:   Know the competition and world leaders.

Xerox manager Robert Camp describes a benchmarking visit to L. L. Bean, the mail-order retailer, to learn what's behind Bean's renown for excellent customer service.[6] Other companies have followed Xerox to L. L. Bean. Another frequently benchmarked company is Federal Express, for its ability to deliver overnight.

Now, though benchmarking is only a few years old, it is in wide use by major hotels, accounting firms, transportation companies, banks, manufacturing companies, and others:

- Marriott Hotels have benchmarked the hiring, training, and pay practices of fast-food companies because hotels hire out of the same labor pool.
- Corporate attorneys at Motorola have even employed benchmarking. Richard Weise, general counsel at Motorola, says, "We began to compile information on how many lawyers and paralegals it takes for each $1 billion in sales. We looked at how other law departments use tools such as computers [and] learned from them. Finally, we determined relative costs of delivering legal services domestically versus internationally."[7]
- Houston's Second Baptist Church, serving 12,000 parishioners weekly, uses benchmarking (e.g., Disney World's parking and people skills) in its customer quality program.

The Benchmarking Process

With so many trying to benchmark the same high-performance firms, the idea of putting benchmarking data into data banks arose. Thus, under the sponsorship of subscribing companies, the American Productivity and Quality Center in Houston has established an International Benchmarking Clearinghouse.

An early Clearinghouse project was to survey current benchmarking procedures. Most benchmarking programs use six common steps, according to the survey. First come planning and organization. The next step is all-important: selecting the process to be benchmarked and the team members. However, the team should not immediately set off to benchmark another company. First they need to benchmark their *own* process, in the following terms:

Metrics (measurements in numbers). For example, a team from accounts payable may find it takes 18 hours average elapsed time and 23 minutes of paid labor to process an invoice.

Practices. The team documents every step in the process, noting delays, sources of errors, departments and skills involved, and so forth.

The third step is collecting information on whom to benchmark and what questions to ask. The fourth is to gain approval and establish plans for exchange visits.

Fifth is the benchmarking itself, including a visit to the benchmarked firms' sites. Information sought must parallel that already gathered by the team for its own firm, namely, metrics and practices. Lastly, the benchmarking team analyzes the data, develops plans for change, and follows through.

Benchmarking is no longer confined to North America, where it originated. Now benchmarking teams criss-cross oceans in the continual quest for competitively valuable process knowledge. Perhaps a portion of the intercontinental travel will dissipate somewhat as clearinghouse information becomes more available. Still, benchmarking seems to have found a solid place in the TQM tool kit. This is especially true in the United States, inasmuch as benchmarking is now one of the criteria used in assessments for the Malcolm Baldrige National Quality Award.

Marks of Excellence

The Baldrige award in the United States is a direct descendant of Japan's Deming Prize for quality, first presented in 1951. Now there are many more descendants. They include the European Quality Award, Canada Awards for Business Excellence, the Minnesota Quality Award, and the Erie Quality Award (Erie County, Pennsylvania), to name a few. Many other states, regions, cities, provinces, counties, and business groups bestow similar awards (e.g., the National Housing Quality Award). Some tilt toward the manufacturing sector, but most award to both manufacturers and services. In the United States, the federal government has its own Quality Improvement Prototype (QIP) Award (with a format similar to the Baldrige), which is given by the Federal Quality Institute. Examples of service organization award winners follow.

- Deming Prize—Florida Power & Light (1990), the first non-Japanese company to win this prize.
- Baldrige Award—Federal Express (1990), Ritz-Carlton Hotel (1992), AT&T Universal Credit Card Services (1992), and Granite Rock Co. (1992).
- Federal Quality Award (United States)—Patent and Trademark Office, Department of Commerce (1992).
- George M. Low Trophy (National Aeronautics and Space Administration)—Grumman Corporation's Technical Services Division (1991).
- RIT/*USA Today* Quality Cup (for individuals and teams)—Sentara Norfolk (Virginia) General Hospital X-ray team (1992).
- Canada Awards—Reimer Express Lines (1988).

These awards are important for some special reasons:

- For profit-making firms, striving to win a quality award can rally the masses. Most people cannot easily relate what they do to company performance as shown in the income statement. But, by definition, TQM involves everybody. Seeking a public prize for everybody's efforts might have more motivational impact than the exhortations of the CEO ever could.
- For nonprofit organizations, there hasn't even been an income statement to look to for overall organizational gratification; a public prize fills a void.

- For service organizations, there is a tangibility problem. As *The Economist* puts it, a service is "anything sold in trade that could not be dropped on your foot." That's pretty nebulous. Service people need things like quality prizes to clarify common purpose.

Whereas winning a quality award is prideful, receiving a quality certification or registration is duty. The best known registration is the ISO-9000 series, which certifies that a company has documented evidence of a companywide quality program. The registration is similar to a diploma. Having it qualifies you in the eyes of a potential employer. In the case of the ISO-9000 series, it qualifies your firm to be considered as a supplier to another company. This way of screening suppliers got its start and is best established in Europe. Increasingly, companies wanting to do business in Europe will need this certification, and its use is growing elsewhere as well.

EMPLOYEE-DRIVEN QUALITY

We have considered the roots and development of the quality imperative. We now turn to implementation, specifically, the need for broad-based human involvement and commitment. Gaining that commitment requires action on three fronts:

1. *Training.* Everyone needs training in the tools of continuous improvement, problem solving, and statistical process control; in addition, people require training in job skills, plus cross-training for an understanding of the bigger picture.
2. *Organization.* People need to be put into close contact with customers (next process) and suppliers (previous process). This calls for organization of multifunctional customer- or service-focused cells, teams, and projects.
3. *Local ownership.* The management, control, and reward systems need to be realigned with the goals of employee- and team-driven, customer-centered quality and continuous improvement.

Time Out for Training

Philip Crosby says that quality is free, but it is not a gift. It pays its own way—but not without an up-front investment. The investment is for training, the essential catalyst for action.

CONTRAST

Management Theories

Theory X
Experts plan; operators do as they are told.

Theory Y
Listen to your people; they are intelligent and earnest.

Theory T (for Training)
Training provides the tools for continual employee-driven improvement; no training, little improvement.

Amid all the evidence that businesses have taken the quality imperative to heart, the elevated commitments to quality-oriented training and cross-training stand out. For example:

- Univar, the largest US chemical distributor, committed $2 million to TQM training and implementation.
- At Xerox, within 90 days of being hired, salespeople receive TQM training.
- At Quad/Graphics, associates spend one day per week in the classroom—a "day a week, forever," as a leader in the firm's educational program puts it.
- Banc One Mortgage in Indianapolis has reorganized into teams averaging 17 cross-trained people who work on all aspects of a loan application at once.
- Carolina Power & Light trains all service specialists in two job areas foreign to them.

Principle 7: Cross-training, mastery, education.

There are thousands more examples like these. Most come from companies—including large, well-known ones—that had been spending virtually nothing on training frontline employees. In the past, only managers and professionals had received company-sponsored training. The old view was that training is an expense that takes away time from real work and is money down the drain when an employee leaves the company. The new view is that it's a necessary investment.

To avoid spending on training, businesses exploited the division-of-labor concept: Break the work down into its simplest elements, bundle a few elements into a job classification, and hire an unskilled person at minimum wage to do it with no training. Many companies still follow those practices—as a result, they have fewer resources (minds) for making improvements, or even for seeing what needs to be improved.

Lack of training also deters teamwork because, at least in Western cultures, people do not seem to be naturally team oriented. Athletic coaches and managers, for example, have to spend years molding lone wolves into wolf packs. In response to the demands of TQM, consultants are out in force providing team-building assistance.

Getting Organized—Team Formats

Team *organization* comes before team building. If a group of angry prisoners received team-building training, they might unite to burn down the jail. And so it is with businesses and agencies. The first priority is getting the right people on the team.

Quality circles.   One useful kind of team is the quality circle (QC). In the late 1970s, Western visitors to Japan were mesmerized by their apparent potency. Japanese quality circles contributed as many as 100 times more suggestions per employee than were typical in Western organizations. In short order, quality circles were organized from Melbourne to Oslo. The results were favorable, but not much more so than certain other programs, such as suggestion plans. It now seems clear that most circles were organized in a way that *avoided* a customer focus—that is, they excluded next processes (see Exhibit 2–2).

Part A of the figure shows two examples of a quality circle composed of five people in a single department. The first consists of four stock pickers and a supervisor, while the second has four order-entry clerks and a supervisor. Those circles could meet every day and never hear a complaint about errors in stock selection or in recording customer requirements. Also, the circles would not be inclined to discuss causes of their own delays. Since their customers are not in the circles, the circles will discuss shared annoyances: room temperature, lighting, company recreation and benefits, work hours, and so forth. While all deserve attention, however, they are only indirectly related to serving a customer. In fact, circles like these may spend much of their time complaining about the demands of customers, instead of teaming up to serve them.

EXHIBIT 2–2
Quality Circles: Gangs versus Teams

A. Gangs: Quality circles composed of employees from same
   department.

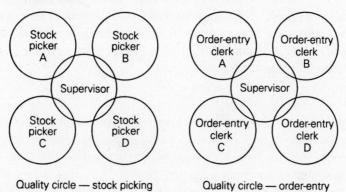

Quality circle — stock picking   Quality circle — order-entry

B. Teams: Quality circle composed of a chain of provider-user pairs —
   formally organized into a work cell.

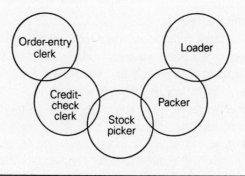

Cells. Part B of Exhibit 2–2 shows how to organize quality circles for effective process improvement. This type of circle is hard to organize because it requires moving people and equipment out of functional departments. Here an order-entry clerk teams up with the customer at the next process, a credit-check clerk. Their desks, files, and so forth, are side-by-side, but not in the sales or accounting department. They move to the stockroom to be close to the next three internal customers. The goals of co-location are to quicken response times, cut out many clerical activities and transactions, eliminate long travel distances, and slash work pileups and related high rates of rework. The cell easily fills every order in less than a day. Any clerical error, such as miscoding a stock number or stock location, is immediately spotted and fixed. Cell members cross-train each other so they can trade jobs, cover for each other, and work meaningfully on improvement projects. The group begins to adopt quality circle-like behaviors whether that was intended or not. And people begin to act like a team whether or not they care to be. Co-location has that effect.

Teams. Like quality circles (a term in declining use), *teams* sometimes employ a *facilitator,* who provides training in process analysis and improvement and may lead problem-solving team meetings. The techniques include process flowcharts, Pareto analysis, fishbone and run diagrams, and other process control tools (all discussed in Chapter 4). Members also study group dynamics methods, including brainstorming, nominal group techniques, role playing, multivoting, cohesiveness building, and consensus attainment, and they learn how to make presentations on proposed improvements. In addition, they may be empowered to interview and choose new employees and to evaluate each other's performance.

While some teams include a supervisor, others are leaderless or are headed by a working coordinator. In some companies team membership is voluntary; in others it's part of everyone's job. Much of the new wave of interest has come from the services sector. In the 1980s, by contrast, circles and cells were of interest mainly to manufacturers, first in the plant and then in support offices.

Unfortunately, teams in service businesses are often organized in the less-effective pattern of Exhibit 2–2A (gangs). But there are numerous notable exceptions. For example, Fidelity Investments has formed several fully staffed units (cells) to perform a complete service. One is Fidelity's Monetary Gate team, which, in its own corner of a single building in Texas, is able to process monetary corrections in 24 hours; formerly, corrections went back and forth among offices in dispersed cities and sometimes took months to complete.

Project teams. What about the many situations in which associates in the work flow are not co-located? They may be out of view, in different departments, or in different cities. Those situations call for still another kind of team: the multifunctional problem-solving or project team. Since most people in a work flow sequence do tend (rightly or wrongly) to be separated, this team form has an important place in total quality management.

In some situations, such as in the transportation industry, it is impossible for people to co-locate and form a cell. Chemical Lehman Tank Lines, a Pennsylvania-based petroleum hauler, creates projects across distance by sending action teams of its employees to customer sites. In an unusual twist to cross-training, Lehman even has initiated exchanges of employees with its customers. Those employees are likely to gain insights that will improve their ideas in any team format.

Principle 1: Team up with customers.

Local Ownership of Control, Improvement, and Results

Unfortunately, smoothly functioning teams don't spring forth directly out of TQM training sessions. Individual behaviors change slowly, and frustration breeds in the void.

It need not be so. An excellent quick outlet for initial TQM enthusiasm is your own *personal quality checklist* (or check sheet), which is a list of a few standout personal defects that you can record by a simple tally stroke on a checklist in your pocket or on your desk. In their book *Quality Is Personal,* Harry Roberts and Bernard Sergesketter explain using their own experiences, plus those of colleagues.[8] Sergesketter, a manager for AT&T's Central Region of Business Network Sales, developed the method, and many of his associates quickly picked it up. His initial list is as follows (plus some health and appearance items):

On time for meetings.
Answer phone in two rings or less.
Return phone calls same or next day.
Respond to letters in five business days.
Clean desk.
Credenza: only same-day paper.

Sergesketter counted his total number of defects monthly. The total quickly fell from about 100 in spring 1990 to 10, then 5. Also, he has implemented changes, such as date-stamping mail, that help with measuring defects and attaining improved performance.

Roberts, a University of Chicago professor, has found that just making the list has resulted in virtual elimination of some defects. Many of his executive MBA students have taken up the personal quality checklist habit in their studies and back on their jobs as well. Experience so far suggests the following:

1. Define the defect unambiguously so it can be recognized easily and tallied.
2. No New Year's resolutions. Focus on attainable defects, especially waste reducers and time-savers. Later refine the list, perhaps including activity expanders to make productive use of the time saved.

As personal quality checklists lead the way and teams follow, everyone needs to feel a sense of ownership. This includes ownership of control, of improvements, and of results. It also means less control from on high and fewer levels of management to review improvement proposals. Further, the company must shift toward rewarding specific results at local levels rather than general ones at high levels.

To support local ownership, managers need to be out of their offices and visible locally, where they admire control charts and process experiments, help remove obstacles, and pass out awards. When local ownership has truly taken root, the evidence is likely to include charts of all kinds—on walls, doors, and partitions—*in the workplace* rather than in managers' offices.

Principle 14:   Retain local ownership of quality, data, results.

There is much more to be said about local ownership and total quality control. We will continue to explore these topics in detail in the remaining chapters.

Chapter Three

Designed-In Quality

When we encounter high-quality, efficient service, it looks elegant, simple, effortless. This happens when overall excellence is designed into service processes.

According to G. Lynn Shostack, however, "Services are unusual in that they have impact but no form," which adds to the difficulty of service development. Still, this is no excuse for a slipshod approach. "There is no way," she says, "to ensure quality or uniformity in the absence of a detailed design."[1]

In this chapter we bring together ideas that lead to effective, detailed service development. Exhibit 3–1 outlines the general approach. The first step is fitting the firm's design strategy to its competitive environment. The next move is pulling people in from different functions to form

43

EXHIBIT 3–1
Effective Product–Process Design

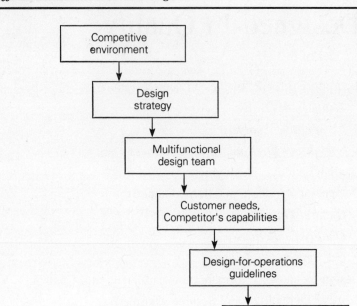

design teams, which systematically collect data on customer needs and competitor's capabilities, and then act on those data while following design-for-operations guidelines. The final follow-through employs a set of relevant measures of design effectiveness.

While each organization must mold its own strategy to fit its competitive environment, an effective strategy should at least address two chronic weaknesses:

1. *Design is too slow.* The new or revised service gets to market late and competitors are entrenched. Often two or more computer software companies are working simultaneously on roughly the same new offering. Perhaps WordPerfect releases first, and WordStar takes a beating in the marketplace for the next upgrade in word processing systems.

2. *Design is fractionated.* A commission or legislative subcommittee may spend a year developing a new program for protecting the forests or housing the poor, and a law is passed. But the agencies

that implement the law were not involved in drafting it. As a result, developing the process for implementation takes many more months, and the implementing regulations turn out to be ineffective.

The remainder of this chapter details ways of avoiding these common weaknesses. The approach described emphasizes getting to market fast with high-quality products that meet customers' real needs.

TEAMING UP FOR EFFECTIVE SERVICE DESIGN

Imagine a hierarchy of chefs in a tony restaurant in which the head chef composes recipes and menus, but never works the kitchen, visits food sellers, or interacts with the serving staff. A food buyer uses the head chef's list to buy ingredients but has nothing to do with other restaurant functions. Others in the restaurant are similarly compartmentalized.

The image is, of course, ridiculous. In larger restaurants, there is a hierarchy—from head chef to sous chef and on down (and plenty of chances for misunderstanding and process variation). However, the head chef works with other key players to a very short plan-do-check-act cycle. Feedback comes quickly (e.g., carrots are tough and tasteless), so that corrective action (drop that recipe and switch to green beans) can be taken for just-arriving diners or at least for tomorrow's customers. The various chefs, servers, managers, and so on, must operate as a team, acquiring and sharing up-to-date information about what's happening. There is no time to dawdle or to pass designs and plans back and forth from department to department.

Principle 1:   Team up with the next and final customer.

Concurrent Design

The last four sentences, with minor changes in terms, fittingly describe good design practices for any kind of organization. Call it team design or concurrent design, in which functional specialists execute their parts of the design as a team simultaneously, instead of in separate departments serially.

The team approach to design and delivery is easy and natural when an organization is new and small. When growth comes, however, people split off into specialties housed in separate departments, and that's the

---

CONTRAST

Design

Over-the-Wall Design	Concurrent (Team) Design
• Becomes common practice as organization grows and splits into functional departments.	• Tends to be common practice in very small organizations and where service redesigns occur often.
• Common, especially, for services with long lives (little urgency to develop new ones).	• Elevated competition has made it common in fast food, consumer credit, and mortgage loans, for example.
• Tends to be slow.	• Is fast and avoids problems (design rework) stemming from poor coordination and lack of shared information.
• Tends to require several costly rounds of debugging.	

---

end of teamwork. Specialists in each department throw the design over the wall to the next group. The final design goes over the last wall to frontliners. The service is difficult or impossible to do right every time, so operations tosses it back for re-design. The changes are costly and time-consuming, and by the time the service is easy to do right, customers have taken their business elsewhere.

Fractionated, stretched-out design cycles become all the more likely in the case of long service lives, whether it's a bank savings plan or new legislation: No urgency, no concurrency.

In some business sectors, shrinking product life cycles have pushed designers into a short loop linked more closely to the do-check-act phases of continuous improvement. New generations of computer software, bank savings plans, and tax laws are announced yearly or more often. Shortened life cycles are fed by high competition, technological advances, and quick compilation and communication of sales trend data.

But even when product life cycles are long, concurrent design has merit. Advantages include the following:

- Concurrent design gets all parties together, including selected customers, suppliers, and frontline associates. Designs should then be more in tune with real customer preferences, more realistic for suppliers to support, and easier for frontline associates to execute.

Hallmark's Holiday Design Teams

Hallmark "lives or dies on new stuff—some 40,000 cards and other items a year, the work of 700 writers, artists, and designers. . . . Developing a new card had become grotesque; it took two years—longer than the road from Gettysburg to the Appomattox Court House. The company was choking on sketches, approvals, cost estimates, and proofs." But now, about half the staff will "work on cards for particular holidays. . . . A team of artists, writers, lithographers, merchandisers, bean counters, and so on, will be assigned to each holiday. Team members are moving from all over a two-million-square-foot office building in Kansas City so they can sit together. Like a canoe on a lake, a card will flow directly from one part of the process to the next within, say, the Mother's Day team; before, it had to be portaged from one vast department to the next."

Source: Thomas A. Stewart, "The Search for the Organization of Tomorrow," *Fortune*, May 18, 1992, pp. 92–98.

- Concurrent design avoids costly misunderstandings and do-overs in the design phase.
- Concurrent design reduces costly bugs, mishaps, rework, and returns. Opportunities for reducing such wastes are everywhere. For example, in a human resources department, "If a bonus system or orientation program needs to be redesigned because employees could not understand it, this is clearly 'rework.' "[2]

Concurrent (team) design has taken root in many companies (see the Hallmark example in the accompanying box). The greatest benefits often come from getting service design and process design people on the same team.

Competitive Analysis

To fully do its work, the design team needs to know the competition. The trouble is, many companies have too few probes into the outside world. Competitive feedback is sparse, late, and narrow gauge—for example, limited mostly to sales totals and anecdotes.

Investigation of competitors' products is called *competitive analysis.* (In contrast, benchmarking, a newer "sibling" of competitive analysis, seeks out best processes of all kinds, rather than just competitors' products. See Chapter 2.) For many services, competitive analysis requires going to the competitor, being served, and taking extensive notes for later use by your own service design group. Example: Warehouse stores (e.g., Circuit City, Home Depot, Sam's, and Office Club) have been expanding into new markets, which brings anxious managers of existing conventional stores in to do a competitive analysis, followed, sometimes, by redesign of their own service practices.

   Principle 4:   Get to know the competition.

Social and Environmental Awareness

On the social and environmental front, businesses have tended to react late rather than plan and design early. The business world's common assumption was that social initiatives are too costly to be in their own or their customers' direct interest.

   Throughout the 1980s, however, tough pollution and recycling laws raised public awareness. Reluctance sometimes changed to willing compliance, translated into planning for recycling and recovery in early design phases. The change in attitude occurred when, for example, paper, once dumped into landfills and now recycled, became a cash generator.

   Competitive one-upmanship can be the attraction that gets social concerns on the design team's agenda. For example, a supermarket chain makes its competitors look bad by being the first to offer bag recycling.

   Sometimes reaction to a social concern opens up a set of promising new design options. For example, in attempting to design self-services easily performed by disabled consumers, designers have unearthed an attractive new approach called *universal design.*[3] It often turns out that, say, easy-to-open doors or easy-to-access information services are popular with young and old, able and disabled. That's good news because it allows the design team to focus intensively on just a few universal designs. With fewer, more universal service variations, designers can focus on better quality. At the same time, however, the design team needs to keep an eye on the big picture.

QUALITY FUNCTION DEPLOYMENT

Quality function deployment (QFD) provides a structured way of viewing the big picture by organizing the details.[4] The structure comes from a series of matrices. The first and most important matrix spells out customer needs—the "voice of the customer"—and compares the company's and key competitors' abilities to satisfy those needs. When the matrix is filled in and "roofed over," it takes the shape of a house—the *house of quality.*

Exhibit 3–2 is a house of quality developed with the aid of the owners of a chain of dry cleaning stores. The owners might use the matrix for improving one or more of their existing stores or for planning a new one. We interpret the QFD matrix as follows:

- The central portion shows what the customer wants and how to provide it.
- Symbols in the central portion show strong, medium, small, or no relationship between whats and hows. A double circle, strong, worth nine relationship points, appears six times. For example, a "perfect press" strongly depends on "firm press pads" and "good equipment maintenance," which account for two of the double circles.
- The five customer requirements are ranked one to five in importance. "Completely clean" is the customers' number one concern; "no delay at counter" gets a five.
- The ratings in each how column add up to an importance weighting. Good training, of medium importance for satisfying all five customer requirements, adds up to 15 points, which is second in importance to equipment maintenance, with 19 points.
- The house's roof correlates each how with each other factor. Only four of the combinations show a correlation. The double-circle indicates a strong correlation between "good equipment maintenance" and "no rust in steam-press lines," meaning that steam-press components are subject to rust and thus must be cleaned out or replaced regularly.
- Target values, in the "basement" of the house, give a numeric target for each how: Change press pads monthly to keep them firm.
- The house's "sub-basement" and right wing show comparisons of the company and key competitors. We see at the bottom that the company is slightly better than competitors A and B in keeping

EXHIBIT 3-2
"House of Quality" Dry Cleaners

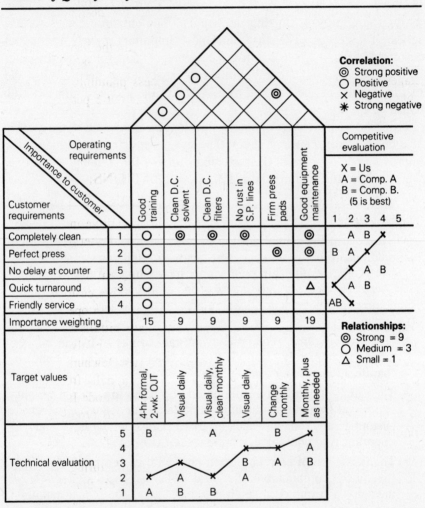

solvent clean, in avoiding rust, and in maintenance. Ratings in the right wing show that both competitors are better on counter delays and quick turnaround.

The tough part for the design team is getting good data to enter into the matrix. Data sources may include focus groups, surveys, studies, comparison shopping, competitive analysis, public information, calculations and reckoning. The emphasis is on relevant data, which may require tapping the minds of leading-edge customers. QFD is (with good data) a structured, inclusive approach. It helps keep the design team from overlooking something important.

The design team uses the basic house of quality in the service planning stage. More detailed matrixes may be developed for three remaining stages of design, that is, service design, process planning, and process control.[5] According to one report, though, only about 5 percent of QFD users go beyond the basic house.[6]

DESIGN FOR SERVICE OPERATIONS: GUIDELINES

A design team with up-to-date customer and competitive information is ready to go to work. Its work is to build quality into the service—and not just on paper.

Service designers can too easily overlook the realities of frontline operations: the moment of truth with an unpredictable customer, or the many sources of surprise, variation, agony, and error in operations. The design team may be able to avoid some of these pitfalls by following design-for-service-operations guidelines, which have evolved from the works of professors Geoffrey Boothroyd and Peter Dewhurst.[7]

In the early 1980s, Boothroyd and Dewhurst (originally from England, now professors of engineering at the University of Rhode Island) began to publish on design for operations for manufactured products. By the 1990s, thousands of design engineers had studied *design for manufacture and assembly.*

Although the guidelines were aimed at manufacturing, they have proven to be general enough to apply well to services; thus, we use the term, *design for service operations (DFSO)*. One version of DFSO guidelines follows.

Design for service operations guidelines

General guidelines:
1. Design to target markets and target costs.
2. Minimize number of operations.

Quality guidelines:
3. Ensure that customer requirements are known and design to those requirements.

4. Ensure that process capabilities are known (those in your firm and of your suppliers) and design to those capabilities.
5. Use standard procedures, materials, and processes with already known and proven quality.

Operability guidelines:
6. Design multifunctional/multiuse service elements and modules.
7. Design for ease of coupling/uncoupling.
8. Design for one-way travel (avoid backtracking and return visits).
9. Avoid offline or misfit service elements.
10. Avoid designs requiring extraordinary attentiveness—or that otherwise tempt substandard or unsafe performance.

General Guidelines

Two guidelines are general, in that they have wide-ranging benefits.

1. Target markets and target costs. Designing to target markets and target costs reinforces the need for marketing and finance representatives to be on the design team. A target cost, carefully set based on target sales and profit, may be a basis for killing a bad project or for stimulating innovation. If it looks as if operating costs are going to exceed target cost, the first response of the design team is to search, strive, and innovate until it can find a way to meet the target. Lack of targets leaves designers to play out their own whims, which may be to see how many new technologies (often costly and risky) they can try out and learn about.

2. Minimize operations. For example, a data-entry terminal may be used to input client data in one operation, instead of several times in several different offices of, say, a college or a clinic.

Principle 5: A few good service operations.

Quality Guidelines

The next three guidelines pertain to quality: quality requirements of the customer (guideline 3), quality capabilities of internal and external processes (guideline 4), and use of standardization to make quality easier to deliver (guideline 5).

3. Customer requirements. Guideline 3 calls for the design team to find out customers' precise requirements, or their best estimates of them, and to keep finding out because requirements can change during the design project. Requirements may take the form of speed of service, minimal waiting time, ability to customize, and so on. The design team must be clear on the matter because one of its jobs is to transform requirements into service specifications.

Principle 10:   Eliminate error and process variation.

Since the design task may be split up among more than one organizational unit, it is important that people from each unit get together on requirements. If they are kept apart, quality problems are likely. Suppliers will cite "ambiguous requirements." They will say, "We followed your requirements [or specifications] and now find out you really want something else."

Such failures to communicate are not just the fault of the customer. Good suppliers, inside or outside the firm, do whatever they can to find out their customers' real requirements, avoid misunderstanding, and make their customers look good.

4. Process capability. Guideline 4, designing to process capability, impacts the design team in two ways. First, the team is held responsible if the service cannot easily be performed using available processes, people, equipment, facilities, and other resources (including those of the supplier). Second, in being held responsible, the design team must become familiar with process capabilities, which usually are measurable to some degree.

Capability measures might include associates' years of experience, degree of cross-training, and educational attainment; documentation of procedures; safety devices in place; and equipment failure rates.

5. Standard procedures, materials, and processes. The fifth guideline advises designers to favor standard procedures, materials, and processes. Related to standardization are questions about creativity, satisfying customer needs for variety, and new opportunities for global marketing. Each of these issues warrants brief discussion.

Standardization.   Nonstandard designs are risky because of lack of knowledge about their performance. Standard designs, such as table settings in restaurants, on the other hand, have known desirable benefits: Supervisors can see at a glance if everything is right, and patrons are more likely to find a complete, familiar-looking table service. In order to achieve standardized services, service associates must be well trained. Thus, service design usually must include design of the training package.

Standardization and creativity.   Some apply the guideline quantitatively. For example, an opinion survey firm may limit the number of questions on a survey form, or a fast-food company may limit the number of allowable operations in a new process for delivering a new food item to a customer. While it might seem that such restrictions could stifle creativity or effectiveness, they may have the opposite effect. By not spending time designing complex multistep forms or fast-food procedures, designers may have more time to be creative or thorough on what counts.

Standardization and personalized design.   Is standardization in conflict with trends toward personalized design? Not necessarily. In fact, standardization may be the only way to make personalized design profitable: Carefully design a small number of standard elements that can be delivered in volume at low cost, and have the flexibility to quickly customize them right in front of the customer.

This formula—personalization but with standard components—is the basis, for example, for Panasonic's personalized bicycle, which starts out with customer fitting in a retail store.[8] The clerk enters customer measurements, color choice, and other specs into a computer. In three minutes a computer-aided design routine produces a customized blueprint at the factory, where assemblers build the bike from standard frames, sprockets, and other components.

Customer-run greeting card machines follow much the same formula. A large variety of customer choices are possible from a few standardized components (plain card, envelope, and inks). According to Edward Fruchtenbaum, American Greetings Corp. president, the CreataCard machine is the "ultimate combination of just-in-time manufacturing and micro-marketing."[9]

Standardization and globalization.   Taken in conjunction with guideline 2 (minimize operations), this guideline has strategic implications. As goods and services are designed with fewer, more standardized operations, costs go down and quality becomes more dependable. In turn, this increases their appeal, sometimes to the point where people around the globe know about and want the item—be it a Big Mac or an American Express card.

More broadly, three trends seem to be interrelated: (1) better designed services (based on these design guidelines) and (2) widespread lowering of political and trade barriers create (3) markets of awesome size. One result is that companies with hot services may be able to prosper through rapid global expansion.

Operability Guidelines

Guidelines 6 through 10 focus on operability—avoiding difficulties in frontline operations.

6. Multifunctional/multiuse service elements and modules. The do-it-yourself industry is alive and thriving. Buy some plumbing modules, shelving components, or mix-and-match clothing, and combine to taste. Good design in accordance with this guideline makes it possible.

Insurance companies, investment funds, health care, and other service companies do much the same thing: Design a self-contained service module (e.g., payroll processing) and offer it to companies that seek ways of cutting their own overhead and getting out of service areas beyond their expertise.

7. Ease of coupling/uncoupling. A salesperson with cellular phone and data diskette can go to work on the road, at home, or in the sales office. This design of the sales process permits easy service coupling/uncoupling as the need arises. Increasingly, facilities in hotels, airlines, and restaurants are designed so that sales or other service people can easily plug in and plug out.

8. One-way travel. Who hasn't had to stand in one line for a certain service element, wait in another line for the next element, and then later go back to the first line? Guideline 8 aims at avoiding that kind of backtracking.

9. Avoid service misfits. This guideline avoids special steps, such as requiring a server to leave a client to fetch a file folder or get an approval.

10. Avoid designs requiring extraordinary attentiveness. Tendencies or temptations to take unsafe shortcuts, to be careless with sensitive equipment, to be brusque with customers, to steal, or otherwise misperform are partly avoidable by using designs that make such tendencies difficult.

A good approach is to design controls into the process. Examples: process designs that maintain strict segregation of personal and business possessions, clearly labeled locations for all files and materials, easy access to backup help, and safety-guard gates to keep associates from blundering into an unsafe area.

DESIGN REVIEW, PERFORMANCE MEASUREMENT, AND CONTROL

Service design is a loop. The design team critiques and improves the preliminary design, critiques again, improves again, and so on. This continues even after service associates are providing the service to customers. Thorough team-based design, with adherence to the DFSO guidelines, aims at getting the design right in the design phase. Systematic design review by a second team helps, and postdesign measures of design performance effectively bring the loop around.

The design-for-service-operations guidelines, listed in the previous section, serve as a good postdesign control. For example, as a check on use of the second guideline, compare the previous version's number of service operations with that of the new design. For longer-term control, track reductions in number of operations (for a given type of service) on trend charts. Broader measures are needed as well. One is speed to market. Another is first-year costs of returns and resolving complaints. Still another is break-even time: total elapsed time until profits from a new service offset all design and operational costs.

Thus far, our discussion of service design has focused on teams, practices, and controls. A special design issue is *service automation,* which has not always lived up to its potential and sometimes meets human resistance.

PROCESS TECHNOLOGY AND SERVICE AUTOMATION

Service automation is of two kinds. One directly involves delivery of a service to a final consumer. Examples are a take-your-own-photo booth, automatic teller service, credit-card devices embedded in the gas pump, and point-of-sale terminals that wand your purchases and debit your bank accounts. Usually it's not hard to assess the payoff from these kinds of service automation. If you, the consumer, don't like the service, you don't use it. The service firm gets the message fast.

The other kind is back-office automation, once or twice removed from a final customer. In 1961, IBM gave the world its first business computer, the 650. That launched the office automation era, which often has failed to yield attractive rates of return. To be sure, there are plenty of clear successes. For example, banks and stock exchanges simply could not handle their huge transaction volumes without their computer systems. However, some processes, such as doing the company payroll on the computer, often are not clear improvements over manual methods.

The success rate goes way down when we consider the many outright failures. For example, nearly every medium-to-large city has at least once spent several hundred thousand dollars on a system—which later failed—to handle court records, process license applications, track police cases, or handle welfare claims. Businesses have had their share of similar failures.

Office automation's time may finally have come. Process analysis by multifunctional teams—detailed in Chapter 4—is a continuous improvement approach that finally leads to automation if the service warrants it. Another approach, *reengineering,* aims more directly at the ills of process automation.

Reengineering

Michael Hammer, a professor of information systems at MIT, pulled several concepts together and called it reengineering. He explains that "heavy investments in information technology have delivered disappointing results—largely because companies tend to use technology to mechanize old ways of doing business." He offers six principles of reengineering:[10]

1. *Organize around outcomes, not tasks.* An example is the redesign at Mutual Benefit Life, where a case worker now can do the entire process of approving an application for a life insurance policy. No more passing pieces of the approval process from office to office.

2. *Have those who use the output of the process perform the process.* This could take Mutual Benefit one step further: Give the insurance agency office the necessary expertise to meet the client, sell the policy, and also approve it.

3. *Treat geographically dispersed resources as though they were centralized.* Mutual Benefit could apply this principle by linking the agent and the home-office case worker by online computer.

4. *Link parallel activities instead of integrating their results.* Hammer uses the example of "a bank that sells different kinds of credit—loans, letters of credit, asset-based financing—through separate units." Each could separately provide credit to the same client, overcommiting the bank in total. The units need coordination. Communication networks, shared databases, and teleconferencing are ways to do it.

5. *Put the decision point where the work is performed, and build control into the process.* Mutual Benefit Life's case workers now make decisions that supervisors once had to make. The case worker has taken on responsibilities that used to be spread out both horizontally and vertically.

6. *Capture information once and at the source.* An example is point-of-sale (POS) store terminals. POS data, in turn, may be fed into an electronic data interchange (EDI) system. EDI forwards the store data to the supplier, who uses it as authorization to ship and bill the store, and maybe initiate funds transfer.

Principle 8:   Reduce variation before automation.

Though these are commonsense principles, they don't occur to people who are divided into departments by specialty. They may occur naturally, however, if the organization realigns itself by type of service or type of customer. In other words, reversing the usual organizational alignment may be the real essence of reengineering. The service- or customer-focused team sees the whole process. It is well positioned, therefore, to remove nonvalue-adding steps before considering service automation. In fact, eliminating the wasteful steps sometimes does more to improve the service than automation ever could.

The Human Element

You get the illusion of . . . an antitechnological mass movement . . . looming up from apparently nowhere saying, "Stop the technology. Have it somewhere else. Don't have it here."[11]

Between 1945 and 1955, the United States suffered over 43,000 strikes.[12] Canada and England had similar labor strife. Japan, Germany, and other countries whose economies had been reduced to rubble in

World War II had their own problems, including unemployment and politically induced labor agitation by Marxists, anarchists, and other groups.

For most of this century, business people have rallied around a technological solution to the labor problem. Replace labor with machines—in other words, automate. How valid is that rationale today? Consider the following:

Strikes: A relatively minor problem throughout the industrial world today. A *Wall Street Journal* headline bears this out: "Work stoppages fell to near record lows last year."[13]

Human relationships: We are progressing from individualism and functional separation to cross-functional teams and improvement projects.

Militant labor: Transformed into an improvement engine in a growing number of companies.

Labor availability: Where labor is scarce or too costly, instead of automating, a business may find competent lower-cost labor elsewhere in the world. Bangalore, India, for example, has become a mecca for software engineers, who electronically interface with home offices in North America and Europe.

Causes of process variability: Instead of blaming labor, the first reaction today (in superior companies) is to look for poor equipment, instructions, training, information, suppliers, and designs.

Productivity and quality: There is a new awareness of potent ways to simplify, cut wastes, upgrade processes, and improve quality with existing equipment and enlightened teams of associates.

Though these points offer an alternative to a vigorous automation strategy, they by no means close the door. There *is* still a labor problem to which automation can respond. That problem is peoples' inherent variability. It is hard for someone to perform a task correctly and in the right amount of time over and over. But variability of method harms quality, and variability of cycle time (time needed to perform a task) hinders staying on time and dependably serving the customer. A particular automation strategy may or may not be worthwhile. We offer below a few observations to help in making an evaluation. They consist of three axioms with three caveats:

1. *Process improvement* is an essential competitive strategy.
2. Automation is one tactic.
   Caveat 2.1: Automation is expensive. Less-costly ways of improving processes ought to be sought first.

3. Humans' inherent variability makes automation desirable.
   Caveat 3.1: Human variability has its good side, namely, flexibility to react to change.
   Caveat 3.2: People have one attribute that makes them superior to any machine: brainpower. Without brainpower in the workplace, further process improvement would come to a halt.

Justifying Service Automation (and Other Improvement Projects)

Because service automation is costly, raises the break-even point, and often breaks new ground—which is risky—company managers usually want to see careful financial justification. Unfortunately many of the expected benefits—such as better quality and quicker throughput—are hard to describe in financial terms, and the finance committee's reaction may well be negative.

Proponents assert that automation is the only way for a high-wage society to compete and that executives should take it on faith that automation projects should go forward. In some cases, that advice has been followed and the results have been good. However, a number of the boldest service automation projects have failed to recover the investment. Reasons include technical troubles, rigidity (difficult to improve or change), designs based on overly optimistic demand forecasts, and automation of mostly nonvalue-adding wastes.

How can the odds of a successful project, whether automated or not, be improved? Some feel that worthy improvement proposals are failing to meet company investment hurdles—and unworthy ones are surviving—mainly because critical costs and benefits are left out, or are treated in an off-hand manner as intangibles. Consultant Michael O'Guin believes that economic proposal reviews usually fail to accurately account for protection of a company's market position. He presents a more thorough kind of economic justification that incorporates sales and market share, plus an overall weighting factor based on five key customer-perceived quality factors: consistency, lead time, training, rate of product innovation, and sales support. O'Guin's system rolls these vital competitive factors into the firm's traditional return-on-investment formulas.[14]

Chapter Four

Quality Control and Continuous Improvement

 The central mission of total quality management is to infuse a quality imperative into the work lives of every employee. This chapter presents a set of relatively simple yet powerful tools that assist in this task. We will see how associates can identify and eliminate causes of poor quality by focusing on process analysis. Before examining these techniques, however, we need to consider the responsibility issue—that is, who does what?

QUALITY IMPROVEMENT—AT THE SOURCE

A. V. Feigenbaum wrote that the burden of proof for quality rests with frontline operatives, not with inspectors.[1] Businesses have broadened this idea and made it action oriented: The *responsibility* for quality rests with the frontliners. That responsibility extends from involvement in service design teams all the way through the transformation processes.

Actions for Total Quality

What should service associates do to carry out their primary responsibility for quality? Six steps in three parts, which repeat in a circular fashion:

A. *Process design and control.* Build quality into the process:

   1. Design a capable and fail-safe, or error-proof, process. The aim is to create a process that prevents mishap from going forward or even happening at all. A *capable* process is one that can and will meet quality objectives.

   2. If the process has not been made fail-safe, the next best response is self-inspection (which of course introduces chances of human error) and correction. Two steps are necessary:

      a. Give each employee authority to correct a mistake on the spot (e.g., placate an angry customer).

      b. Make every work group responsible for correcting its own errors; avoid passing problems on to a separate rework or complaint group.

B. *Inspection and early warning.* When the process cannot be fully controlled, we're pushed into the poor practice of inspection at a later process. Since delayed detection is costly and damaging, let's not compound the error by allowing long feedback delays as well. Strive for quick and specific feedback on the problem—an early warning system tapping these two error discovery points:

   3. Inspection in a later process in the same organization.

   4. Inspection and use by the final customer.

C. *Process improvement.* Process improvement requires collection and use of data about process problems. This requires:

5. Training supervisors and service associates in how to measure and collect quality data, and how to analyze quality statistics in order to isolate causes.

6. Formally organizing teams that carry out process improvement projects, applying data analysis and problem-solving techniques. Projects aim at making deficient processes capable and fail-safe; so back to step one.

Principles 2 and 15: Dedicate to continual improvement. Involve front-line associates in problem solving.

Time–Quality Connection

Timing is a critical element in the total quality process. Robert Galvin, Motorola's executive committee chairman, says that "one can focus on time and improve quality" and that "one can focus on quality and accomplish time."[2] The following points explain this apparent contradiction:

- *Quicker response.* Improving quality eliminates delays for rework, process adjustments, and placating customers, thus providing quicker response.

- *On-time.* Quality the first time—every time—removes a major cause of delays and unpredictability, thereby improving on-time performance.

- *Quick feedback.* All efforts to cut out delays provide quicker feedback on causes of bad quality, allowing earlier process improvement efforts. To quote from Western Electric's classic handbook on quality control, "It is an axiom in quality control that the time to identify assignable causes is while those causes are active," and further, "delay may mean that the cause of trouble is harder to identify, and in many cases cannot be identified at all."[3] In other words, anything that reduces delays is a powerful technique for process quality improvement.

Principle 10: Make quality easy to achieve.

- *Enough time for quality.* The time saved by removing delays and making quality right must not be squandered. It needs to be reinvested in training, design collaboration, inspection and on-the-spot correction, feedback and consultation with people in earlier and later processes, data collection, and improvement projects. If those activities are neglected, for example, under pressure for more output, quality suffers, and a chain reaction of delays and variations results in *less* output and *slower* response.

Quality as a Specialty

When frontline associates assume primary responsibility for quality, is there still a need for a quality assurance (QA) department? Usually there is, except in very small organizations. However, the quality movement changes the role of that department, probably toward greater professionalism.

The new breed of quality professionals has high-level responsibilities. They lead companywide quality planning, coordinate quality training, arrange for facilitators to assist improvement teams, provide quality consulting, and monitor overall results. Old-style inspection is still needed on a limited basis. For example, the QA professional may spot-check a new service or new supplier. Overall, however, the QA department shrinks in number of employees but grows in prestige and value. But please note that quality analysis no longer belongs to the professionals—everyone needs to learn and use the quality improvement methodology, which we review next.

PROCESS IMPROVEMENT OVERVIEW

The systematic approach to process improvement follows the scientific method. Briefly, the sequence is to find and study a problem, generate and evaluate possible solutions, implement and review the chosen solution, then repeat for a new problem.

The scientific method provides an overall plan of attack. In following the plan, the improvement team makes use of several tools. Some of the common ones are listed in Exhibit 4-1. Two are in the general category. Team building and group interaction tools, with deep roots in the social sciences, have a new home in team-based TQM programs.

The specific process and technology tools relate or apply to a certain work specialty. They might include a computer spreadsheet, stethoscope, accident claim form, or customer satisfaction survey card—anything that helps improve process output.

EXHIBIT 4-1
Tools for Process Improvement

General Tools	Coarse-Grained Tools	Fine-Grained Tools
1. Team-building and group-interaction tools. 2. Specific process/technology tools.	3. Process flowchart.* 4. Check sheet.* 5. Pareto analysis.* 6. Histograms* 7. Fishbone charts.* 8. Fail-safing. 9. Scattergrams.*	10. Run diagram. 11. Process control chart.*

*Sometimes called the seven basic tools of statistical process control (SPC).

Coarse-grained tools are useful for broad planning and analysis and for sifting through data to find promising targets. The fine-grained tools deal with a single quality characteristic; they aim at the process elements most responsible for the behavior of that characteristic.

COARSE-GRAINED ANALYSIS AND IMPROVEMENT

Process improvement often begins with studying work flows and finding promising targets for improvement. Tools for this analysis include process flowcharts, check sheet, histograms, Pareto analysis, fishbone diagrams, fail-safing, and scattergrams.

Process Flowchart

Process flowcharts (also called process maps) pictorially show how people or things move through a series of transformations. Flowchart symbols portray the process step by step. A big O represents a value-adding service operation, while all other symbols stand for non-value-adding activities. The improvement team works on perfecting the value-adding steps; it seeks ways to perform them faster, more accurately, and more consistently. Nonvalue-adding steps, on the other hand, are targets for elimination.

Exhibit 4–2 is a process flowchart that describes a company's travel approval procedure, both before and after improvement. In the improved version, delays, inspections, and unnecessary operations have been eliminated. Occasionally an improvement team can complete its project using the process flowchart as the sole process analysis tool. More often, the flowchart maps the process for further analysis.

Check Sheets, Pareto Analysis, and Histograms

Process improvement activities thrive on data, especially data collected and maintained close to the process being improved. Most useful are tools that allow quick data collection and tell their story at a glance, which is the case for check sheets and Pareto charts.

Principle 14:   Record process and problem data at the workplace.

Check sheets are the simplest of all—just make a checkmark. Busy employees needn't be delayed, yet they gain valuable process knowledge. We noted one version, the personal quality checklist, in Chapter 2. Exhibit 4–3A is a portion of a check sheet for a mail-order house. A multifunctional improvement team would have held meetings to define commonly occurring mishaps. The sheet (or chalkboard) lists the mishaps, 24 types in this case. When anything goes wrong, an associate judges why and records a tally mark beside that mishap category. For example, mishap 1, "missing data on order form," occurred five times in the week of October 5–9.

Periodically—perhaps once a week—someone counts the mishaps. A good place to record the counts is on a Pareto chart, which is a form of bar chart with the bars arranged highest to lowest. Each bar stands for one of the mishap categories, and the bar's height equals the frequency count. Thus, the Pareto chart prioritizes each successive improvement project.

We see in Exhibit 4–3B that mishap 10, "truck delivery failure," is first in line for improvement. The process improvers will want to focus first on that problem and save the others for later rounds of improvement.

A histogram combines features of the check sheet and Pareto chart. Like a check sheet, the histogram counts occurrences of each quality characteristic. But instead of check marks, the counts plot as bars; it's like a Pareto chart, except the bars are not arranged in descending order.

Pareto analysis often precedes—and feeds a problem to—fishbone analysis, our next topic.

EXHIBIT 4–2
Flowchart: Travel Authorization Process

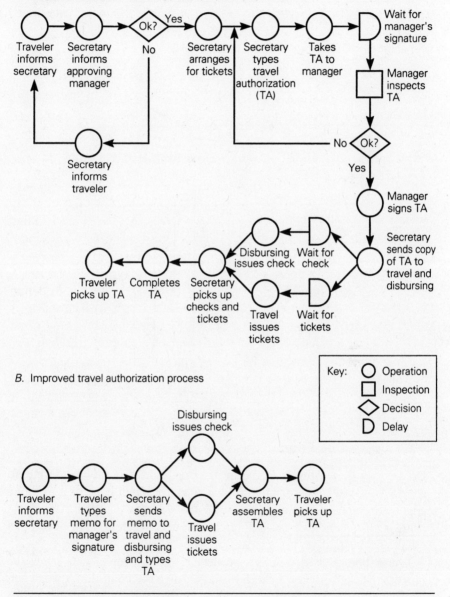

A. Original travel authorization approval/preparation process

Traveler informs secretary → Secretary informs approving manager → Ok? → Yes → Secretary arranges for tickets → Secretary types travel authorization (TA) → Takes TA to manager → Wait for manager's signature

Ok? → No → Secretary informs traveler

Manager inspects TA → Ok? → No / Yes → Manager signs TA → Secretary sends copy of TA to travel and disbursing

Disbursing issues check → Wait for check → Secretary picks up checks and tickets → Completes TA → Traveler picks up TA

Travel issues tickets → Wait for tickets

B. Improved travel authorization process

Traveler informs secretary → Traveler types memo for manager's signature → Secretary sends memo to travel and disbursing and types TA → Disbursing issues check / Travel issues tickets → Secretary assembles TA → Traveler picks up TA

Key:
○ Operation
□ Inspection
◇ Decision
D Delay

Source: Adapted from Dennis C. Kinlaw, *Continuous Improvement and Measurement for Total Quality* (Homewood, IL: Business One Irwin, 1992), pp. 214–15.

EXHIBIT 4–3
Check Sheet and Pareto Chart

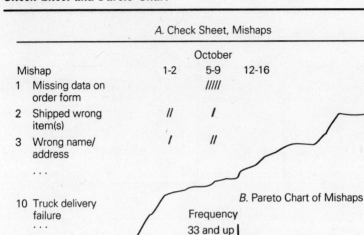

A. Check Sheet, Mishaps

Mishap	October 1-2	5-9	12-16	Remarks
1 Missing data on order form		/////		
2 Shipped wrong item(s)	//	/		
3 Wrong name/ address	/	//		
. . .				
10 Truck delivery failure				
. . .				
24 . . .				
. . .				

B. Pareto Chart of Mishaps

Frequency

| 33 and up |
| 29 – 32 |
| 25 – 28 |
| 21 – 24 |
| 17 – 20 |
| 13 – 16 |
| 9 – 12 |
| 5 – 8 |
| 1 – 4 |
| 0 |

Mishap Category: 10 6 5 11 20 15 3 . . .

Fishbone Chart

Delivery to the customer is the most error-prone process on the Pareto chart. Thus, truck delivery failure becomes the spinal bone of a *fishbone chart,* so named because it looks like the skeleton of a fish. (Fishbone chart is also called a cause-and-effect diagram, where a main bone is an effect and a sub-bone is a cause.)

The fishbone chart must be produced by the people who know the process: trucker, packer, material handler, material controller, dispatcher, and supervisor. The team brainstorms backwards from the target for

EXHIBIT 4–4
Fishbone Chart—Truck Delivery Failures

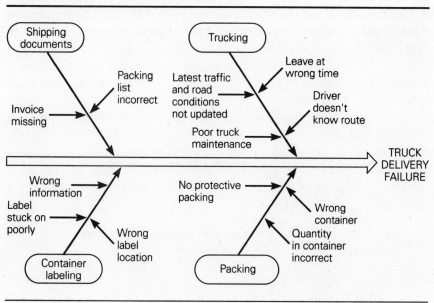

improvement (truck delivery failures). It treats that problem as an effect, then identifies its probable causes and continues down through the "bone structure" until the most likely root causes appear as extremity bones on the chart.

Exhibit 4–4 is the full fishbone chart, as the shipping-area team might develop it. The main causes are deficiencies in trucking, packing, shipping documents, and container labeling. Each main cause is influenced by secondary causes. For example, trucking failure has four secondary factors, shown as small bones: rush-hour traffic and bad road conditions, poor truck maintenance, wrong departure time, and driver's failure to learn the route.

The team might post the chart in the shipping area and begin thinking about the root causes. Sometimes the mere presence of the chart (if done in enough detail) stimulates ideas for fixing root causes. At other times the improvement team elects to conduct further analysis—perhaps another round of Pareto analysis and fishbone charts at a more detailed level.

What happens when the team feels that the chart breakdown is fine enough? Perhaps 50 or 100 detailed end-points (possible root causes) demand attention. The vast majority, however, will not require extensive data collection and fine-grained analysis. Rather, a simple change in procedure, equipment, materials, or design is usually the answer. For example, to ensure correct label placement, the packer decides to use a template that makes a window for the label at a measured distance from two corners of the box.

Consider, also, the sub-bone "quantity in container incorrect." If team members have been well trained, they will know about a solution that many other companies have adopted for getting the right quantity into a container: egg-crate-like partitions inside the container, serving as a simple, visual control that makes it difficult not to pack the correct quantity.

Principle 10:   Make it easier to make goods without error
or variation.

Fail-Safing

We have just seen two simple examples of fail-safing: a template to assist in labeling and egg-crate dividers so packers always fill the box correctly.

Fail-safing is a realistic view of people, processes, and mishaps. It acknowledges that people need to be protected from their natural inclinations to vary. To illustrate, if the packing crew had been trained in the fail-safing concept, they might have held a process improvement session to discuss the truck delivery failure.

First packer:
Anybody is going to put the label on wrong or put the wrong quantity in the container once in a while. This process is an error waiting to happen!
Second packer:
Yeah. Let's find a way to fail-safe it. Otherwise, people will blame us, instead of the poor process design.

This is an excellent attitude. If people are unaware that processes should and can be fail-safed, their tendency is to hide the error when it occurs to avoid the possibility of blame.

Unlike other tools of improvement, fail-safing does not depend heavily on process data. Rather, it is a mind-set that can help direct people, positively, toward fixing a process. It is best applied at the root-cause level of analysis—for example, a third- or fourth-level sub-bone of a fishbone chart.

Scatter (Correlation) Diagram

A *scatter diagram*—or *scattergram*—is useful for plotting what happens in an experiment. For example, a team of window washers may wonder how quickly window cleaner should be wiped off after spraying it on. The experimenter notes how long it takes to clean a window pane when the spray is left on for 2 seconds, then does it again for 4 seconds, 6, 8, and so forth. The spray-wipe interval is plotted on the X-axis and clean time on the Y-axis of an X–Y chart. If the pattern of plotted points rises to the right, it indicates that longer spray-wipe intervals require more wiping. That would suggest the best method is spraying and wiping one small patch at a time. Other plot patterns would tell different stories.

These examples illustrate the value of the seven coarse-grained process analysis tools. Most of the time, this analysis yields an acceptable answer to the team's problem. When it doesn't, it is at least likely to point the way to further study using fine-grained tools.

FINE-GRAINED ANALYSIS AND IMPROVEMENT

Exhibit 4–1 lists two tools that give improvement teams a closer look the behavior of specific quality characteristics: run diagram and control chart.

Run Diagram

Consider a patient hooked up to an electroencephalograph. Brain waves emerge on a running roll of paper. This is a run diagram. A run diagram plots points continuously or at each successive instance. The analyst or improvement team studies the variation and trend and draws conclusions. To help with the interpretations, the run diagram may include upper and lower limits. For example, a company offering a "two-hour" sightseeing tour might set and publicize specification limits of 130 minutes and 110 minutes. These upper and lower spec limits allow for variable traffic and other conditions. Operation beyond those limits, however, can become too costly to the company and unacceptable to sightseeing clientele.

Process Control Chart

Whereas the run diagram plots every running point (e.g., every sightseeing tour's duration), the process control chart just plots samples from the process (perhaps using four tours from each day's schedule). Also, it isn't a control chart unless it has a center line and upper and lower control limits. The center line is at the average; here, the average sightseeing tour duration. Control limits are statistically set based on the variation of the process, as recorded over a test period; control limit lines usually go at three standard deviations (of the sampling distribution) above and below the center line. Thus, while 130 and 110 minutes might define limits of acceptable service performance, control limits for a certain test period might be narrower or wider than that. Specification limits show preference; control limits show actual variation.

Most quality experts, notably Dr. Deming, hold the process control chart in high esteem. As total quality management takes root in ever more kinds of enterprise, new ways of using process control charts follow. For example, the transitional care unit at Northwest Hospital in Seattle now has a control chart in every patient's record (this is probably a first in the field of medicine). Daniel Sloan, author and consultant largely responsible for the hospital's adoption of control charts, has this to say about it:

> Traditionally, a doctor comes onto the floor and asks "how's my patient doing." And the nurse says "pretty good" or "not very good" and proceeds to tell a story about the patient. [Now] at Northwest, the nurse might say, "Well, the correlation analysis we've done on these clinical measurements indicates a possible relationship of the following—blank, blank, and blank.... Additionally, we've done a time series analysis on the control chart, and the pattern of variation would suggest blank, blank, and blank about the process. What do you think, doctor?" ...
>
> Physicians respond well to this higher level of professionalism and better information from the staff.[4]

Control charts are of two general types: One type is for *variables* data. It tracks a quality characteristic that varies continuously and thus requires a measurement or reading. Examples are everywhere in services—patient vital signs and blood chemistry in medicine, financial ratios in banking and investment services, and response times or duration times in most services. The second type of control charts is for *attributes* data. It tracks a factor that is simply counted, such as number of dishes broken in the cafeteria. Control of a variable usually requires a pair of control charts, a measures chart and a range chart (formally known as $\overline{X}$—pronounced *X-bar*—and *R* charts). Sample averages go on the measures chart, and the range (high value minus the low value) within each sample goes on the range chart.

The control chart procedure is basically the same for both variable and attribute control charts. In view of the importance of process control charting, we'll review the basic procedure with two examples. The examples also demonstrate two different kinds of attribute charts, which are simpler than $\overline{X}$ and *R* charts.

EXAMPLE 4–1 *p* Chart—Bills of Lading at P*I*E Nationwide[5]

The first use of process improvement tools at P*I*E Nationwide, fourth largest trucking company in the United States, was for billing errors. In bringing the billing process into statistical control, a P*I*E improvement team was able to eliminate all inspectors and cut the error rate from 10 percent to 0.8 percent in one year.

In the spirit of continual improvement, the team's next step was to use process control charting to track the proportion, *p,* of defective bills per day. That attribute, a defective bill, was defined as one having any type of error.

Phase 1: The first step with a *p* chart, as with any process control chart, is to make some decisions. The team decides on a sample size *(n)* of 50, to be taken every day for 20 days. The collected data are summarized below.

Day	Defective Bills	Proportion Defective	Day	Defective Bills	Proportion Defective
1	25	0.50	11	30	0.60
2	22	0.44	12	32	0.64
3	33	0.66	13	35	0.70
4	25	0.50	14	33	0.66
5	37	0.74	15	30	0.60
6	25	0.50	16	30	0.60
7	35	0.70	17	35	0.70
8	33	0.66	18	40	0.80
9	35	0.70	19	35	0.70
10	35	0.70	20	25	0.50
				Total 630	

Phase 2: Next, a team member calculates the chart center line $(\overline{p})$ and control limits $\pm\, 3\sigma$ from the center line. Since the p chart plots proportion defective, there are only two values for the attribute: good or bad (defective or nondefective). Thus, the binomial (two numbers) distribution applies. Sigma (σ) in the binomial distribution is:

$$\sigma = \sqrt{\frac{\overline{p}(1 - \overline{p})}{n}}$$

where

$\overline{p}$ = Average (mean) fraction defective (or percent defective)
n = Number in each sample

Therefore, the control limits, at 3σ from the center line, $\overline{p}$, are:
Upper control limit (UCL):

$$UCL = \overline{p} + 3\sqrt{\frac{\overline{p}(1 - \overline{p})}{n}}$$

Lower control limit (LCL):

$$LCL = \overline{p} - 3\sqrt{\frac{\overline{p}(1 - \overline{p})}{n}}$$

The average fraction defective, $\overline{p}$, *is total defectives divided by total items inspected, where total items inspected equals number of samples, k, times sample size, n:*

$$\overline{p} = \frac{\text{Total defectives found}}{kn}$$

Since 630 defectives were found in 20 samples of 50 bills,

$$\overline{p} = \frac{630}{(20)(50)} = 0.63$$

The control limits are:

$$UCL = \overline{p} + 3\sqrt{\frac{\overline{p}(1 - \overline{p})}{n}}$$

$$= 0.63 + 3\sqrt{\frac{(0.63)(0.37)}{50}}$$

EXHIBIT 4–5
Chart of Proportion of Defective Bills per Day

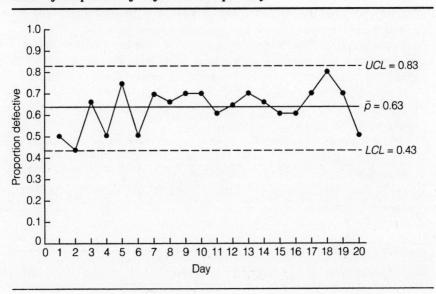

$$= \ 0.63 \ + \ 0.20 \ = \ 0.83$$
$$LCL \ = \ 0.63 \ - \ 0.20 \ = \ 0.43$$

Phase 3: The team member plots the points back on the chart. Exhibit 4–5 shows the resulting *p* chart. All points are within the control limits and show no startling patterns. If the process were out of control, bill processing associates would undertake a search for a special cause. For example, they might find an incomplete address for a major customer in computer memory. An address correction could reduce errors on days when that customer places several orders, or an associate may trace a pricing error back to a previous process, such as in sales.

Phase 4: Associates use the charts daily, watching them for an out-of-control condition that requires investigation and action. Meanwhile, the team employs other tools of process improvement in keeping up the attack on causes of defective bills and process variation. (With the aid of fishbone charting and Pareto analysis, the actual P*I*E team found "that 77% of the errors could be corrected by drivers during pickup and that only 23% were actual billing errors. The original error rate of 63% fell in less than a month to [below] 20% and was approaching 8%.")[6]

EXAMPLE 4-2 *c* Chart—Hotel Suite Inspection

A luxury hotel has five suites for visiting dignitaries and other VIPs. As part of a TQM program, the housekeeping supervisor has implemented daily inspection of those five suites immediately after housekeeping duties are performed. Housekeeping associates alternate inspection duties and record any deviation from established standards of excellence (a ruffled towel, wilting flowers, unstocked bar and refrigerator, etc.) as a defect. Daily the inspector records on a control chart the number of defects (*c*) found during the five-suite inspection.

Phase 1: As always, decisions about data collection are mostly defined by the circumstances. In this case, suites may be cleaned only at the guests' convenience, and the inspector must follow shortly thereafter. Defect totals apply to the entire five-suite inspection; those totals for a 26-day period are as follows.

Day	Defects	Day	Defects	Day	Defects
1	2	10	4	19	1
2	0	11	2	20	1
3	3	12	1	21	2
4	1	13	2	22	1
5	2	14	3	23	0
6	3	15	1	24	3
7	1	16	3	25	0
8	0	17	2	26	1
9	0	18	0		Total 39

Phase 2: Calculate center line and control limits. The center line ($\bar{c}$) is the sum of the defects found divided by the number of inspections (*k*, which should be at least 25). Here:

$$\bar{c} = \frac{\Sigma c}{k} = \frac{39}{26} = 1.50$$

To get control limits, the supervisor needs to know the standard deviation. Since the basis for the *c* chart is the Poisson statistical distribution, rather than the binomial or normal, the formula for the standard deviation (σ) is very simple:

$$\sigma = \sqrt{\bar{c}}$$

Thus the 3σ control limits are:

$$UCL = \bar{c} + 3\sqrt{\bar{c}}$$
$$= 1.50 + 3(1.22)$$
$$= 5.16$$
$$LCL = \bar{c} - 3\sqrt{\bar{c}}$$
$$= -2.16, \text{ or } 0$$

(There cannot be a negative control limit on attribute control charts.)

Next, the housekeepers construct the process control chart (in much the same fashion as would be used with a p chart). They draw the center line and control limits and plot the 26 data points. The process is within limits and shows no unusual pattern, so the group concludes that the process is in control. The housekeeping supervisor and the staff, however, aren't satisfied with control; they want perfection.

Phase 3: Process improvement efforts continue. The group's ideas might include checklists to avoid forgetting, a closer supplier of freshly cut flowers (maybe just outside the hotel's front door), and prestocked bar and refrigerator shelves that are inserted each day and refilled at night.

VARIATION STACKUP—RATIONALE FOR CONTINUOUS IMPROVEMENT

The never-ending mission in TQM is continuous improvement. But what if the customer never complains and keeps coming back smiling? What if the premises always meet cleanliness standards, the food is always fresh and tasty, and the truck always arrives within allowable time limits?

Continuous improvement is still necessary, for two reasons:

1. In each of the cases just cited, the quality is within acceptable limits *for that particular process.* But a process doesn't stand alone. It interacts with other processes. The acceptable limits allow a range of variability, and that variability interacting with variability at a related process will sometimes yield a bad result. Interacting process-to-process variation is what we call *variation stackup.* The accompanying box contains an example.

2. Quality is on an incline. What a customer finds acceptable today may not measure up tomorrow. Rising expectations breed more of the same. Moreover, as more service organizations embrace TQM, the slope of the quality incline increases. The rate of continuous improvement must exceed (*a*) the rate of rising expectations and (*b*) competitors' rates of improvement.

In Part Two we've established quality—in planning, design, and operations—as the foundation for *synchroservice*. Part III, in five chapters, targets the usually misaligned elements of service demand management with the aim of synchronized service delivery.

Variation Stackup

Isn't meeting specifications enough? Not really. Output that meets specs may be unsatisfactory when the customer has to put it to use with other outputs. Variation stackup occurs when two or more outputs that must be used jointly each lie at the extremes of their spec limits.

Consider a municipal bus system's specifications:

- Commuters (riders): Get to bus stop up to five minutes before scheduled departure.
- Bus arrival time: Arrive at each stop no more than five minutes behind schedule.

If the commuter is five minutes early and the bus is five minutes late—which "happens all too often," according to commuters—it's bad service. Just-in-time commuter plus early-departing bus? "Those @#&$%* buses!!!"

The best cure for these and other variation stackup problems is reduction of process variability. Put enough slack in the bus schedule so that buses are rarely late and set a rule that a bus may never leave a stop early. Northwest Airlines did exactly that in 1991 and went from being chronically late to having the best on-time performance of the major airlines operating in the United States.

P A R T

III

PLANNING FOR SERVICE DEMAND

Service demands enter the organization in assorted forms, some less specific than others. *Synchroservice* requires the organization's planners to sort out these demands and restate them as internal services or service orders so that they can be executed without confusion or error. The five chapters of Part III detail the steps necessary for demand sorting and service planning.

Chapter 5 examines overall service demand management and specific demand forecasting techniques, and Chapter 6 addresses master planning to set overall capacity and service output levels. Chapter 7 describes how orders should flow under careful control through the system, from order entry to delivery. Chapters 8 and 9 explain the many details of buying and managing purchased services, supplies, and for-sale materials.

Chapter Five

Demand Management and Forecasting

Service Sequence
Demand Forecasting
  Purposes of Demand Forecasts
  Forecast Error
Forecasting Techniques
  Mean and Trend
  Seasonal
  Patternless Projection by Moving Average
  Associative Projection by Leading Indicator

 Demand is the lifeblood of any enterprise and it deserves good management. A customer-oriented approach to demand management and forecasting requires long-range vision as well as focus, and it includes:

- Planning for demand (developing readiness and flexibility).
- Recognizing all sources of demand.
- Processing demand.

Success in these and supporting activities is a shared demand management responsibility that includes the total service sequence. We examine that sequence next and complete the chapter with a close look at demand forecasting.

Demand Management at Sea-Tac Airport

The governing council for Sea-Tac Airport (Seattle-Tacoma area) has approved a plan to evaluate demand management strategies. The plan includes assessment of "increasing landing fees during peak travel times, ... use of more efficient aircraft sizes and types for the number of existing passengers, [and] increased use of Stage 3 [quieter] aircraft. ... 'Until a decision is made on adding physical capacity, demand management has to be a part of what happens,' " said Port Commissioner Paige Miller.

Source: *Sea-Tac Forum*, July 1993, p. 1.

SERVICE SEQUENCE

When things go well, operations is able to keep up with customer demand. To keep things going well, associates must play an active role in monitoring customer activities and being prepared. In most cases it is poor policy for a company to go for maximum customer traffic if that traffic just ends up in backlogs and waiting lines. Instead, the planning team needs to devise a responsive customer- and order-processing system. In this section, we discuss the service sequence, which is sometimes by appointment and sometimes immediate and may or may not require purchasing.

Exhibit 5–1 details common elements in the service sequence. In compressed form the demand or sale, order entry, and service delivery occur all at once—1 to 2 to 7 in the exhibit. When the service is booked in advance, the service sequence is longer, involving checking the appointment book (3), making the order promise (4), and finally delivering the service (7). A still longer sequence includes planning for (5) and buying (6) needed supplies (e.g., blood for a surgery) or materials (e.g., for a mail-order sale).

Sometimes a service process consists of several subprocesses. In that case, parts of the service sequence repeat a few times. Consider, for example, a medical clinic. You, the patient, are an order. When you go to X-ray, the technician assigns an X-ray order number. When you go to the lab, lab people create several lab orders. After more stops, you are finished, and there will be a billing order (or invoice) with its own

EXHIBIT 5–1
The Service Sequence

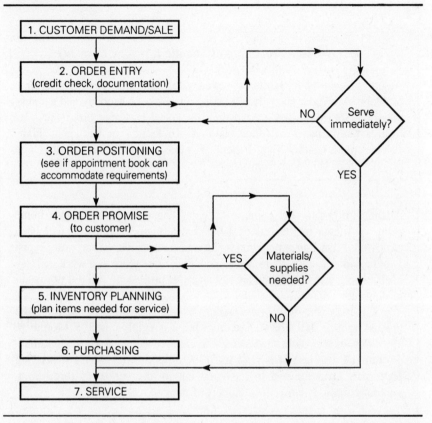

number for total services rendered. Thus, the question, "Where's the customer?" or "Where's the order?" does not always have an easy response; the answer is in a chain of several service steps.

Some organizations make hard work of the service sequence by stretching it out and failing to be ready for customers or orders. Departmental walls chop up the sequence and hinder unified preparation. Superior firms, however, rely on team-based service planning that combines or avoids certain steps. (See the box, "Speedy Order Processing at Atlantic Envelope Company.") And to avoid surprises, they *plan* for demand; that is, they forecast.

Principle 2: Dedicate to continual, rapid improvement in quality, cost, lead time, flexibility, and service.

Speedy Order Processing at Atlantic Envelope Company

Atlantic Envelope Company's seven sites had the same back-office problem: slow order entry. It was taking a week or so (nobody had actually measured it) from when salespeople booked a customer order (such as from a retail chain, an office supplies wholesaler, or perhaps a high-volume mail handler like Federal Express) to the start of envelope production or shipment from stock.

Stage 1, 1990
Atlantic's effort to streamline order entry began at the company's home plant in Atlanta in the fall of 1990. Earlier, office partitions had been removed so that four order-processing associates (order editor, order typist 1, order typist 2, and order checker) could operate more as a work cell. By itself, working in a common area as an order processing cell did not result in noticeable changes.

As a base line for improvement, it was necessary to measure the processing time. It averaged five days, but was highly unstable. Moreover, all orders, except those designated for special routing, were treated alike. No rational priority system existed. One quick result: Merely measuring processing time resulted in its being cut to an average of three days, without conscious efforts on the part of the cell associates.

Stage 2, 1992
Then the team went to work. By fall 1992, they had cut average processing time from five days to about eight hours (and reduced their team from four to three associates). They made the following primary improvements.

- An order-entry associate screens incoming orders and puts them into color-coded folders: one color for standard manufacturing orders, a second for rush orders, a third for "jet" orders (overprinting on existing envelope stock using a jet printer), and a fourth for orders filled through purchasing from another Atlantic plant or an outside printer. Color-coding sets the stage for separate, focused treatment of each type of order.

- Jet orders, for example, are processed by a jet coordinator (a new position), who is able to get a sample to the art and composition department in about an hour (formerly it took one day). She determines which jet press to use, assigns the completion date, and returns the jet

---

Speedy Order Processing (*continued*)

order to the order-entry cell for final processing (price, commissions, etc.) and forwarding to the jet press department. Jet orders are now processed in 5 days (15 days formerly).

- Large, split-lot orders and stock replenishment orders, both involving inventory actions, go directly to the inventory planner for more specialized handling.

- Order-entry associates now hold regular order review meetings with raw materials and scheduling people; these meetings resolve order-processing problems faster and reduce errors.

- Order entry now sends incorrect and incomplete orders to sales service associates, who are better able to take corrective action with sales people and customers.

- Associates are becoming cross-trained, which allows people to help at another order-processing desk and across department lines, as needed to handle surges in certain types of orders.

In the spirit of continuous improvement, further innovations are being considered. At the same time, Atlantic's other sites are involved in their own order-entry streamlining, mostly by adapting the Atlanta system.

DEMAND FORECASTING

Every service manager forecasts demand. The forecast ranges from a vague idea, based on experience, that "tomorrow will be like today" to computer routines that statistically project from demand history. The best forecasts make use of experience and demand history, plus close connections with present and potential customers. Our discussion of the subject begins with the general—purposes and accuracy—and it proceeds to details on some of the common forecasting techniques.

Purposes of Demand Forecasts

The obvious purpose of demand forecasting is to project final customer activity: sales for the profit-making firm, and client contact hours in public services. That short-term forecast is the basis for planning hours of operation and the scheduling of service associates. Medium- and long-term forecasts are also necessary. A medium-term forecast translates into planning staff (e.g., hiring) and acquiring supplies and materials, and a long-term forecast projects needs for facilities (e.g., sites, buildings, and furnishings).

Since the workloads of the support departments do not necessarily rise and fall with whole-company demand patterns, each support service needs to do its own demand forecasting. Example 5–1 illustrates why.

EXAMPLE 5–1 Apex Bus and Limo Charters

O. R. Guy is the new president of Apex. One of his first acts is to create the department of management science and assign corporate forecasting to it. Corporate forecasting applies to the firm's revenue-earning services: its charter bus rentals.

Management science department analysts arrive at a forecast of a 10 percent increase in total bus charter sales for next year. Mr. Guy informs key department heads that they may consider 10 percent increases their targets for planning departmental budgets. Mr. Guy hears the following protests at the next department head meeting:

Engineering chief: O. R., I hate to protest any budget increase. But I'd rather wait until I need it. The engineering workload often goes down when bus charters go up. That's because marketing pressures us less for new bus cabin customization designs when sales are good. But then, in some years of good sales, we have a lot of new design and design modification work. This happens when several bus interiors are in the decline phase of their life cycles. So you can see that our budget should not depend strictly on corporate sales.

Director of human resources: We are the same way, O. R. The personnel workload depends more on things like whether the labor contract is up for renewal. Sure, we need to do more interviewing and training when corporate sales go up. But we have bigger problems when they go down. Layoffs and reassignments are tougher. Also, when sales go down, we may get more grievances.

Marketing chief: Well, I hate to be the crybaby. But it's marketing that bears most of the load in meeting that 10 percent forecast sales increase. I was going to ask for a 20 percent budget increase—mainly for a stepped-up advertising campaign. I don't dispute the management science projection of a 10 percent sales increase. The market is there; we just need to spend more to tap it.

Based on those three comments, Mr. Guy rescinds his note about a 10 percent targeted budget increase. He then informs managers at all levels that they are expected to formally forecast their key workloads. That becomes the basis for their plans and budgets. A management science associate advises those managers requesting help.

To explain what is meant by key workloads, Mr. Guy provides each manager with a simple forecasting plan developed by the director of human resources:

Workloads	Forecast Basis
1. Hiring/interviewing.	Number of job openings is based on data from other departments. Number of job applicants is based on trend projection and judgment.
2. Layoffs and reassignments.	Number of employees is based on data from other departments.
3. Grievances.	The number of stage 1, 2, and 3 grievances, estimated separately, is based on trend projection and judgment.
4. Training.	The number of classroom hours, and the number of on-the-job training hours; both are based on data from other departments.
5. Payroll actions.	Number of payroll actions is based on number of employees and judgment on impact of major changes.
6. Union contract negotiations.	Number of key issues is based on judgment.
7. Miscellaneous—all other workloads.	Not forecast in units; instead, resource needs are estimated directly based on trends and judgment.

Eventually Mr. Guy may want to amend his direction on forecasting. He doesn't need to know how they do the forecast; what is more important is forecast accuracy, which he may ask them to track. Following the same logic, we'll look at forecast accuracy, usually stated as forecast error, before considering demand forecasting techniques.

Forecast Error

There are several popular ways of measuring forecast error. All, however, are after the fact; that is, a manager must wait one period (sometimes longer) to unearth the error in the forecast.

Forecast error for a specific item in a given time period is:

$$E_t = D_t - F_t$$

where

E_t = Error for period t

D_t = Actual demand that occurred in period t

F_t = Forecast for period t

The period t depends on the purpose of the forecast. It might be a year for forecasting demand for a new facility (e.g., new motel units), or it might be 15 minutes for a hot prepared fast food (e.g., a hamburger). There is little value in knowing the error for just one period. Average error over several periods, however, indicates the validity of the forecasting method.

Mean absolute deviation. Among the ways of calculating average error, one of the simplest and widest used is the mean absolute deviation (MAD). The MAD is the sum of the absolute values of the errors divided by the number of forecast periods; that is:

$$MAD = \frac{\Sigma |Et|}{n}$$

where n is number of periods.

Example 5-2 shows the calculation of the MAD for eight business days in a small service firm.

EXAMPLE 5-2 Forecast Error—Résumés-a-Glow, Ltd.

Kathy and Kyle have just opened their new business, a résumé preparation service. As part of their business plan, needed to secure start-up financing, they forecast a level daily demand of 10 customers. After the first eight days of business, they evaluated the wisdom of the level forecast. Exhibit 5-2 shows the demand pattern and the error. The table below shows the day, actual demand (number of customers), and forecast in the first three columns. In column 1, -8 is the first business day, -7 is the next, and so on through the eighth business day.

Error, in column 4, is column 2 minus column 3, and column 5 is the absolute value (ignore the minus signs) of column 4. The sum of column 5 provides the working figure needed in the formula:

$$MAD = \frac{\Sigma |Et|}{n} = \frac{16}{8} = 2.0$$

EXHIBIT 5–2
Demand and Forecast Plot—Résumés-a-Glow, Ltd.

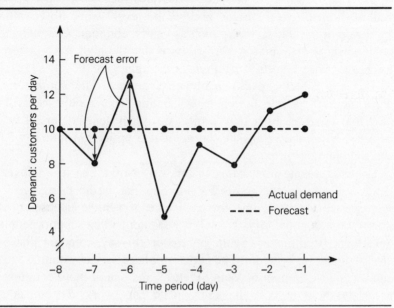

(1) *Period* *(Day)* *(t)*	*(2)* *Demand* *(Customers)* *(D_t)*	*(3)* *Forecast* *(Customers)* *(F_t)*	*(4)* *Error* *(E_t)*	*(5)* *Absolute* *Error* *$|E_t|$*
−8	10	10	0	0
−7	8	10	−2	2
−6	13	10	3	3
−5	5	10	−5	5
−4	9	10	−1	1
−3	8	10	−2	2
−2	11	10	1	1
−1	12	10	2	2
		Sum:	−4	16

Is an error of 2.0 too high? If so, does it suggest changing the forecast (e.g., raising it to 11) or the forecasting method? Kathy and Kyle decide to watch closely for another week or two, then decide.

Forecasting specific versus aggregate services. Forecast error is likely to be high for a specific service, such as number of vanity vehicle license plates. Error is less, however, when forecasting the aggregate of several services, such as vanity, common, commercial, and government vehicle plates. The reason is that the high and low forecasts for each service tend to cancel out in the aggregate.

This can effect capacity planning. Example: The human resource department of vehicle licensing is planning labor requirements for the next four quarters. First they project historical demand for all types of licenses. Next, they translate the aggregate projection into labor hours and then number of people.

Using aggregate forecasting in this way works fine if employees are flexible. If not, the method is a sham. Say that the licensing agency has four service counters, one for each type of vehicle license. If vanity plates surge in popularity, that service counter and its support people will need help. If employees at the next counter—say, common plates—are cross-trained, no problem. The common-plates service counter puts up a sign saying "Common or Vanity Plates," and one or more common plate associates help process the vanity-plate paperwork. Service does not degrade, and the aggregate forecast has done its work well.

Rolling forecasts. The method just described works best for forecasting the near future. Any forecasting method deteriorates in accuracy as we look farther into the future. Thus, a forecast should be re-done, or rolled over, at regular intervals. The licensing agency might project aggregate demand and labor requirements for the next four quarters. Then each quarter it drops off the old quarter and adds one more future quarter. The forecast for next quarter is the basis for actual hiring and other personnel actions. The less-reliable forecast for outlying quarters is less for action and more for rough planning.

FORECASTING TECHNIQUES

A good forecast—one with low forecast error—relies on demand records. Larger service firms are likely to have profuse data on past demand. Minimal or no records at all might be the case, however, especially with start-ups, small firms, or smaller departments within organizations.

Where sufficient records don't exist, the manager uses experience to decide what future demand to expect. Inaccuracies in these rough

---

Fashion and Fast-Food Forecasting

Insiders at Limited, Inc. (retail fashion apparel), speak reverently of the "Weiss calendar." Michael Weiss, vice chairman, developed the calendar during his 12-year presidency of Express, Limited's most profitable retail chain. The calendar—really a forecasting aid—pinpoints what stores and what days of the year to run test-marketing of a new garment. The method is highly accurate in predicting success for the garment across the entire chain. The calendar also "marks optimum dates for ordering fabric, beginning production, and starting markdowns."

Source: Teri Agins, "Limited Puts 'Weiss Methodology' to Test," *The Wall Street Journal*, August 9, 1993.

McDonald's ARCH system, "in theory, will enable a store manager to have a customer's food ready when he or she walks through the door. . . . [It] tells the manager how many fries, hamburgers, or cheeseburgers he or she can expect to sell over the next 10 minutes. It indicates how many packages of tartar sauce or Big Mac sauce the manager should have on hand for the day. It recalls the store's history for, say, the four most recent Friday afternoons with regard to Filet-O-Fish sandwiches. Or, if a particular store normally gets a bus load of customers every Friday afternoon at 3 PM, ARCH . . . 'knows' that, too."

Source: Chuck Murray, "Robots Roll from Plant to Kitchen," *Chicago Tribune*, October 17, 1993, section 7, p. 3.

---

forecasts could result in idle resources at some times and failure to meet demand at others—the twin risks. Recordkeeping is essential even for small firms. The high rate of failure among small businesses illustrates the danger of misjudging (really, mismanaging) demand.

A reliable forecast must allow for several types of demand variation:

1. Trend, or slope.
2. Seasonal variation (seasonality).
3. Cyclical pattern, usually spanning several years.
4. Random events of two types:
    a. Explained, such as effects of natural disasters or accidents.
    b. Unexplained, for which no *known* cause exists (UFDs: unidentified flying demands).

EXHIBIT 5-3
Arithmetic Mean and Trend Projection—Data Services, Inc.

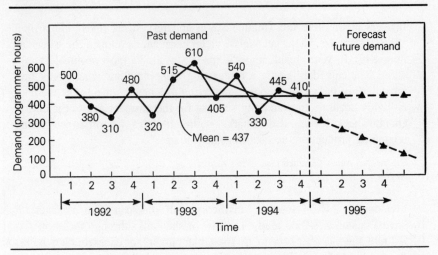

We cannot do much about random events, but trend, seasonality, and cyclicity show up by examining demand history. Forecasting methods are available for each variation pattern. We consider these techniques next, along with a method for the situation when history reveals no apparent pattern of variation.

Mean and Trend

The simplest demand projection uses the arithmetic mean. When historical demand lacks trend and is not seasonal, the simple mean may serve well. More often there is at least some upward or downward trend, which could even be projected as a curve. Exhibit 5-3 illustrates the mean and trend for Data Services, Inc., which offers commercial computer programming.

Three years of past quarterly demand in hours of programmer time are plotted. A first impression might be that there is no strong trend, and a bit of study shows no seasonal pattern either. If a certain quarter's demand is high one year, it looks as likely to be low the next. The up-and-down movement seems random. Also, one would not consider programming to have a seasonal demand pattern. What should the forecast be for upcoming quarters in 1995? Perhaps the mean (which works out to be 437) is the best way to minimize forecast error for such a nondescript demand; see the level dashed line.

EXHIBIT 5–4
Twenty-Quarter Eyeball Trend—Data Services, Inc.

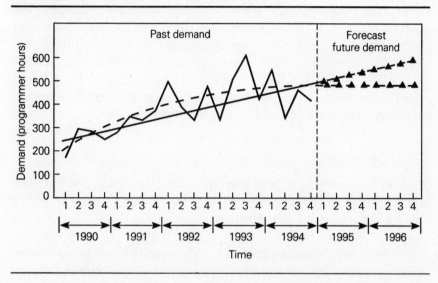

Alternatively, we might look at only the most recent data, say, the last seven quarters. The trend is downward; see the "eyeball" projection (done by eye with a straightedge) slanting downward in Exhibit 5–3. Data Services's analysts may consider the projection to be valid for one or two quarters into 1995. They do not accept it for the longer term since it is trending toward out-of-business status! If they know the business is strong enough to carry on and prosper, the analysts would look for a more realistic way to project the future.

For a better forecast, better demand data might help. Let us assume that 20, not 12, quarters of past demand data are available; see Exhibit 5–4. Quite a different pattern emerges. The long-run trend, projected two years (eight quarters) into the future, is definitely upward. The 1995 quarterly forecasts are now in the range of 500 programmer-hours instead of the 300 to 200 range resulting from the 7-quarter downward trend projection in Exhibit 5–3.

Another interpretation is that the 20-quarter demand data describe a slow curve. The exhibit shows such a curve (dashed line) projected by the eyeball method through 1996. The 1995–96 forecast is now between the two previous straight-line forecasts. This projection is for a leveling off at about 450.

The curving projection looks valid. In other cases, of course, a straight-line projection may look valid. In any event, forecasting teams may use the graphic projection only to sharpen their own judgment. For example, Data Services's people may know something about their customers that leads them to a more optimistic forecast than the projected 450 programmer-hours. As Al Ries and Jack Trout point out, "Trends change very slowly. It's only a fad that is fast-moving."[1] Even where outside information, perhaps about a fad, seems to overrule historical projection, it is worth doing. It is quick and simple.

Seasonal

Often an item showing a trend also has a history of demand seasonality. In fact, perhaps most services exhibit at least some seasonality, which calls for the *seasonal index* method.

Seasonal index: an example. The moving business is seasonal, so let's consider how a mover might make use of seasonal indexes. Exhibit 5–5 shows four years of demand data, in van loads, for Metro Movers, Inc. Since moving companies experience heavy demand surges during summer school vacations, Metro groups its demand history into three-month seasons—summer, fall, winter, and spring.

From the demand graph, summer demand is clearly the highest and fall demand is generally the lowest. (Note: Besides seasonality, there appears to be a slight upward trend over the 16 periods, but we'll ignore that for now.)

Using fall 1991 as an example, we calculate the seasonal index as follows:

1. Find the seasonal average. Fall 1991 is in the middle of a year that includes half of spring 1991, all of summer, fall, and winter 1991, and half of spring 1992. Thus, the seasonal average demand for the year that surrounds fall 1991 is:

$$\frac{(90/2) + 160 + 70 + 120 + (130/2)}{4} = 115 \text{ van loads}$$

2. Find the seasonal index by dividing actual demand by the seasonal average. Since actual demand for fall 1991 is 70, the seasonal index is:

$$\frac{70}{115} = 0.61$$

EXHIBIT 5–5
Seasonal Demand History—Metro Movers

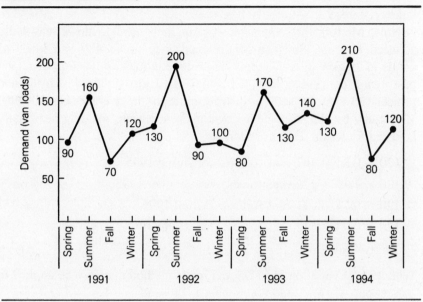

In other words, the fall 1991 demand was only 61 percent of an average season's demand for the surrounding year.

By the same two-step procedure, the four years of demand history yield the following seasonal indexes:

Fall 1991	0.61	Spring 1993	0.70
Winter 1991	0.96	Summer 1993	1.36
Spring 1992	0.98	Fall 1993	0.95
Summer 1992	1.51	Winter 1993	0.95
Fall 1992	0.73	Spring 1994	0.89
Winter 1992	0.88	Summer 1994	1.52

The final step is to reduce the three indexes for each season to a single average value. For the three summer indexes the average is:

$$\frac{1.51 + 1.36 + 1.52}{3} = 1.46$$

The other three average seasonal indexes are: 0.85 for spring, 0.76 for fall, and 0.93 for winter. (These numbers are rounded so that the four indexes sum to 4.0—exactly four seasons.)

Now, Metro's forecasters have what they need to do a seasonally adjusted forecast. Suppose Metro expects to move 480 van loads of goods in 1995, which is simply an arithmetic mean projection of recent past years' demand. It would be foolish to just divide 480 by 4 and project 120 vans per season. Instead, multiply the average-season value, 120 loads, by the seasonal index for each season, yielding seasonally adjusted forecasts. The procedure is:

$120 \times 0.85 = 102$ vans forecast for spring 1995

$120 \times 1.46 = 175$ vans forecast for summer 1995

$120 \times 0.76 = 91$ vans forecast for fall 1995

$120 \times 0.93 = \underline{112}$ vans forecast for winter 1995

Yearly total $= 480$

With a slight variation, the seasonal index method may also be applied to projections when a trend component is present.

Cyclical patterns—natural and induced. Cyclic and seasonal demand patterns are alike, except for the wavelength—the time it takes for the pattern to make a complete cycle. Thus, forecasters can treat seasonality, whether with a standard one-year wavelength or one that recurs, say, every 5, 10, or 15 months, in much the same way. Other tricks of seasonal or cyclic demand management depend somewhat on whether the cause of the pattern is natural or artificial.

Naturally occurring seasons are sometimes accompanied by extraordinary events that affect the magnitude of seasonal peaks. For example, a summer heat wave might raise temperatures from the seasonally normal high 80s to record 100-degree heat and create unusual demand for electricity. Accountants know that every spring is income tax season; newly revised tax laws, however, can further increase the peak demand for their services. In both cases, extra capacity will be needed beyond that associated with the usual seasonal surge. A public accounting firm that saw a 17 percent increase in its tax-related business following the 1986 US tax law change, for instance, plans on an additional 15 to 20 percent demand surge when new changes occur.

Other seasonal patterns are artificial. For example, some firms fall into a pattern of inflating current sales totals—by various means—to meet some sort of goal. Where such artificial demand patterns are a fact of life, seasonal analysis can and should account for them. That should not stop people from attacking the problem directly in an effort to eliminate the causes of spikey demand patterns.

Patternless Projection by Moving Average

Sometimes there is no clear demand pattern. Those cases call for *patternless projection* techniques. The best known are the moving average, to be explained below, and exponential smoothing. The two are similar in result. They project only one period forward. In practice, however, forecasters extend the single-period forecast a few more periods into the future, and roll over the forecast each period.

The *moving average* is simply the mean or average of a given number of the most recent actual demands. Exhibit 5–6 demonstrates the method for our moving company, Metro Movers, except that this time the demand history is in weeks instead of quarters. Demands, in van loads, for the last 16 weeks are in column 2 in the exhibit, where −1 means one week ago, −2 means two weeks ago, and so forth. Column 3 shows three-week moving averages; a sample calculation is at the bottom of the table. The average of weeks −16, −15, and −14 becomes the forecast for the next week, −13.

Since actual demand in week −13 was 11, the forecast error is 11 − 9 = 2. That is a shortage or underestimate of two vans for that week. The moving average for weeks −15, −14, and −13 then becomes the forecast for week −12. The forecast error is 11 − 10.7 = 0.3. The process continues, the average moving (or rolling over) each week, dropping off the oldest week and adding the newest; hence, a moving average.

The three-period moving average forecast results in a forecast error (MAD) of 3.0 vans per week (see calculation at the bottom of Exhibit 5–6). But the choice of three weeks was arbitrary.

Suppose forecasters decide to try a different time span, say, six weeks. Using the same demand data, we find that the MAD becomes 2.4 (calculations not shown). The mean error of 2.4 is better than the previous 3.0 value. They could try other moving average time spans and perhaps further reduce the error. In a larger firm with many services, searching for the best time span is a job for the computer.

EXHIBIT 5-6
Three-Week Moving Average and MAD—Metro Movers

(1) Week	(2) Actual Demand	(3) Forecast Demand (Three- Week Moving Average)	(4) Forecast Error [(2) − (3)]	(5) Sum of Absolute Values of Forecast Errors
−16	6			
−15	8			
−14	13			
−13	11	9.0	2.0	2.0
−12	11	10.7	0.3	2.3
−11	16	11.7	4.3	6.6
−10	11	12.7	−1.7	8.3
−9	8	12.7	−4.7	13.0
−8	7	11.7	−4.7	17.7
−7	15	8.7	6.3	24.0
−6	10	10.0	0.0	24.0
−5	11	10.7	0.3	24.3
−4	5	12.0	−7.0	31.3
−3	9	8.7	0.3	31.6
−2	12	8.3	3.7	35.3
−1	12	8.7	3.3	38.6

Sample calculation for weeks −16, −15, and −14: $\dfrac{6 + 8 + 13}{3} = 9.0$

$MAD = \dfrac{38.6}{13} = 3.0$ vans per week

Moving average time spans generally should be long where demand is rather stable (e.g., groceries) and short for highly changeable demand (e.g., white-water rafting). The time span resulting in the lowest MAD is the best choice for actual use in forecasting future demand. But keep in mind that the forecasters relied on past data. As long as they think the future will be similar to the past, that is fine. If the future will be different, however, there is little point in expending much time analyzing past demand.

Associative Projection by Leading Indicator

In all of the preceding techniques, forecasters track demand over time. Associative projection tracks demand not against time but against some other known variable, perhaps student enrollment or inches of precipitation. The associative techniques are the leading indicator and correlation.

Few service firms are able to discover a variable that changes with demand but leads it, which is the definition of a leading indicator. The reason probably is that demand for a service usually depends on (is led by) a number of variables rather than a single dominant one. The search for such a variable can be costly and futile. Therefore, most of the work with leading indicators has centered on national economic forecasting instead of service demand forecasting. Nevertheless, the leading indicator is a valued predictor in those cases where it can be isolated.

One story about leading indicators has been widely circulated. It is said that the Rothschild family reaped a fortune by getting advance news of Napoleon's defeat at Waterloo. Nathan, the Rothschild brother who lived in England, received the news via carrier pigeon. On that basis he bought depressed war effort securities and sold them at a huge profit after the news reached England.

The leading indicator in this case was news of the war, and it led prices of securities. The Rothschilds's astuteness was not in realizing this, for it was common knowledge; rather, it was in their development of an information network with which to capitalize on that knowledge. A costly information system like that set up by the Rothschilds can provide highly accurate information rapidly. In contrast, personal judgment as a basis for action is cheap but tends to be less accurate and to be hindsight rather than foresight; that is, personal judgment often does not lead events.

In sum, leading indicators should have long lead times as well as accuracy. That requires good information systems. Example 5–3 illustrates.

EXAMPLE 5–3 State Jobs Service and Leading Indicators

Mr. H. Hand, manager of the Metro City office of the State Jobs Service, sees the need for better demand forecasting. The problem has been that surges in clients tend to catch the office off guard. Advance warning of demand is needed in order to plan for staff, desks, phones, forms, and even space.

One element of demand is well known: Many of the job seekers are there as a result of being laid off by Acme Industries, which is by far the largest employer in Metro City. Hand is able to obtain Acme records on layoffs over the past year. He plots the layoff data on a time chart, along with the Jobs Service office's data on job applicants, in Exhibit 5–7. The chart shows the number of job applicants ranging from a high of 145 (period 8) to a low of 45 (period 20). Layoffs at Acme range from a high of 60 (periods 6 and 7) to a low of zero (several periods).

EXHIBIT 5–7
Layoffs at Acme and Job Applications at Jobs Service, with Time Scale

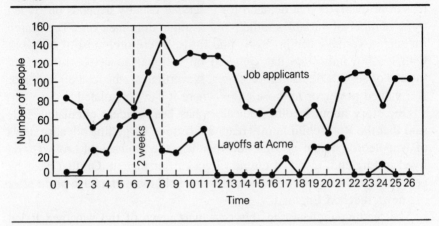

Plotting the points seems well worth the effort because Hand notes a striking similarity in the shapes of the two plots. Further, the layoffs plot seems to lead the applicants plot. For example, the high of 145 applicants occurred two weeks after the high of 60 layoffs and the low of 45 applicants occurred two weeks after layoffs spiked downward to zero. Weeks 1, 3, 17, 21, and 22 are other places on the layoff plot in which a two-week lead appears; the lead is close to two weeks in weeks 11 through 15.

Does a two-week lead make sense, or could it be coincidence? Hand feels that it makes sense. He bases this on the impression that laid-off Acme people tend to live off their severance pay for a time—two weeks time seems reasonable—before actively seeking other jobs. Hand therefore takes the final steps. First, he establishes an information system. This is simply an agreement that every two weeks Acme will release the number of its laid-off employees to the Jobs Service office. Second, he establishes a forecasting procedure based on that layoff information and the two-week lead pattern in Exhibit 5–7.

In setting up a forecasting procedure, Hand regraphs the data from Exhibit 5–7. The new graph, shown in Exhibit 5–8, is a scatter diagram. It plots layoffs at Acme for period $T-2$ and applicants at the Jobs Service for period T as the two axes of the graph. For example, the first point plotted is (0,50), which is taken from Exhibit 5–7, where for period 1 layoffs are 0 and two weeks later applicants are 50. Every other point is plotted in the same way. The points tend to go upward left to right, clustering around the dashed line.

EXHIBIT 5–8
Correlation of Layoffs at Acme (T – 2) with Demand at Jobs Service

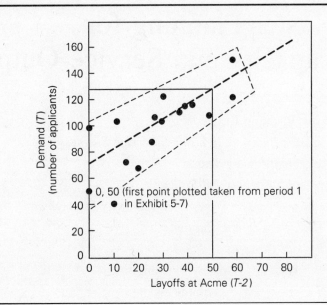

Hand uses the dashed line for forecasting. Suppose, for example, that he learns today that Acme is laying off 50 people this week. In Exhibit 5–8 a solid vertical line extending from 50 to the dashed line and leftward yields a forecast demand of about 125. This tells Hand to plan for 125 applicants in two weeks.

How good is Mr. Hand's leading indicator? By one measure—the supporting information system—it is very good! The layoff data from Acme are cheap to obtain and highly accurate. But in terms of lead time, it is not so good. Two weeks' notice seems insufficient for the purpose of adjusting resources on hand. In terms of validity, the leading indicator looks good. The points in Exhibit 5–8 tend to cluster along the broad, shaded band running upward at about a 30-degree angle. This is the pattern of a positive correlation. While a correlation coefficient could be mathematically found, the visual evidence is convincing enough in this case.

Chapter Six

Master Planning for Capacity and Service Output

Master Planning Basics
   Master Planning in a Small Service Business
   Master Planning Teams
Capacity Strategies and Policies
   Chase-Demand versus Level-Capacity Strategies
   High-Performance Staffing
   Special Capacity Policies
Group (Family) Capacity Planning
Reservations and Appointments

 "How's business?"
    "Great! Demand's up 15 percent! Only problem is, they can't keep up in operations. I've noticed quite a few angry customers."

That reply—to a common question—reflects one side of master planning: strong demand, but inadequate *capacity* to serve it. This means service delays and probable loss of customers to the competition. The other side of master planning, excess capacity and output, raises costs and prices, which can also send customers to the competition.

MASTER PLANNING BASICS

Grappling with capacity options is called *master planning,* and it occurs both broadly and narrowly (see Exhibit 6–1):

- At a broad level, the master planning team balances aggregate customer demand and the capacity to process demand. The result is a capacity plan.

EXHIBIT 6–1
Master Planning

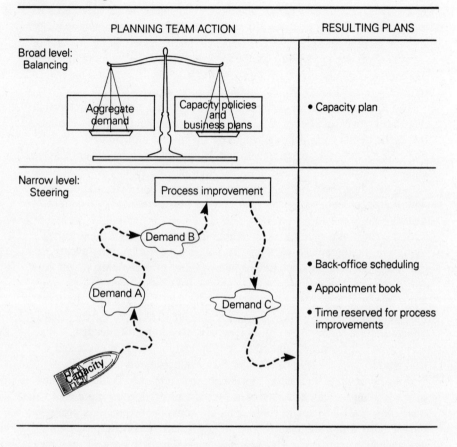

PLANNING TEAM ACTION	RESULTING PLANS
Broad level: Balancing	• Capacity plan
Narrow level: Steering	• Back-office scheduling • Appointment book • Time reserved for process improvements

- Master planning's narrower role includes ensuring capacity to meet short-term commitments and allowing capacity for continuous improvement. The result of this planning is an appointment or reservations book (if applicable); flexible, cross-trained associates; and time in people's schedules for training, improvement projects, housekeeping, and so forth.

Master Planning in a Small Service Business

An example will show how master planning weaves itself into managing even a small service business, Anita's Studio.

EXAMPLE 6-1 Master Planning—Photography Services

Anita's Studio is a professional photography business. Anita specializes in individual and family portraits. She shoots in her own studio and does her own developing and printing. Demand may be expressed as the number of customers or, more precisely, the number of photos. But to Anita, demand has another, equally important meaning: demand for capacity. What capacity does she need to satisfy the demand for her services?

The first capacity item is Anita's time, which includes hours in the studio, developing, packaging, recordkeeping, management, and so forth. Second is the demand for paper, developing chemicals, film, and other supplies. Next, she needs certain tools and equipment, such as cameras, lights, backdrops, enlargers, drying racks, and light meters. Finally, she needs the facility (studio) itself. As long as demand is stable and the studio sticks with portraits, Anita's capacity plan may be just to maintain the current plan.

But what if she wants to change her business plan, say, by expanding into event photography—weddings and other social or sporting events? For one thing, demand for photographs and capacity to process them will grow, which requires further capacity planning. Also, while some capacity items are common to both portrait and event photography, others must be separately planned. Event work will require new kinds of capacity: travel and on-site shooting time. Also, Anita may have to purchase faster lenses, battery packs, film winders, and other special equipment. Both event and portrait work, however, require capacity for developing and printing.

Another issue is seasonality. Weddings, anniversaries, graduations, and proms pile up in May and June. Anita may consider buying more equipment, hiring assistants, and contracting out some developing and printing. On the other hand, she may choose simply to limit business, reasoning that any added springtime capacity will be unused during the rest of the year. She might wish to avoid the unpleasant task of dismissing assistants when there is not enough work. The point is that she has options in planning capacity.

Anita's business plan, including goals, strategies, and policies, will affect her thinking about capacity options. What she wants to do influences what she plans to do.

In developing an appointment book, Anita must consider demand for her services as well as her capacity to provide them. Total (aggregate) demand for all photography services will determine the load on developing and printing, as well as capacity to cover demand for billing and other clerical operations. The mix of portrait and event photography (major subgroups of aggregate demand) will determine the capacity requirements for studio shooting and travel/site-shooting times, respectively. Finally, planning for each capacity item, such as each type of film and each size of printing paper, will require forecasts of each type of photography assignment, including number of shots, size and number of prints desired, and so forth. Actual customer bookings and ensuing print orders will most accurately help predict capacity needed, by type.

On the other side of the coin, the capacity plan Anita selects will determine how much and what type of demand she can satisfy. She might have to revise her appointment book, perhaps more than once, as she juggles demand and capacity, seeking a fit.

It is easy to see that inattention to demand for photography services might lead to investment in too much or too little capacity. Likewise, failure to consider capacity could lead to overbooking and promising more than can be delivered. Adverse effects may include delays, customer dissatisfaction, lost business, and overall careless and hurried business practices.

Several items emerge from the Anita's Studio example:

1. Capacity is needed in order to meet demand—without panic or shortcuts.
2. The business plan (including plans for expansion or contraction) influences capacity choices (equipment quantity, staff size, etc.).
3. Greater variety of services offered (portrait photography, event photography, etc.) complicates capacity planning.
4. Demand planning and capacity planning set limits on what the appointment book can accommodate.
5. In a given period, one or more revisions of the appointment book might be required.

These points also apply to master planning in large firms, with the extra difficulty of developing consensus among the many manager-planners.

Master Planning Teams

Except in very small businesses, like Anita's Studio, master planning is a team effort. Members of the team should come from each key function and meet regularly. All too often, unfortunately, master planning is fractionated. Each department has its own views on capacity planning and scheduling, and master planning becomes political, not customer serving or right for the firm as a whole.

For example, finance may push for greater capacity utilization to gain a higher return on existing fixed assets, while sales wants more capacity (never mind utilization) to meet peak demands. At the same time, senior management, fretting about high overhead costs, commissions a benchmarking study, which zeros in on the human resource department's budget. The study points to an abnormal amount of hiring/ training to handle demand peaks, followed by layoffs and terminations when demand wanes—and the cycle repeats. Meanwhile, the vice president of operations bemoans layoffs of well-trained employees, who later are replaced by green new hires who aren't productive. These and other managers all have different views about capacity, utilization, and meeting demand. Decision making boils down to behind-the-scenes combat.

There are no magic formulas for resolving the conflict. However, divergent views on capacity stem from being out of touch. The best cure is regular teamwork, which forces each decision maker to confront the big picture.

Principle 3:   Achieve unified purpose.

Besides amount of capacity and output, master planning has a time component. Plans must cover a medium-term planning horizon, from a few weeks to a few months out. For example, Anita and her associates would want to plan labor and equipment needs at her studio a few weeks in advance of need. (By contrast, any associate could go out and buy film and paper, which is short-term planning, not our concern here.) Also, Anita schedules her photographic assignments in an appointment book, which reserves a block of time. On-demand customers (who arrive occasionally, mainly to buy prints) are not an element of this medium-term scheduling effort.

As noted in Chapters 3 and 5, readiness and flexibility reduce planning lead time. Thus, Anita can avoid the hazards of capacity planning in the distant future—where demand forecasting is poor—by being flexible and well prepared. She might obtain flexible equipment (e.g., a highly versatile camera and lenses), have on-call backup assistance, and make sure everything is well placed and orderly in the studio.

Anita must also do long-term planning for fixed assets, such as her studio and fixtures.

CAPACITY STRATEGIES AND POLICIES

A capacity plan provides the inputs (resources) to achieve a certain level of service outputs. To illustrate, Anita's Studio might want to plan for 10 portraits per day. She translates that service output level into a capacity plan. The required daily capacity, she estimates, is five hours of her studio time and two and one-half hours of darkroom time for her or her assistant. Of course, demand might be greater or less than 10 portraits, and there are prints for previous customers' portraits to consider. Options for excess demand include overtime, a temporary employee, and subcontracting some of the printing to another studio. She needs a strategy for sorting out these and other options.

Chase-Demand versus Level-Capacity Strategies

Capacity strategy often is a matter of finding a competitive niche. At a tax preparation service, for example, the owner's strategy might be cost leadership, or keeping salary costs low. The owner might employ mostly part-time tax advisors, brought in only when required by current demand. This bare-bones labor-capacity strategy is known as *chase demand:* Hire when demand is good, lay off when demand is poor.

An alternative labor strategy is known as *level capacity:* Try to retain people through thick and thin. Level capacity is favored in labor-intensive operations when quality is a vital competitive factor. This is especially so if employees' skill qualifications are high or skills are scarce.

The level-capacity strategy sometimes governs backlogs as well as labor. A *backlog* is an accumulation of unfinished work or purchase orders.

Consider, for example, ABC, Inc., a Wall Street brokerage firm.[1] ABC handles transactions coming in from branch offices around the country. Securities and Exchange Commission regulations require all transactions to be settled within five days; that gives ABC managers time to smooth out the daily volume fluctuations so that transaction-handling capacity will not be strained one day and underused the next. But stock market volume can swing dramatically overnight. For example, a rumor about a peace agreement somewhere in the world might cause volume to soar. This could tax ABC's capacity to process stock transactions. How would ABC cope? Here are what two ABC managers might propose:

Manager A: Our capacity should be set at 12,000 transactions per day. This will allow us to meet demand most days. Last year we had a few hot periods when demand ran at 14,000–15,000 per day, and we probably will this year, too. We can handle those problems by overtime for a few days—until new clerks can be hired. Our labor turnover rate is high, so when transaction volume drops we can ease capacity down by not filling vacancies.

Manager B: I think we should keep capacity right at 17,000 transactions per day. That will be enough to handle the spurts in volume, which are very hard to predict.

Who is right? In this case both are—and here's the rest of the story. Each is managing a different end of the business of handling the stock transactions. Manager A is in charge of cashiering: processing certificates, cash, and checks. Clerks and messengers with uncomplicated tasks are the workforce. Manager B, on the other hand, runs order processing. The workforce has higher skills: data entry, data processing, programming, and information analysis. Equipment is expensive, and lead times to change information processing procedures are long.

Manager A is advocating chase demand, which seems rational for A's department. Manager B prefers a level-capacity strategy, which is logical for B's department. Since A's lower-skill people cannot handle the work in B's department, A and B should have different capacity plans based on separate aggregate demand forecasts. One plan for the whole transaction processing operation won't do.

Conditions often dictate the strategy. Businesses that employ low-wage, low-skill people in possibly unpleasant working conditions use the chase strategy. With low skill levels, training costs are low per employee but could be high per year, since turnover tends to be high. Turnover also means high hire–fire costs and, along with low skills, contributes to high error rates. Forecasting and budgeting may be short-term since lead times for adding to or cutting the workforce are short.

Level capacity has opposite features. To attract more skillful people, pay and working conditions must be better. Training costs per employee are high. The attractions of the job are meant to keep turnover and hire–fire costs low, and high labor skills hold down error rates. Forecasting and budgeting must be longer term, since hiring and training skilled people takes time.

These contrasting points about the two strategies are summarized as follows.

	Chase Demand	*Level Capacity*
Labor skill level	Low	High
Wage rate	Low	High
Working conditions	Erratic	Pleasant
Training required per employee	Low	High
Labor turnover	High	Low
Hire–fire costs	High	Low
Error rate	High	Low
Type of budgeting and forecasting required	Short term	Long term

Is global competition making companies flip-flop on capacity strategies? Sometimes it seems so. Service firms long admired for their level-capacity strategies (e.g., banks and insurance companies) have been shutting down or moving business units, laying off people, and cutting wages—which sounds like chase. These chase strategies are not always well advised. Eric Greenberg, a research director for the American Management Association, says that "US companies keep trimming workers even when it doesn't make their businesses any more stable, or competitive. . . . Less than half the companies that have downsized since 1988 have improved their profits, and only one-third . . . have seen better productivity."[2]

Other companies' competitive response is to stick with, but improve, their level-capacity strategies. The improvement is based on elevated training and process improvement. They had been paying high wages to employees who lacked the skills necessary to deliver world-class quality. By not spending enough on, or allowing time for, training and quality, the companies had not followed through with the full level strategy. Strategic correction, including a policy of underscheduling resources (explained next), is part of that follow-through.

High-Performance Staffing

High performance staffing allows time for training, getting the quality right, meeting quick-response targets even on busy days, and holding team improvement project meetings. Such a policy requires *undercapacity scheduling*. The policy usually applies just to the labor resource, but it presumes—and requires—that equipment will also be underscheduled. If equipment is too heavily scheduled, it won't be properly maintained, checked, set up, and improved; quality and response-time goals will not be met.

As a labor policy, undercapacity scheduling may be set numerically. A dental clinic, for example, might use a 15 percent undercapacity scheduling policy. If clinic capacity (measured in dentists' time, dental technicians' time, etc.) is 100 patients per day, the clinic will schedule 85 patients per day.

Is this practice wasteful of capacity? Not when TQM is active. When the schedule is met early (which is most of the time) the policy calls for data analysis, project work, preventive maintenance on equipment, training, and other activities aimed at reducing errors, rework, equipment trouble, and variation of all kinds. When the office plans fewer patients per day, there are valuable compensations: fewer unplanned stoppages, greater staff efficiency, lower operating costs, time to fit in emergency patients, time for unexpected patient problems, less rework, and happier customers. Happier customers lead to better customer retention, thus avoiding the costs of patient turnover or, worse, too few patients to keep the staff busy.

Special Capacity Policies

While underscheduling labor provides time, other specific capacity policies are needed to guide the attainment of specific strategies. Suppose, for example, that Anita's Studio follows chase demand. Her customer-oriented policy is to promise finished prints no later than 72 hours after portrait photos are taken. To meet that commitment, her capacity policy is to make extensive use of subcontracting (to a friend's studio) for developing and printing. Other examples of specific policies are:

- A municipal power company has a strategy of providing high employee security in order to gain a stable workforce (low employee turnover). Its enabling policies include (1) maintaining excess linespeople and installers in order to meet surges in demand and (2) subcontracting (to local electric contractors) extraordinary maintenance, especially repair of downed lines.
- A bowling lane proprietor's strategy is one of high utilization of bowling lanes. To act on that strategy, the proprietor offers lower prices for daytime bowling.

- At a food wholesaler, planners have adopted a competitive strategy of very fast service to retail grocers. Its supportive policies include shift work, weekend hours, overtime, cross-trained office associates who can help out in the warehouse or drive delivery vehicles, and large inventories.

Pitching In—From Green Eyeshade to Eyewear

At Knighton Optical, help-your-neighbor work practices jump across department and business-unit lines. Accountants in the head office (in Ogden, Utah) are cross-trained to fit glasses. A spurt in customer demand at Knighton's retail optical shops will bring accountants out to help. In turn, opticians in the retail stores are cross-trained to work in Knighton's optical laboratory, where they help out with lens grinding and polishing or fitting lenses to frames.

Examples of these capacity policies, plus several other common ones, are listed as follows:

Hiring and layoffs.

Overtime and extra shifts.

Part-time and temporary labor.

Cross-training and transfers (of people or work) among departments.

Service pools (e.g., a typing pool).

Quick changeover techniques to make capacity flexible.

Maintenance work as a filler.

Use of marginal facilities.

Renting space or tools.

Refusing, back-ordering, or postponing work.

Building backlogs.

Peak/off-peak price differences.

Setting capacity policies is, properly, a responsibility of top officers. These might include the general manager and the vice presidents (or department managers) of finance, operations, marketing, human resources, and scheduling.

Capacity policies may be expressed generally, such as "Avoid overtime and keep backlogs low." Or they may be expressed numerically, with minimums, maximums, or ranges, and may be priority ordered. For example, a set of priority-ordered policies aimed at maintaining a level permanent workforce might be:

1. For insufficient demand:
   a. Keep employees busy by building backlogs—maximum of 10 percent buildup above predicted demand.
   b. Lay off employees only after a 10 percent backlog is on hand.
2. For excess demand:
   a. Use temporary labor for the first 5 percent of excess demand.
   b. Use overtime for the next 5 percent.
   c. Reduce customer service (serve best customers fully, but for lesser customers, postpone or even refuse the work, offer partial service, etc.)

With such specific policies, master planning is straightforward; managers just follow the policies. Usually, however, a company will not hem itself in so explicitly. For example, "no layoffs" may be stated as a goal rather than an explicit policy.

While capacity strategies and policies apply to organizations, other master planning tools apply to units of service output. The most important of these is aimed at natural capacity groupings, our next topic.

GROUP (FAMILY) CAPACITY PLANNING

Group-based capacity planning, a commonsense partner of aggregate forecasting (discussed in Chapter 5), requires three steps:

1. Group services into natural families and select units for aggregate capacity planning. A family consists of services that employ units of capacity going through roughly the same processes. It is a natural family only if capacity (skills and equipment) is flexible enough to process all the services within the family.
2. Project aggregate customer demand for each capacity group. This forecast is in the units of measure chosen in step 1.
3. Develop an output plan (output units), and convert to capacity units if necessary. This step aims at having the right amount of aggregate resources on hand.

Example 6–2 illustrates the 1-2-3 procedure. The idea for the example (but not the data) comes from Ashton Photo, Salem, Oregon. Ashton's professional photo-processing business has been organized into 16 U-shaped photo finishing cells. Each cell has about nine cross-trained members, focuses on one type of photo (e.g., sports teams or school photos), and processes the entire job from incoming film to outgoing finished work and invoice.

Principles 6 and 7:   Form focused chains of customers. Cross-train for multiple skills.

EXAMPLE 6-2 Capacity Planning—FastFotos, Inc.

FastFotos is a large photofinisher, handling both consumer and commercial film processing (including some contract work for Anita's Studios, especially in the school graduation season).

The capacity-planning team (the personnel director and the operations manager) plans a number of weeks in advance. Since there is plenty of equipment, the plan includes labor only: the right skills, hiring, and training. Their day-to-day fine-tuning includes reasonable overtime and labor borrowing.

The capacity team uses the three-step method:

Step 1. They conclude that consumer and commercial photo processing make up separate capacity groups: consumer processing is routine; commercial customers usually require special processing. Routine processing and special processing take place in different areas of the building. The team agrees that number of orders is an appropriate capacity measure for both groups. The team plans capacity for its all-important commercial accounts first.

Step 2. They use recent past demand (number of orders) as a simple, reasonable projection of demand for the next eight-week capacity planning period.

Step 3. Exhibit 6-2 is the team's capacity-planning work sheet for commercial business. It includes recent demand data (second column) and two capacity options, both tight on capacity (team members are very cost-conscious). Option 1 provides enough capacity to process 1,800 orders per week (100 less than the mean recent demand of 1,900 per week). Projected deviations range from +700 (excess capacity) to −1,000 orders per week. Since negative deviations signify backlogged orders, consecutive negative values carry over to the next week. The projected backlog grows to −2,100 orders in week 7, then falls to −1,500 in week 8. The capacity shortage in week 7 is over a week's backlog (2,100 orders /1,800 orders per week = 1.17 weeks), which won't do in FastFoto's competitive business.

Option 2 provides for 300 more orders per week than option 1. This results in projected excess capacity in the first four weeks, but insufficient capacity in the second four weeks; the backlog grows to a high of 1,050 orders in week 7. Since 1,050 orders are less than one week's backlog, the capacity planning team considers the plan workable (with the potential of marshalling additional labor hours during peak weeks).

EXHIBIT 6-2
Capacity/Backlog Options at FastFotos, Inc.

Week	Recent Demand Orders	Option 1: 1,800 Orders per Week				Option 2: 2,100 Orders per Week			
		Orders	Deviation	Backlog	Excess Capacity	Orders	Deviation	Backlog	Excess Capacity
1	1,800	1,800	0			2,100	0		300
2	1,100	1,800	+700		700	2,100	+1,000		1,000
3	1,800	1,800	0			2,100	0		300
4	1,950	1,800	−150	−150		2,100	0		150
5	2,300	1,800	−500	−650		2,100	−200	−200	
6	2,800	1,800	−1,000	−1,650		2,100	−700	−900	
7	2,250	1,800	−450	−2,100		2,100	−150	−1,050	
8	1,200	1,800	+600	−1,500		2,100	+900	−150	
Total	15,200								

Mean demand $= \dfrac{15,200}{8} = 1,900$ orders per week

CONTRAST

Capacity Planning

Reactive
Poor; hampered by functional organization and lack of service focus.

Service-Group Based
Good, but dispersed capacity for each group hampers communication, cross-training, labor borrowing, and so on.

Service-Group Based, Capacity Focused
Very good; co-locating capacity and service groups simplifies planning, problem-solving, and adjusting to wrong forecasts.

Does this method of capacity planning assume that future demand will be like past demand? No. While total demand may be fairly close, the week-to-week demand pattern is sure to be different. Thus, maximum backlogs can be much more or less than projected. Still, the method can work quite well because overtime, job transfers, and other flexible responses are available in weeks when the plan goes wrong.

Put another way, capacity planners generally should reserve their flexible options for when the plan does not work out. If they build overtime, subcontracting, and so forth, into the capacity plan, there is no room for correction when actual demand patterns don't follow the plan.

In some businesses, such as transportation, restaurants, and lodging, an unmet order is lost; backlogs are not carryable. The method of Example 6–2 needs to be modified in those cases. The altered method treats demand as noncumulative so that negative deviations are lost sales, not backlogs.

RESERVATIONS AND APPOINTMENTS

Reserved-seat business and professional services require a detailed appointment book or reservation listing that schedules a time slot for each client or order. At Anita's Studios, the appointment book schedules customers into Anita's available time slots. A bigger service business such as a medical clinic would have a separate appointment book for each physician, and might also have appointment books for scarce, high-cost facilities like CAT scan.

While appointment systems are simple in a small firm, they can involve several steps in a large organization. Example 6–3 shows how a department within a college does appointments, which in this case are student registrations for courses.

EXAMPLE 6–3 Class Schedules and Student Registrations
                  in Department of Management—
                  Funk University

Each department chairperson in the College of Business Administration at Funk University must plan for student registrations for each course and covering the next few terms. They prepare the plan twice each term. One version is based on preregistrations; an updated version is based on general registration data.

The procedure is illustrated for the Department of Management in Exhibit 6–3. The steps are the same for all other departments, but the aggregate forecast groups (block 2) would be different. The Department of Management's courses (30 to 40 offerings) cluster neatly into three capacity groups:

1. Service management/production management.
2. Behavioral/human resources.
3. General management/business policy.

Those groups are not intended to correspond to clusters of demand (though student demands may cluster that way). Rather, the purpose is to form natural units of capacity; that is, the courses in any given group should be similar enough to enable the group's faculty members to trade off teaching assignments. The groupings shown would not be perfect. Someone whose specialty is human resource management may, for example, have a second-ary interest in general management instead of in behavior. Still, the group-ings should be all right for the purpose: to arrive at a capacity plan (out of block 3) that matches up reasonably well with total course requirements (block 6), leading to a trial plan of course offerings (block 7).

The budget (education plan) and strategies and policies (block 1) are controls on the capacity plan. Policies are for class sizes (faculty-student ratios), classroom space, teaching loads (per faculty member), use of teach-ing assistants, and utilization of faculty skills (the extent to which faculty teach in stronger or weaker areas of expertise).

EXHIBIT 6-3
Courses and Student Registrations—Department of Management

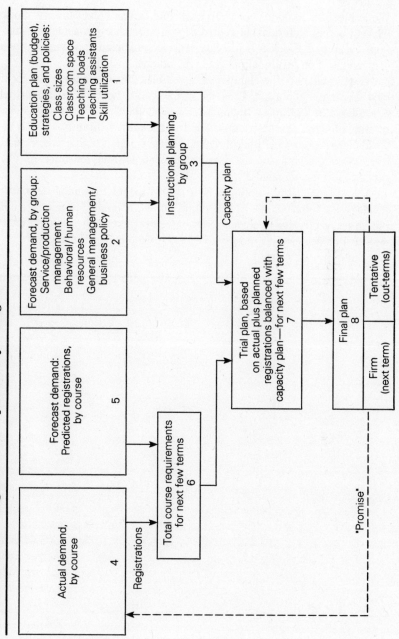

While blocks 1 through 3 concern aggregate demand and capacity, blocks 4 through 6 deal with demand course by course. Block 4 is actual registrations by course. Block 5 is forecast demand: predicted registrations, by course, based on historical patterns plus other knowledge.

Next, in block 6, the chairperson assembles course requirements for the next few terms into a list. Then she matches this shopping list against what is available in the capacity plan. The result is the trial schedule of course offerings for the next few terms. The feedback arrow from block 8 to block 7 indicates closed-loop control. By adjusting the plan until scarce resource overloads are eliminated, the plan becomes an accurate reflection of capacity to meet demands.

A final plan emerges at block 8. It is firm for the upcoming term and tentative for future terms. At this point, Funk University's registrar sends out an order promise to students who have registered. The registrar either confirms or denies their registration for a given course. If denied, a substitute may be offered.

Chapter Seven

Flow Control and Quick Response

 Flow-control failures destroy timeliness of service. Since service companies gain or lose customers based on raw speed or being on time, flow control is at the core of time-based competition.

A flow-control system in human services is a customer processing system. In wholesaling and retailing, it is that plus an inventory system. In all cases, flow control is also an information processing system. The same flow-control problems arise, however, in customer, inventory, and information processing. Our task in this chapter is to isolate and deal with root causes.

SYSTEM VARIABILITY

In any organization, multiple process elements can vary from target performance at the same time, and the combined variations can result in extreme mistakes, delays, failures, and total shutdowns. The variabilities are not pluses (goods) and minuses (bads) that cancel out over the long run: One uncooked cake and one burned cake do not add up to great baking. All variabilities are bad, and combining them only makes matters worse: We don't forgive a team member for being late yesterday if she is early today.

Principle 10:   Eliminate process variation.

Additive process variability annoys, both because it yields bad results and because it equals uncertainty. If a bus is late by 10 minutes dependably, we might be able to live with it. But if it's 10 minutes late on average—sometimes much later, on time, or early—we may give up on bus riding.

Keeping buses on time requires controlling just a few sources of variability. But flow control in a complex organization involves many interacting sources of variability, such as multiple internal processes using many different external services and other resources. Reducing interacting variability requires a three-pronged attack:

1. System designers avoid complexity so that there are fewer sources of variability.
2. Every associate and team finds ways to control process variation.
3. A cross-functional team develops the flow-control system so that the team can detect and plan around or adjust to sources of variability, thus producing a satisfactory result.

Developing the flow-control system is this chapter's focus, and it requires a basic understanding of how to cope with variabilities in demand and capacity. Coping methods include queue limitation, readiness, company-to-company synchronization, constraint avoidance, and measuring responsiveness. The remainder of the chapter addresses these topics.

FLOW CONTROL: AVOIDING SLACKS AND GLUTS

A tailor, a tax advisor, or a ticket-taker each seeks a steady flow of customers to and through the processes. This means avoiding both slack resources and customers waiting impatiently for services. To be successful, these businesses must keep their cloth, tax forms, and ticket revenues flowing.

In wholesaling and retailing, for-sale materials must be kept flowing while avoiding slacks that anger customers and gluts that raise the costs of carrying the inventories. Inventories are a major cost, typically over 70 percent of expenditures in retailing and 90 percent in wholesaling. In these businesses, controlling inventories is a key to success. Highly efficient Wal-Mart spends less on inventory mistakes (too much or too little inventory), which enables it to spend more (85 percent) of its expenditures on the revenue-earning inventories themselves.

Control does not mean elimination. Inventories, documents, or customers must flow. But like life-giving rivers, they should neither dry up nor flood too often.

The world's best retailers team up with freight carriers and producers at several echelons in the supply chain in order to keep goods flowing. In any business, planning and timing do not work out if equipment is down. Thus, equipment maintenance is part of flow control. Also, long get-ready and setup times disrupt the flow and thus must be reduced.

Quality is especially important. If quality is erratic, service may be timely but end up at the complaint department.

Principle 10: Eliminate error and variation.

The point should be clear—poor flow control has diverse causes, including disconnection between supply chain echelons, long get-ready times, erratic processes, and poor quality.

These causes are commonly addressed defensively or reactively. Common defenses include flooding distribution warehouses or internal processes with extra, just-in-case inventories. Common reactions are rescheduling or "making it right" for the customer.

Failure to solve problems causes flow control, as a separate function and cost center, to become highly complex. Indeed, the costs of managing the delays and changes may rival the direct costs of the operations being controlled. For example, office people sometimes spend more time searching for a document than working on it; then, often enough, the work isn't done right and must be done over. To those costs we could add costs of control systems (e.g., progress meetings and rescheduling) that are necessary only because of chronic delays and do-overs. In human services, customers waiting in line bear their own costs of idleness, which, they may estimate, sometimes exceed the value of the purchase or service received.

Costly systems to monitor and control wastes and delays deal, of course, with symptoms. It is far better to treat root causes. Earlier chapters gave us techniques for attacking causes of poor quality. Next we look at a simple, yet powerful way to keep wait-for-service delays in check.

QUEUE LIMITATION

Reining in the direct costs and the control system costs of delays requires enforceable queue limitation rules. A queue limiter is any device, method, or rule that limits the waiting line (queue) or waiting time (queue time). For example, a bank might allow no more than three personal loan applications on any desk. Each department along the approval route must abide by the rule. Formerly, in the same bank, every desk held stacks of applications; loan processing time averaged many days and ranged from a few days to a few weeks. Setting the queue limit at three cuts processing time to under a day *every time*. The bank heavily advertises its distinctive competency—dependably fast personal loan processing—which brings in many new customers.

Queue limitation has a subtle but powerful added benefit: It tightly links each pair of service associates along the processing route. They come to feel a sense of interdependency (which does not exist when large queues and long queue times separate one subservice from the next). Even if processors are in different rooms, they begin to feel like a team. A problem that slows down anybody in the flow soon affects everybody else. The stage is set for them to form problem-solving teams and become cross-trained so that an overload at one process brings help from another. Dependably quick response delivered by associates teamed up for continuous improvement is our recipe for synchroservice.

Examples

The following are examples of queue limiters:

Queue limit rule or policy. To be effective, the rule should be prominently displayed and hard to ignore. Ernst Home and Garden stores have signs above cashier stations proclaiming the Three-Person Promise (queue limit equals three). The signs explain that if a fourth customer gets in line, an Ernst clerk comes immediately to open another cashier station. Ernst extensively cross-trains its staff so they can stock shelves, unload trucks, or work the back room when business is slow, but go to the cash registers when business is brisk.

Ernst had been successful in the Pacific Northwest for years, but the arrival of Eagle Hardware and Home Depot—low-priced warehouse stores—created a new threat. Ernst's queue limit policy was one of several new ways of keeping a competitive edge. However, Ernst needed to cut costs at the same time. If it were to do so by reducing staff, peak business periods would overwhelm the small number of on-duty cashiers. At that point, the Three Person Promise falls apart. It remains to be seen whether Ernst can stay with and profit from its queue limitation strategy.

Timer or warning light or bell.   Each Seafirst Bank has a clock at the place where customers line up for a teller. A sign beside the clock says the bank will pay $5 to anyone who waits more than five minutes (queue limit equals five minutes). Since customer arrivals are extremely uneven, Seafirst uses part-time and flexible labor to keep queues below the limit. Some tellers work only the noon rush, some only on Mondays, Fridays, paydays for the area's biggest employer, and so forth. Supervisors take a turn as a teller as needed.

Desktop queue limiters.   These apply in processing documents, such as insurance claims, license applications, invoices, and purchase orders. The rule, (e.g., no more than three documents on any desk) needs an enforcer. A simple one is three plastic trays on the edge of the desk or an adjacent table. Each tray may hold just one document. When all three trays are filled, work temporarily stops at that desk. The employee might go help the associate at the following desk, who is not keeping up.

Randy Benson, a Seattle-based consultant, has devised a training simulation game that employs desktop queue limiters. The setting is a mock office with a mail room and several desks. Players process the mail, desk to desk, first in the no-queue-limit mode. Total processing time is very long. The next two rounds of processing introduce a queue limit of three documents, then one. With a limit of one, total throughput time is very fast. In this game the plastic trays hold the documents vertically on edge, which takes up less space than flat trays. The trays are modular, so that converting from three to one tray just requires detaching two modular trays.

People from banks, utilities, hospitals, and manufacturing back offices have played Benson's game. Thousands of others—mainly from manufacturing company offices—have played similar games that employ paper folding or Lego building at each station instead of document processing. As organizations put the lessons of the games to use, most are able to cut average throughput times by a factor of 5 or 10. This puts heavy pressure on competitors to do the same. Perhaps the day will come when failure to use queue limitation in office work and human services will be thought of simply as bad management.

Spatial queue limitation in inventory-intensive services. Since inventory takes up space, spatial queue limitation often makes sense in inventory-intensive services. In grocery stores, there is a limit on shelf space for each item. The space limit translates into a certain number of units. The replenishment system can be as simple as just filling the empty spaces or as automatic as sending bar-coded sales data to distributors. Distributors may have authority to refill shelf space and bill the grocer, which cuts out several of the usual purchasing processes. Distributors, in turn, may give the same kind of authority to manufacturers: Just fill the racks in the distribution warehouse as they empty.

Spatial queue limitation also works well in some fast-food restaurants. At a McDonald's, for example, when the chute for Quarter Pounders is full, the cook quits making them. When a customer buys two, only then may the cooks make two more. This is sometimes called the *pull system:* The customer pulls the string, which causes a clerk to pull two burgers, which causes the cook to cook two. (In a push system, cooks keep frying, oblivious of demand, and push the burgers forward. Vendors load their insulated totes and fan out hawking the already cool and stale burgers. People in the arena are dubious but some buy anyway—and have a standard reaction: "Yuk!")

In most businesses, spatial queue limitation can work well for consumable supplies. At Microsoft's headquarters, each building has a supplies room with labeled shelves for each item of office supplies. Two suppliers have contracts to enter the buildings, fill the shelves, and issue a single invoice monthly. Spatial limits can make replenishment that simple.

Queue limitation plus electronic data interchange (EDI). Counting how many boxes of Tide remain on the shelf is the hard way. The easy way is keeping track via point-of-sale bar-code tallies. Many stores link up electronically to distributors, who fill orders based on the bar-code data, not purchase orders. Increasingly, stores bypass distributors and EDI-link directly with factories. (Queue limitation is well-known in manufacturing, where it usually goes by the name *kanban,* from the Japanese.)

Reducing the Queue Limit (Continuous Improvement)

A special attraction of queue limitation is its continuous improvement feature: Just cut the queue limit. Of course, you would do this only when it will not cause the system to become undependable. The following example is realistic.

EXAMPLE 7–1 Queue Limit/EDI Service Agreement— Medivice, Inc. and Muny Hospital

Last year, Muny Hospital contracted with Medivice, Inc., to provide medical devices under a queue limit/EDI contract. The initial, trial agreement included 30 high-use items. Included were bar-coded cartons of H1 disposable hypodermic needles.

For that item Muny Hospital's stores manager and a Medivice salesperson agreed to an initial limit of eight cartons. Whenever Muny's demands for H1 needles require a stores clerk to break open another carton, the clerk uses a wand to scan the carton's bar code. That sends an EDI message to Medivice, authorizing shipment of one carton next time the truck goes to the hospital. If the hospital has used, say, three cartons since the previous delivery, Medivice learns about it through EDI and ships three cartons instead of one.

But was eight the right queue limit? Experience quickly provided the answer. In the midst of a serious flu epidemic, Muny Hospital quickly went through all eight cartons of H1s and experienced a stockout. The medical staff was in a panic until Medivice made a special midnight needle delivery. That seemed like an isolated exception, but several more stockouts occurred in the next two months, caused by various system failures (miscount of cartons, a late truck, a stockout at Medivice's warehouse, and a defective lot of H1 disposable needles). As a result, the stores manager and the salesperson increased the queue limit on H1 needles to 10 cartons.

On I1 intravenous solution (IV) bags, the opposite happened. The initial limit, 14 containers, proved to be more than enough. Despite a few startup problems in getting I1-IV bags on queue limits, they were always available at the hospital. The service rate on this item was 100 percent, which spelled too much inventory to the stores manager and called for cutting the limit. The manager and the salesperson reduced the quantity to 10 containers of IV bags. (More reductions followed, primarily because hospital improvement teams, including representatives from the freight carrier and the supplier, implemented overall improvements in the system.)

Principle 11:   Cut wait time and inventory.

EXHIBIT 7-1
Queue Limit and Stockout Check Sheet—Hospital

Items on Queue Limits	Last Year		This Year							
Hypodermic needle, H1		J	F	M	A	M	J	J	A	S ...
Limit	8 → 10	8	8	7	6	6	6	6		
Stockouts	5				//					

Comments: April problem (damaged needle packages—two stockouts) quickly resolved by supplier; no need to increase queue limit.
*
*
*

IV Bags, I1										
Limit	14 → 10	10	10	10	9	8	8	7		
Stockouts	0									

Comments: No stockouts last year or this year to date.
*
*
*

Nurserver carts									
Limit	30 → 25	25	25	25	22	22	22	22
Stockouts					/				

Comments: June late delivery (8:30 AM instead of 5:30) due to large turnover of drivers (e.g., graduation of student drivers). Freight co. has set up backup driver system, so no change in queue limits.

Note: Data shown for only 3 of 30 queue limit items.

Stores associates wanted a simple, easily noticed record of stockout incidence for H1 needles, I1 bags, and the 28 other queue limit items. They developed a large wall chart check sheet with preprinted categories of problem causes. A stores clerk makes a check mark beside the probable cause whenever a stockout occurs. Improvement teams later investigate the most frequently checked causes.

Stores associates treat reduction of limit quantities as one measure of success; response ratios, in pieces rather than boxes, are another useful measure. Associates make check marks for stockouts, and they track limit reductions on the same wall chart, shown in part in Exhibit 7-1. Out of Muny's several thousand stockkeeping units (SKUs), only 30 are currently on queue limitation, so it's feasible to chart them all.

Exhibit 7–1 includes two individual SKUs (H1 hypodermic needles and I1-IV bags) and the Nurserver cart, a shelved cart filled with common supplies (tape, swabs, tongue depressors, etc.). Medivice takes Nurserver carts away each day for restocking and return.

The exhibit shows a pattern of few stockouts (high fill-rates), which is to be expected since queue limitation is a disciplined, highly reliable system. The exhibit shows that the limit quantity for H1 needles rose from 8 to 10 last year, but was reduced three times this year. The stockout problem that occurred twice in April this year was quickly resolved, but Muny's cautious associates agreed to keep the limit at six cartons for awhile. Good service experience has led to intermittent limit reduction for both I1 IVs (14 to 10 to 7) and Nurserver carts (30 to 25 to 22; a single late Nurserver delivery problem causing the June stockout was successfully resolved).

We've seen that queue limitation won't perform without cross-trained, flexible labor. It will also break down for lack of readiness. That is, if it takes too long to get ready for the next customer or to respond to a change in what the customer wants, customer waiting lines will lengthen and exceed queue limits.

READINESS AND QUICK SETUP

How long does it take an Indy 500 pit crew to change four tires, fill the tank, clean the windshield, and squirt Gatorade into the driver's mouth? Fifteen seconds? Less? Regardless of how long, the workings of an efficient pit crew capture many concepts of quick-change teamwork and readiness. Those concepts can be expressed as guidelines for action.

Principle 12: Cut setup, get-ready, and start-up times.

Guidelines

Although some businesses are famous for their quick changeover expertise (e.g., stage crews and airline caterers), most organizations give the matter scant attention. But elevated competition in many businesses demands quicker, error-free service and enhancing the firm's ability to continually reduce setup and get-ready times. The training materials that address these concerns are based on the following guidelines.

Changeover avoidance:

1. A dedicated, single-purpose process.

Be-ready improvements—developed by teams of associates:

2. External (offline) steps performed while process is active.

3. Setup implements close, clean, in top condition, and ready.

4. For costly equipment, trained crew and clockwork precision.

Modifications—technical assistance on improvement team:

5. Eliminate/immobilize unneeded devices and adjusters.

6. Add positioners and locators.

7. Simplify/standardize software, equipment, and service options.

8. Employ extra work-element holders.

Changeover avoidance. Guideline one is the special case of a single service, product, or type of customer that gets its own dedicated process. If, say, three quarters of McDonald's customers wanted a Big Mac and a medium Coke, the restaurant would set up a dedicated Mac-and-a-Coke line, with no flexibility or changeovers to worry about. All companies would love to have services or products that popular. The simplicity, low cost, and uniformly high quality of this mode of processing yields high profits and large numbers of loyal customers.

Be-ready improvements. The next three guidelines provide natural, low-cost improvement projects for teams of associates.

Guideline two is doing all possible get-ready steps while the process is engaged on its previous type of customer or service. That minimizes the time the process is stopped and unproductive. At a laundromat, for example, have your next load sorted and the detergent and other additives measured out before the machine stops.

Guideline three provides the discipline of "A place for everything, and everything in its place." Have you had to wait to sign something while a clerk looks for a 49 cent pen? Or has one but it won't write? By contrast, an Indy pit crew is ready with gasoline hoses, tire-changing devices, and tires correctly positioned and in tip-top shape. Surgical teams in operating rooms adopt the same kinds of readiness habits and discipline.

Where equipment is expensive—a race car or a surgical room—a sizable, well-trained changeover crew is justified. Guideline four is deftly applied, for example, in well-managed conference centers: Dozens of people assemble the minute a conference ends, and acting quickly in parallel, they dismantle the speaker's platform, remove water pitchers and other tabletop items, fold and stack tables and chairs, clean the area, and set up for an evening banquet or wedding party.

Modifications. Guidelines five through eight generally require that the improvement team call on an expert for technical assistance. Since the modifications may be costly, these guidelines would usually take effect after the be-ready guidelines (two through four).

Guideline five calls for eliminating or immobilizing devices and adjusters that come with the equipment, or that were once part of the process but are no longer needed. For example, an overhead projector has a focus knob, but if the projector stays in the same classroom anchored to a table facing the same screen year after year, the focus adjustment unit is an invitation for unnecessary, nonvalue-adding tampering and variable image quality. In one company, a conference room user had wound strapping tape around the adjustment knob at the right focus setting so that other users could skip the adjustment step.

Why not just order the projector with a fixed focal length to suit the room layout? Because it would be a costly special order, and the manufacturer would have to charge a higher price. Equipment designers usually include many adjustment features; this practice broadens appeal, increases demand, produces economies of scale, and lowers the price. After the sale, however, teams of users should work on removing or immobilizing unneeded adjustment devices.

Guideline six is the opposite of five: adding special features not usually provided. For example, to make recycling easier, a team might come up with a plan to equip all the firm's pop machines with a bin that receives, crushes, and holds empty cans.

Guideline seven calls for simplified, standardized designs. Too many different word processors, computers, or service options expand exponentially the array of supporting devices and sets of instructions needed for getting started.

Guideline eight specifies having extra holders for the work elements, such as tools or paper feedstock. Think of a fondue party where each person loads a backup fondue fork while having another already loaded fork in the hot oil.

Quick Setup Projects

The eight guidelines assist project teams organized specifically to improve readiness and cut setup times. In practice, by cutting setup time, the project team usually also improves process consistency, quality, safety, maintenance, ease of operation, housekeeping, and other factors for the target process. Similarly, a team organized to reduce process variation will often also cut setup time. In other words, many of the goals of continuous improvement and competitiveness overlap and are largely inseparable.

This inseparability can be bothersome to veteran managers and technicians, who are used to seeing the work subdivided into many specialties and allocated to specialty departments. However, superior companies have discovered the power of continual improvement led by teams of frontline employees, who call on experts only as needed and usually after several rounds of low-cost improvements have already been implemented.

Principle 15:   Improvement led by front-line teams.

While queue limitation and readiness help synchronize internal processes, synchroservice requires flow control with external partners as well. Quick-response programs (QRPs) bring external partners into the loop.

QUICK-RESPONSE PROGRAM FOR INTERSECTOR FLOW CONTROL

QRP links different companies in several stages of supply and freight hauling to final points of sale (see Exhibit 7–2). The ultimate aim is tight synchronization: Pick the cotton that's spun into thread that's woven into cloth that's dyed and finished into fabric that's cut and sewed into a shirt that's delivered to the store just before you walk in to buy it—all of this, and transportation, too, in synch. Synchronization at each stage affects scheduling, purchasing, storage, logistics, capacity, and cash flow planning. The accompanying box gives examples.

Principle 13.   Operate at the customer's rate of use.

QRP's unofficial kickoff was in June 1986 in Chicago. A few dozen retailers and apparel and textile companies met to discuss how they could, together, respond to foreign competition. Bennetton's and The Limited's homegrown versions of QRP provided a model. Within a few years, QRP had become a competitive necessity among major retailers. An international conference, Quick Response 91 (an annual event), drew

---

QRP at Wal-Mart

"A manufacturer like Gitano can access Wal-Mart's point-of-sale terminals to track sales of its jeans. This way, Gitano knows when to crank up production to resupply a Wal-Mart store before the store runs out of merchandise. Wal-Mart's electronic data interchange system enables it to electronically place orders with a manufacturer."

"But Wal-Mart goes further. It works with its suppliers and with its suppliers' suppliers. For example, with a company like Gitano it will work with the fabricmaker and even the fiber producer. According to David Glass, Wal-Mart's president and CEO, 'We just tie everyone into the loop. You won't call the apparel manufacturer and have them say, "Gosh, we'd make that for you, but we don't have any fabric."'"

Source: "Cutting Out the Middleman," *Forbes,* January 6, 1992, p. 169.

QRP at Luxottica Group SpA of Italy

"Luxottica [the world's largest eyeware manufacturer] reorganized its [US] sales staff and started sharing with customers the advantages of computer power. It is equipping [independent] retailers with software that checks Luxottica's stock and orders goods for overnight delivery. In the past, delivery took days or weeks."

Source: Bill Saporito, "Cutting Out the Middleman," *Fortune,* April 6, 1992, p. 96.

---

participants from companies dealing in hand tools, furniture, greeting cards, hardware, floor sweepers, household cleaners, batteries, cosmetics, toys, consumer electronics, office equipment, motor oil, and others, as well as textiles and apparel.

Technology is part of the QRP equation: universal product codes, scanning equipment at the retailer, data communications hardware, and electronic data interchange software. However, according to one executive, "Technology is 10 percent of the issue." The other 90 percent, he says, involves tight "relationships with trading partners," plus assorted process improvements.[1]

BOTTLENECKS AND CONSTRAINTS

If you're standing in line waiting to buy a ticket and the ticketing machine or computer breaks down, you get annoyed. You are idled at a

EXHIBIT 7-2
Smart New Way to Get Goods to Consumers

Top Row: Consumers lose when manufacturers periodically stuff excess goods into distributors' warehouses (sometimes called trade loading). Here a typical grocery item takes 84 days to go from factory to store shelf.

The manufacturer stockpiles in-gredients and packaging supplies to meet peak production levels.

Plants prepare huge runs. Sche-duling is chaotic, with more over-time and temporary workers.

Freight companies charge premi-um rates for the manufacturer's periodic blow-out shipments.

No more panic purchases are nec-essary. The company cuts down on inventories, freeing up cash.

Factories run on normal shifts. The company cuts down on over-time pay and supplemental workers.

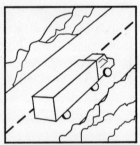

The manufacturer eliminates peak-and-valley distribution. That helps it save 5% in shipping costs.

bottleneck, which is any process (office, work cell, machine, manager, etc.) that impedes the flow of work. Generally, we say that demand exceeds capacity at a bottleneck. Repair of the ticketing computer removes the bottleneck.

When you finally buy your ticket and surrender it to a ticket taker, you may head for the restroom only to find a long queue there. In this case, the bottleneck stems from failing to plan enough restroom capacity.

Bottlenecks are serious and costly and they drive off customers. The cause of a bottleneck must be fixed, but that takes time; meanwhile, the flow-control system must go to work to minimize damages.

EXHIBIT 7–2
Smart New Way to Get Goods to Consumers (continued)
Bottom Row: Speeded-up cycle is more efficient, improves company's cash flow, and gives consumers a fresher product at a better price.

Distributors overstock as they binge on short-term discounts. Cartons sit for weeks inside warehouses.

At distribution centers, the goods get overhandled. Damaged items go back to the manufacturer.

Twelve weeks after the items leave the production line, they may not be fresh for the consumer.

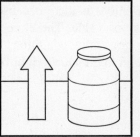

Wholesalers' inventories get cut in half. That means storage and handling costs decline 17%.

Retailers receive undamaged products. Their perception of the manufacturer's quality improves.

The consumer gets the goods 25 days earlier, and—even better news—at a 6% lower price.

Source: Patricia Sellers, "The Dumbest Marketing Ploy," *Fortune*, October 5, 1992, pp. 88-94. Used with permission.

Avoiding Avoidable Constraints

First, the organization should learn to avoid constraints of its own making. No single department can do this. It takes what can be called a multifunctional service strategy team, whose members are senior people from marketing, finance, human resources, operations, and sometimes one or two more. When business is light, the team oversees initiatives having long-term impact, such as training programs and new-service development. When business is brisk, the team meets more often. Its main agenda is potential bottlenecks and constraints.

When sales soar, demand for certain services bumps up against capacity limits—a constraint. If nothing is done, service slows, becomes shoddy, and turns away customers. In nearly every case, however, some of the overheated demand is for unprofitable services or from difficult customers. The firm may sell at a loss and welcome pain-in-the-neck customers when demand is light; the revenue offsets fixed costs. It's illogical, however, to follow the same policy when capacity is pushed to the limit. The team therefore alters business strategy to favor high-margin services and existing, loyal, major customers. It cuts advertising and other promotions, especially for least-profitable services and for new, small-potatoes customers. Another option is giving best customers higher priority service ("to the front of the line")—and worst customers lowest priority.

Each team member has a special role. The finance/accounting member helps sort out the profitable from the unprofitable services, customers, and sales channels. Marketing knows which customers the firm should protect, and what services it might want to provide to good customers even if unprofitable. Human resources is on the team because they hire, train, and assign capacity. And operations is there because they *are* capacity.

The point is, a sale is not a sale. There are good sales and there are not-so-good sales. In a constraint condition, it's time to analyze the components of demand and to do what's right for the whole organization and its best customers.

Capacity Cushions

Lowering demand is one way of dealing with a constraint. While the multifunctional team works on that, others should be working on the opposite: squeezing out more, or more effective, capacity. Together these approaches create a small capacity cushion. Without a cushion, plans and schedules unravel and efficiency deteriorates.

Ernst stores make their capacity more effective by cross-training everybody. Seafirst Bank does some of that, too, but it also relies on assorted part-time labor. The US Civil Service has long had a labor designation for part-timers called WAE—when actually employed. Part-timers and on-call temporaries provide a pool of extra capacity, which can be scheduled to match rising and falling patterns of demand.

Increased use of casual labor has been a worldwide phenomenon, except where restrictive labor laws make it difficult. In the United States, lax laws allow firms to escape paying benefits to casuals, which creates a moral dilemma. It seems probable that new legislation will provide more rights and benefits to part-timers. Costs to employers will rise, but the need for this form of capacity cushion will remain.

Another approach is improvement projects. Whether aimed at quality, speed, or safety, most improvements usually also increase capacity. Better quality cuts rework and returns, along with the extra administrative workload entailed, thus freeing up capacity. Quicker setup does the same. Greater safety means less lost time.

To sum up, the organization may enhance its capacity and avoid constraints by the following:

1. Less service (and therefore less demand on capacity) for less-profitable services or less-valued customers.
2. Cross-training and faster process setups to gain capacity, flexibility, and speed.
3. Maintaining capable standby capacity, including trained on-call labor.
4. High involvement in improvement projects that cut capacity losses due to breakdowns, lack of materials or information, rework, and cancellations.

RESPONSE RATIO

Mishap and error rates, do-overs, and returns are fine for measuring quality. We need, as well, good measures of flow control. In human services, waiting-line length, waiting time, and throughput time are naturals. In multistep services, such as department-to-department order filling, we need measures of flow control at every step along the way. Each process then becomes accountable for its own flow control improvements. The *response ratio* fills the need—and serves well in human services, too.

The response ratio relates throughput time to value-adding time (it is also called a value-added ratio). At peak voting times, for example, voters may wait 58 minutes for a booth and then spend 2 minutes voting. The response ratio is 60 minutes (throughput time) divided by 2 minutes (value-adding time), which equals 30 to 1. Thirty to 1 might still be okay in the former Soviet Bloc countries. Western Europeans might tolerate 5 to 1 or 10 to 1. Americans and Canadians get edgy at 3 to 1, which seems to be a norm that many stores shoot for in competitive metropolitan areas.

We get the same ratio by counting work units, instead of timing. Say that at the same voting place 290 people are waiting for 10 voting booths, eac h with one person inside. The response ratio is 300 to 10 or, again, 30 to 1. A buyer in a purchasing department calculates the ratio by counting requisitions instead of people. If a buyer typically has a stack of 29 requisitions in her in-basket and one "under pencil" on her desk, the ratio is 30 to 1. A mail-order house might have 29 orders in a typical stack for every one being worked on in the boxing, wrapping, and addressing work centers—again, 30 to 1.

Response ratios apply even in project work: It is pointless for an architect or road repair crew to be assigned five projects. At any given time just one will be active, and the other four will be idle (response ratio = 5 to 1). The architect or crew will flit back and forth from one project to the next, stretching out all of them. Average project duration will be five times longer than the minimum, in which we start and finish one before taking on another project (a 1 to 1 ratio).

Actually, in restoration services, there may be times when it makes sense to trade back and forth between two projects (ratio = 2 to 1). When lack of materials interrupts one, work on the other. Or on sunny days the paint crew is outside, and on rainy days they paint inside. Similarly, in any kind of intellectual work (e.g., doing a report or writing computer software), the ideal ratio may be 2 to 1. That allows gestation time: When stuck on one project, put it aside and work on the other for a while.

Holding to a response ratio of 2 to 1 requires changes in the way projects are scheduled and released for action. Those responsible for releasing—the master scheduling team—must withhold release of a new project until a current one is completed.

High ratios mean long queues of documents, idle materials, customers, or projects. Team members may calculate the ratio, post it in the workplace, and then work to lower it. But they cannot do so without making improvements: cut setup times, limit the queues, have a system for borrowing labor when lines get too long, eliminate disruptive rework by doing it right the first time, keep all areas clean and well organized, and so forth.

Following an improvement, the new ratio can be posted on the graph for all to see. The process continues, one improvement at a time, with 1 to 1 or 2 to 1 as the ultimate (though sometimes unattainable) goal. It is often a good idea to post before-and-after photos or schematic drawings showing waiting-line reductions as the ratios drop. Use of the ratios helps instill the habit of improvement at the operator level so that improvement becomes primarily a line, not staff, responsibility.

Some firms use response ratios for an entire sequence of operations (total lead time to theoretical minimum time). This overall ratio can be a useful scorecard for senior managers. But it is not very meaningful for frontliners, who should be concentrating on their own process responsiveness, measured by their own local response ratio.

A main advantage of the response ratio is that it is unitless, devoid of numbers of minutes, clients, truckloads, and so forth. The goal of 1 to 1 or 2 to 1 is the same for any kind of work, and it enables comparison of improvement rates across the enterprise. In short, the ratio is promising as a universal measure of service speed and flow control.

Chapter Eight

Purchasing
Quest for High-Quality Suppliers

Toward Supplier–Customer Partnerships
   Tenure
   Type of Agreement
   Number of Sources
   Prices/Costs
   Quality
   Service Design
   Order Conveyance
   Documentation
   Transportation
   Relationship Openness
Purchasing and Contracting Policies and Practices
   ABC Analysis
   Purchasing and Contracting Procedures
   Performance and Compliance: The Tangibility Factor
Sourcing Outside or Staying Inside

Improving supplier quality is the number two strategic objective for the 1990s, surpassed only by that of improving quality in one's own organization. That is the consensus of opinion among top executives participating in one study.[1] This is in sharp contrast with the formerly prevalent single-minded focus on cost of purchased services and materials.

CONTRAST

The Purchasing Associate

Traditional	Modern
Commodity-oriented.	Captain of a purchasing team of
Burdened with paperwork.	colleagues and suppliers.
Out of touch with suppliers.	Quality-oriented and challenged by
	task variety.

The shift in opinion follows from the realization that higher quality begets lower cost. Whether buying services, items for resale, or supplies, the one sure way to cut costs is better quality in the supplier base. Thus, the isolated buyer placing one phone call after another in search of the best price is obsolete. In its place are multifunctional supplier development teams working toward partnerships for quality with a few preferred suppliers.

The shift toward partnerships reduces the number of suppliers per item. At the same time, many organizations are choosing to buy certain services that had been performed in-house. Information processing, security, food service, landscaping, and building maintenance are a few examples. The idea is that the service experts can do a better job at less cost. Growth in contracting for services raises new issues, because measuring quality of intangible services is difficult, as compared with measuring the quality of goods.

In the first part of this chapter, we examine some details of supplier partnership (or, when initiated by the supplier–customer partnership). In the remainder, we match up purchasing practices with cost and degree of tangibility of items to be purchased.

TOWARD SUPPLIER–CUSTOMER PARTNERSHIPS

Distance and *distrust*. These two words describe typical old-style supplier–customer relationships. Buyers had no real contact with suppliers except by remote communication. It was an adversarial system, with no loyalty on either side.

Today, synchroservice, extending to supplier partners, is strongest among major retailers, such as Dillard, Wal-Mart, and McDonald's. Some are calling the new approach partners in profit, and a few companies are adopting new job and department titles, such as Frito-Lay's vice president of supplier development.

Exhibit 8–1 contrasts the old and new approaches. The second column describes adversarial relationships. Few companies have been totally adversarial with suppliers, but most have been that way to some degree. By contrast, certain leading-edge companies have embraced nearly all of the partnership items, and many others have adopted them in part. The extremes of adversary and partnership are anchors for discussion of the 10 dimensions in Exhibit 8–1.

Tenure

Under the adversarial approach, it's supplier musical chairs. A new supplier's price list might catch a buyer's eye and trigger a switch from the old to the new supplier. For larger volume (or big-ticket) services or items, buyers request bids from several suppliers at least yearly; the low bidder (often not the present supplier) usually gets the contract.

The partnership approach calls for staying with one supplier and letting the learning curve work for the benefit of both parties. Suppliers who get to know a customer's real requirements are valuable participants on improvement teams, quality function deployment, and other continuous-improvement efforts.

Type of Agreement

In the adversarial approach, sporadic purchase orders are the norm, and orders for a single item may rotate among 5 or 10 suppliers. Special, one-time buys will probably always require a purchase order. For regularly used items, however, the trend is toward one-year or longer contracts.

Some contracts specify the quantity for the next few months and provide a forecast for the rest of the year. Also, the contract may grant exclusivity to a supplier but not stipulate exact quantities.

Number of Sources

Having several sources for each purchased item is common practice among adversarially oriented buyers. Government regulations require it

EXHIBIT 8–1
Supplier Relationships

	Adversary	*Partnership*
1. Tenure	Brief	Long-term, stable
2. Type of agreement	Sporadic purchase orders	Exclusive or semiexclusive contracts, usually at least one year
3. Number of sources	Several sources per item for protection against risk and for price competition	One or a few good suppliers for each item or commodity group
4. Prices/costs	High on average; low buy-in bids (below costs) can lead to unstable suppliers	Low; scale economies from volume contracts; suppliers can invest in improvements
5. Quality	Uncertain; reliance on receiving inspections	Quality at source; supplier uses statistical process control and total quality management
6. Service design	Customer developed	Make use of suppliers' design expertise
7. Order conveyance	Mail	Long-term: contracts. Short-term: queue limitation, phone, fax, or electronic data interchange
8. Documentation	Packing lists, invoices, and count/inspection forms	Sometimes no count, inspection, or list—just monthly bill
9. Transportation	Late and undependable; stock missing or damaged	Dependably quick, on-time, and intact
10. Openness	Very little	On-site audits of supplier, concurrent design, visits by frontline associates

for certain classes of goods and services for reasons of price competition and the "fairness doctrine." In most cases, however, fear of supplier failure accounts for the many-supplier rule.

Over time, multiple sourcing has effects opposite to what is intended. It raises each supplier's costs and thus costs to the customer. But sole- or preferred-supplier sourcing gives the supplier confidence that demand will continue. This encourages supplier investment in process and service improvements.

Multiple sourcing is also costly to buying organizations: Costs of supplier selection, evaluation, certification, data processing, communications, and administrative and clerical activities are obvious examples. A less tangible cost is the loss of the opportunity to get to know and take advantage of suppliers' capabilities.

Principle 5:   Cut the number of suppliers.

Cutting number of sources reduces these wastes. The trend in that direction is strong among leading producers and has spread to fast-food companies, hotels, retailers, and wholesalers. Wallace Company, a distributor of oil-drilling repair parts and a winner of the Malcolm Baldrige Quality Award, cut its number of valve suppliers from 2,500 to 325.[2]

McKesson Corp., a pharmaceutical distributor, reversed the process. In the early 1980s it developed a total service plan that led to its becoming sole or preferred distributor to many small drug retailers. The services are EDI based and include inventory and shelf management, pricing, credit, insurance claims, and others. These services have created a strong dependency relationship between the retailers and McKesson.[3]

Despite the obvious cost benefits of vendor-base reductions, some companies fear that the sole supplier might fail. Sole-sourcing is not always the answer; often firms maintain two suppliers for each commodity group but just one for each item within a group. For example, they buy business forms 1, 3, 5, 7 and so on, from supplier A, and forms 2, 4, 6, 8 and so on from supplier B. If disaster strikes one supplier, the other is able to help, without the expense of developing new supply channels.

Prices/Costs

In the adversarial approach, price is dominant. Buyers attempt to play suppliers off one another on price. Sometimes a supplier will buy in with a discount or a bid price that is below costs, but it then must overcharge on other contracts in order to stay in business. Also, when big customers with clout are able to force suppliers into making recklessly low bids, the suppliers become unstable and financially unable to invest in improvements. That instability, along with frequent changing of suppliers, introduces high change costs for both parties. Thus, while the adversarial approach focuses on getting good prices, it often causes the opposite.

By contrast, the partnership approach, offering stable high-volume contracts with opportunities for economies of scale, is attractive to suppliers. It persuades them to try to improve and do their best for customers.

Quality

When suppliers are distrusted, customers must protect themselves. The insurance may be a sizable staff of inspectors at the receiving dock or in a holding area. Sometimes it takes days to clear incoming inspection, while users watch their own schedules slip. For purchased services, the distrusted supplier's work must be checked, reports and claims must be filed and reconciled, and sometimes the service must be re-done.

Instead of spending so much time discovering postreceipt errors, firms need to partner up and send customer teams to visit, develop, certify, and then nurture suppliers. Some companies furnish training and technical assistance to suppliers to prevent mistakes (fail-safing) or to help the supplier discover and correct them (process control).

Principle 10:   Make it easy to provide goods and services without error.

Service Design

If the customer buys packaged designs, the supplier clearly has control of the design specifications. However, the customer often wants special features. In the adversarial approach, the customer typically develops the service specs, passes them on to the supplier, and expects them to be followed. But that approach has come under attack from wise customers. Programs such as early supplier involvement, design-build teams, and quality function deployment tap suppliers' expertise and can reduce development time significantly.

Order Conveyance

Exhibit 8–2 illustrates the order conveyance and documentation aspects of purchasing. We deal with order conveyance here and documentation in the next section. In traditional delivery systems, a mailed purchase order from the customer or an order booked by a salesperson starts the ball rolling in the supplier's plant (see the top portion of Exhibit 8–2A).

Under partnership with frequent deliveries, mail is too slow. New, faster methods of transmitting order information include phone, facsimile copier, and electronic data interchange (see Exhibit 8–2B). EDI dates back to the early 1960s when American Hospital Supply began using it to link up with its hospital customers.[4]

EXHIBIT 8–2
Purchasing—Order Conveyance and Documentation

A. Traditional approach

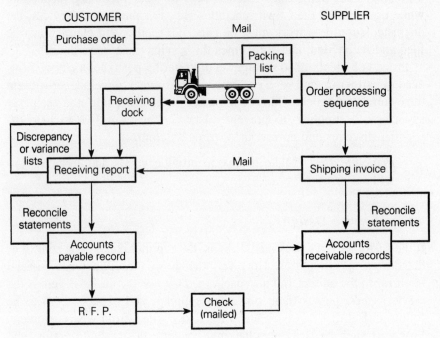

B. Partnership approach

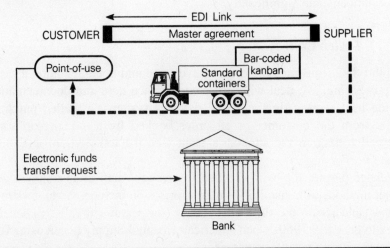

The simplest order conveyance method is recirculating containers in the queue limitation mode. A label on each container tells what the item is, number of containers, quantity per container, supply point, and use point. Return of the container directs the supplier to fill and ship another. Alternatively, the label is a removable queue card (or kanban card). First withdrawal from a container initiates replenishment: The customer faxes the queue card to the supplier, which authorizes shipment of one more container-full.

Documentation

The partnership approach tries to eliminate or simplify paperwork. In an ideal system based on a master agreement (see Exhibit 8–2B). There is no purchase order, packing list, or receiving report. A bar-coded label or queue card identifies standard containers as to contents, quantity, and so forth. Inspection isn't needed; supplier and item are certified. When an associate scans the bar code upon receipt of the order, accounts payable receives payment authorization. Alternatively, frontline associates scan the bar codes, thus recording the receipt in appropriate inventory accounts and stock records. A monthly bill and electronic funds transfer may complete the process.

Principle 16: Cut transactions and reporting.

Transportation

Synchroservice requires that freight haulers be partners, too. Trucking deregulation has helped pave the way. In turn, a can-do trucking industry drives the railroads to become customer-sensitized. And overnight air freight keeps the others honest. Intermodal linkages among these competitors are part of the equation as well.

Dependably quick, on-time, no-damage deliveries are what customers require. The new breed of carriers meets the challenge in many innovative ways, ranging from TQM to high tech. As noted in Chapter 2, Chemical Lehman Tank Lines, a Pennsylvania petro-hauler, sends action teams to visit clients and even initiates exchanges of employees with customers. Within Lehman, teams of terminal managers, dispatchers, and hourly employees tackle improvement projects.

High technology includes satellite communications and navigation systems for truckers. "Every truck in industry-leading Schneider National's fleet has sprouted a jaunty little satellite antenna. . . . You look in the cab and see generally not a Teamsters truck driver but an 'associate' with a merit pay plan and an on-board computer that links him with headquarters.... When Schneider's tractor-trailer pulls up with a cargo of appliances, for example, Sears' home delivery trucks are lined up across the loading dock, scheduled to bring them to customers expecting delivery that day."[5] This approach, called cross-docking, eliminates many nonvalue-adding steps and greatly reduces warehouse space needs.

Relationship Openness

In the adversarial approach the buyer, in the office or at trade shows, sifts through suppliers' offerings and finally selects a few; from then on, communication is by mail and fax (except in times of materials scarcity, when the suppliers put their customers "on allocation"—1,000 Nintendo game sets to this store chain, 1,200 to that one, and so forth).

The partnership approach requires the buying organization to send teams to the supplier's site. The visitors get to know people at the supplier's facility and acquire an understanding of the supplier's culture, skills, processes, nagging problems, and potential sources of misunderstanding. They invite the supplier's people to reciprocate the visit.

Some buying companies, in what is called supply-chain management, actively seek to extend the partnership to the supplier's suppliers and beyond. Sometimes the catalyst for such linkages is a supplier's trying to forge partnerships with customers and their customers. Such companies as Baxter Healthcare, Wal-Mart, and Levi Strauss & Co. have engaged in this form of customer development or customer-chain management.

Buying companies also should do formal audits of the supplier's quality and processes. Failure to visit and perform audits invites misunderstanding, bad feelings, and a return to adversarial relationships. It is perhaps like gardening: Till the soil, or weeds will grow.

PURCHASING AND CONTRACTING POLICIES AND PRACTICES

Supplier partnerships thrive when followed by correct policies and practices. Good policies must consider annual cost, degree of tangibility, and outside sources of purchased items. We consider each of these items— cost, tangibility, and outside sources—in the remainder of the chapter.

ABC Analysis

It makes sense to manage costly services and goods tightly and to manage cheap ones loosely. That logic is the basis of *ABC analysis,* an old and still important tool of materials management.[6]

ABC analysis begins by classifying all stocked items by annual dollar volume (or annual demand times cost per unit). Class A items, those needing close control, are the high-dollar-volume group. They may include 80 percent of total purchase cost but only 1 percent of total items bought. Class B is a medium-dollar-volume group, perhaps 15 percent of cost and 30 percent of items. Class C is the rest, say, 5 percent of cost and 69 percent of items.

ABC analysis may be used as follows (the details will vary from firm to firm):

1. *Purchasing.* Have each contract or purchase order for a class A item signed by the president or chief financial officer, for a class B item by a department head, and for class C item by any buyer.
2. *Physical inventory counting.* Count A items weekly or daily, B items monthly, and C items annually.
3. *Forecasting.* Forecast A items by several methods on the computer with resolution by a forecasting committee, B items by simple trend projection, and C items by buyer's best guess.
4. *Safety stock.* No safety stock for A items, one week's supply for B items, and one month's supply for C items.
5. *Quick response.* Deliver A items frequently, perhaps daily in a quick response program. Deliver Bs weekly, and Cs monthly.

While this list is conventional, some firms find ways to outdo the list. At Microsoft, for example, each group assistant (serving a group of software engineers) gets a company credit card for buying class C items. They buy innumerable computer supplies, software, and special office items using the cards, and Microsoft gets billed monthly. This eliminates the usual costly purchase-order processing sequence for nearly 40 percent of the firm's purchases. A TQM team came up with the suggestion in a breakout session at a seminar in 1991. It took a year for Microsoft to find a bank that was willing to administer this new use of credit cards. Now other companies have implemented similar systems.

Like many other companies, Microsoft also consolidates certain class C items so that they deserve class A treatment. Two suppliers have all of the company's business for routine office supplies. The volumes are large enough that the suppliers can come to Microsoft as often as daily. The supplier just fills the bins in each Microsoft building and sends a monthly bill.

ABC applies well to wholesaling and retailing (see Example 8-1).

EXAMPLE 8-1 ABC Analysis—Wholesaler

At Universal Motor Supply Company, the buyer has arranged 10 inventory items in order of annual dollar volume. His ordered list is shown below, with dollar volume expressed in percentages.

Stock Number	Annual Demand	Unit Cost	Annual Dollar Volume	Percent
407	40,000	$ 35.50	$1,420,000	59.53%
210	1,000	700.00	700,000	29.35
021	2,000	55.00	110,000	4.61
388	20,000	4.00	80,000	3.35
413	4,400	10.00	44,000	1.84
195	500	36.00	18,000	0.76
330	40	214.00	8,560	0.36
114	100	43.00	4,300	0.18
274	280	1.00	280	0.01
359	600	0.25	150	0.00
			Totals $2,385,290	100.0%

The buyer examines the list to arrive at an ABC classification of the items, which is shown in Exhibit 8-3. The groupings seem natural: the three B items account for over seven times as much annual volume as the five C items, and the two A items account for about nine times as much as the three B items. It is clear that A items should receive major attention. Have them delivered often in small quantities, store them in flow racks at or near the receiving/shipping docks, and carefully monitor and control them. Class Bs should receive moderate attention, and class Cs little attention; for example, handle them manually and store them in conventional racks in a remote part of the warehouse.

EXHIBIT 8-3
ABC Classification—Universal Motor Supply Company

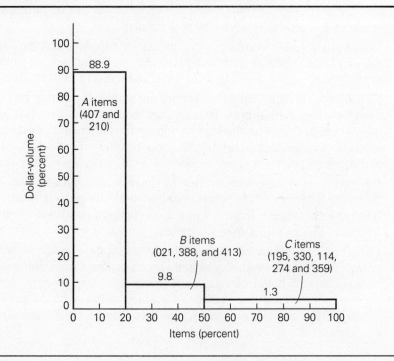

Purchasing and Contracting Procedures

Besides ABC analysis, there are other common purchasing practices and terms that service managers should know. They have to do with arranging the supplier–seller agreement and the terms of that agreement, and they group fairly well into the A, B, and C categories.

Class A items. A class A item may be a service contract, an expensive, seldom-ordered item, or a low-cost item ordered often or in large quantities. Common purchasing measures are:

Soliciting competitive bids on specifications. Specifications may be necessary because the item is nonstandard or because the buying firm wishes to exclude low-quality suppliers. Also, specifications provide a basis for determining compliance with the buyer's requirements. Governments, especially the federal government, intermittently buy based on publicly available specs. Regulations require that for many types of purchases the invitation to bid be published in a widely circulated government document.

Certification. Many companies quality-certify suppliers and their services or goods. Quality-certification sometimes includes such factors as quality of design, training, lead-time, and delivery performance.

Negotiation. Where sources of supply are stable, there may be no need to solicit formal bids. Instead, purchasing teams may just periodically negotiate with the regular source for better price or delivery terms. Typically, negotiation applies to nonstandard class A goods and services.

Buying down and speculation. Buying down means trying to buy an item with a history of cyclic price swings when its price is down. It is a form of speculative buying. In pure speculation, purchases are made for price reasons rather than for meeting an actual need for the goods.

Hedging. Hedging applies especially to commodities, such as wheat, corn, silver, and lumber. Organized futures markets exist for some commodities. A buyer can pay cash to buy a commodity now and at the same time sell a like amount of a future delivery of the commodity. Price changes will mean that losses on one order are offset by gains on the other.

Class B items. Class B goods and moderate-cost services usually warrant less purchasing effort. That applies to many kinds of standard off-the-shelf goods, such as maintenance, repair, and operating (MRO) supplies, as well as standard services, such as those of a plumber or auto body shop. For nonstandard items in the class B cost range, specifications might be necessary, but the expense of soliciting bids is harder to justify than for class A items. Order procedures for the class B category include the following:

Approved supplier lists. Companies like to buy from proven suppliers. Buyers rely on the approved supplier list, especially for class B items, though it also is used for class A and class C buying. The approved supplier list may be based on an old-style performance rating or on a full certification study.

Catalog buying. Perhaps the most common purchasing procedure for off-the-shelf MRO goods is buying out of current catalogs, sometimes with the help of salespeople. Most buyers have shelves full of suppliers' catalogs for this purpose.

Blanket orders. An ongoing but varying need for an item with class B annual volume may call for a blanket-order contract. The blanket order covers a given time period, and deliveries are arranged by sending a simple release notice to the supplier. Price and other matters are covered in the contract.

Systems contract. A systems contract is similar to a blanket order, but it is longer-term and more stringently defined. The purchasing department negotiates the systems contract; purchasing then typically monitors, but does not participate in, ordering. The contract may name certain responsible employees who may order, by mail, phone, or other means, directly from the supplier.

Class C items. Class C or low-cost items are worthy of little attention by purchasing specialists. Buying such items from a supplier on an approved supplier list provides a measure of control. For many items even that is too much control and red tape, and to avoid these, using departments buy out of petty cash funds. Until recently, petty cash buying has been restricted to office employees. Now a few progressive North American companies provide each improvement team with a petty cash fund for purchasing low-cost items that can improve performance.

Performance and Compliance: The Tangibility Factor

One more way that buying companies must look at things to be bought is by their degree of tangibility. The issue is one of accountability. The buying firm needs to ensure that the supplier complies with the contract or purchase order. While this is straightforward for highly tangible goods, it is less so for highly intangible services. Exhibit 8–4 describes eight degrees of tangibility, each of which is discussed briefly below.

- Highly tangible items include simple parts like screws, diodes, and switches. Quality is easily measured.
- Commodities (corn, iron ore, bananas, etc.) are tangible but some of their properties are costly to measure. These may require a certain amount of subjective eyeball judgments to grade quality.
- Simple finished goods are less tangible than commodities. Books, furniture, and fabrics, for example, have several measurable physical properties, but visual inspection for scratches, flaws, and so on, may be more important.

EXHIBIT 8-4
Tangibility of Purchased Goods

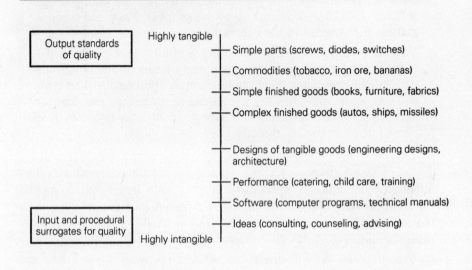

- Complex finished goods (autos, ships, mobile homes) have thousands of measurable physical properties of *form* (e.g., dimensions) and *function* (such as turning radius and speed). Nevertheless, partly subjective judgments of effectiveness (how well a destroyer protects the fleet, or a mobile home keeps the elements out) are also important. For complex goods aimed at consumer markets, even more subjective judgments—about style, comfort, and even status—come into play.

- Designs for tangible goods, such as those rendered by architects and engineers, are harder to judge until the end result (the tangible good itself) becomes reality. If a bridge caves in or a door handle keeps breaking off, we can (in hindsight) judge the design to be bad. The engineer might even be liable for damages. Perhaps the best *up-front* help for buyers of these items is design expertise on the buying team.

- Contracting for performance is growing explosively; catering, child care, and employee training are examples. The end products or outputs are good food, well-adjusted children, and requalified employees. It is difficult to write standards for those outputs into a

contract. Consequently, there is growing use of measures of compliance such as mean number of customer complaints and opinion
polling involving customers, experts, or impartial panels using
some form of Likert scale (a rating scale from 1 to 5, 1 to 7, etc.).

- Software (computer programs, technical or training manuals, operating instruction booklets, etc.) is slightly more intangible. Buyers
of these items must distinguish between the quality of the item
specified—a television set, for example—and the quality of the
software (operating instructions manual) being purchased. A
benchmark-class health care package may not impress employees
because the benefits description booklet is poor. Buyers may set
contract limits such as number of pages or lines of code, but these
hardly measure quality, and the supplier is likely to receive full
pay (even for a shoddy job) just by meeting those limits.

- Highly intangible items, at the bottom of Exhibit 8–4, have no
physically measurable properties. Therefore, purchase contracts
may be based on input and procedural factors. In a contract with a
consultant, input factors may include level of education and years
of experience of the consultants sent out on the job; procedural
factors may include number of people to be interviewed and number of pages on the final consultant's report. Those factors themselves do not account for the quality of the consultant's services,
but they are often treated as surrogates for output quality.

We can conclude that the most serious measurement and compliance
assessment problems occur when buying performance, software, and
ideas, items at the intangible end of the scale. Buying from certified
suppliers, or at least from those with good reputations, helps. But
performance service providers tend to come and go rather than stay and
build clientele and reputation. Software firms and consulting firms are
somewhat more stable. Ironically, poor software or consulting is not
notably destructive to firms' reputations. The reason is that dissatisfied
customers may not admit their displeasure (1) because of the risk of
defamation suits (bad quality is difficult to prove) and (2) because
dissatisfaction would be an admission of having wasted time and money
on poor software or consulting services.

On occasion, however, service providers' failure to perform is publicly
recognized, especially when those providers charge stiff fees for their
failure. An example is the attempted leveraged buyout of UAL Corp.
(United Air Lines' parent) that fell through on October 13, 1989. Already

reeling from plummeting stock values, UAL shareholders nevertheless received a bill for $58.7 million for professional services rendered by the lawyers and bankers hired to complete the deal. Irked by this high price for failure, shareholders and other observers criticized the banks and law firms involved and questioned the wisdom of the UAL Corp. board for its purchase of the services.[7] Even large corporations can have problems in buying service performance.

Public and corporate officials rely increasingly on consultants to help them with sticky decisions. But the inability to write tough contracts leaves the officials at the consultants' mercy. Fortunately, most consultants are professionally dedicated and motivated to maintain self-respect. Still, contracting for intangibles is a major challenge for buyers, one that permeates all organizational transformations. Clearly, trust, openness, and a few good suppliers are key to meeting the purchasing challenge.

SOURCING OUTSIDE OR STAYING INSIDE

Buying from outside sometimes doesn't seem worth the trouble and the cost. However, services provided within the organization can begin to look too costly or unprofessional. The cost side of whether to switch is a classical make-or-buy question. Often, other critical factors besides cost bear on the decision. We'll consider some of those factors after a make-or-buy example.

At some volume of business, the costs of buying outside equal the costs of doing it inside. That volume is the break-even point. Three costs are involved: fixed cost of setting up inside, variable cost per unit inside, and variable cost per unit outside.

Say, for example, that a large company is thinking of setting up its own travel department to save on airline ticket commissions. The current average variable cost of airline tickets is $423 per trip. (The cost varies directly with the number of trips.) With an internal travel department, the estimated cost per ticket would fall to $405 per trip. The company's fixed costs, for salaries and expenses in the new department could come to $80,000 per year. How many trips per year would be required to break even?

A simple break-even formula has fixed cost in the numerator and savings in the denominator. Thus

$$\text{Break-even point} = \frac{\$80,000}{\$423-\$405} = 4,444 \text{ trips per year}$$

This means that if fewer than 4,444 trips are likely, don't set up a travel department. Instead, "stick to your knitting."

The heyday of *not* sticking to one's knitting was the recent era of rampant mergers and acquisitions. One type of acquisition is backward integration—acquisition of a supplier. There can be many reasons for doing so. Short-term financial reasons include tax, stock price, and foreign exchange benefits. Chasing low labor costs (store coupon processing in Haiti, computer programming in India) is also fairly short-term.

A worthy long-term factor is ownership of key technologies or processes. At one time, department stores made lots of money on their own credit cards. Ownership of credit-card processing was vital to the store. Today, the chief guardians of credit-card processing are banks, which are happy to supply credit card services for department stores, airlines, auto companies, or professional societies.

Sometimes poor supplier quality is what triggers thoughts of backward integration. When a company launches a TQM effort, its suppliers' performance might suddenly look inferior. Taking over a supplier's business, however, is usually an overreaction. The mature TQM way of thinking is: It's just as much our fault. We helped create an adversarial relationship, which discourages good supplier performance. The best response is to work with, instead of against, our suppliers—in a true partnership for quality.

CONTRAST

Competitive Sources

Out-Sourcing	*In-Sourcing*
1980s: Not cost competitive? Search the globe for lowest cost and then move.	1990s and beyond: Not cost competitive? Slash nonvalue-adding wastes and stay (or return) home. Not quality competitive? Adopt TQM.

Chapter Nine

Managing Service Materials and Supplies

 Whether it is a store full of goods for sale or a stockroom full of supplies, service inventories deserve good management. Flow control (Chapter 7) and supplier partnerships (Chapter 8) are part of it. In this chapter we continue with some of the fine points. They involve inventory costs, quantities, timing, and performance measures.

CARRYING COSTS

If a store buys a coat and sells it the same day, its only inventory cost is the purchase cost. If maintenance buys 10 fluorescent tubes and installs them the same day, same thing. Usually, we aren't that good at matching inventory in and inventory out. Long spells of idle stock are the norm. And anything sitting around tends to collect dust—and cost.

We are talking about inventory carrying costs. As the following list shows, some of these costs are obvious, some semiobvious, and others hidden.

Obvious carrying costs:
  Capital cost—interest or opportunity costs of working capital tied up in stock.
  Holding cost—stockroom costs of:
    Space.
    Storage implements (e.g., shelving and stock-picking vehicles).
    Insurance on space, equipment, and inventories.
    Inventory taxes.
    Stockkeepers' wages.
    Damage and shrinkage while in storage.
Semiobvious carrying costs:
  Obsolescence.
  Inventory planning and management.
  Stock recordkeeping.
  Physical inventory taking.
Hidden carrying costs:
  Inventory transactions and data processing support.
  Management and technical support for equipment used in storage, handling, and inventory data processing.
  Scrap and rework.
  Lot inspections.
  Lost sales, lost customers because of slow processing.

Obvious Costs

In order to be a true inventory carrying cost, a cost must rise with the growth, and fall with the reduction, of inventory. *Capital cost,* first on the list, clearly qualifies. Company financial managers frequently attempt to secure bank loans or lines of credit to pay for more inventory. Banks often use the inventory as collateral for loans.

Only in abnormal situations can a company avoid capital costs. For example, a store may buy a coat with 30 days to pay the supplier and sell it the same day to a customer who pays cash. On the books, the effect appears as negative inventory.

Next on the list is *holding cost,* which is mainly the cost of running stockrooms. While the accounting system may consider space and storage implements as fixed costs, they exist only to hold stock; therefore, they are true carrying costs. The other more or less obvious holding costs are insurance, taxes, material department wages, damage, and shrinkage costs.

Semiobvious Costs

Semiobvious carrying costs include inventory obsolescence and costs of inventory management and clerical activities. People involved in inventory planning, stock recordkeeping, and physical inventory counting do not actually handle stock, and their offices often are far from stockrooms. Perhaps for these reasons, some companies include those costs as general or operating overhead. Clearly, however, they are inventory carrying costs.

Obsolescence cost is nearly zero when materials arrive just in time for use, but it can be high if companies buy in large batches and then find that the need for the items has dried up. High-fashion stores are acutely aware of obsolescence as a cost of carrying inventory. Other organizations (e.g., military and civil defense agencies) often pay too little attention to it.

Hidden Costs

Carrying costs that commingle with other costs tend to be hidden. These include the cost of associates' time for entering inventory usage and scrap data into terminals plus the cost of the terminals, usually treated incorrectly as operating costs. Much greater are the associated central processing costs (hardware, software, and computer operations) and the costs of corrections and report processing. In inventory-intensive firms, inventory management is the dominant computer application; its costs have been conveniently bundled into the information system department's total costs, but they are actually hidden inventory carrying costs. Costs of management and technical support for storage, handling, and data processing equipment are also carrying costs, but they are rarely treated as such.

Principle 11:   Minimize idle inventory.

Scrap and rework costs also fall with decreases in inventories, including decreases in lot sizes. This is true in processing perishables (such as cutting off rot from food items), in wholesaling and retailing (e.g., an entire lot of garments missing a buttonhole), and in information processing.

As an example, suppose telephone sales associates send sales orders forward once a day in batches averaging 800 orders. Order-entry clerks in the next department might find numerous defects, such as missing quantity, incomplete address, or lack of a promise date. Sometimes, especially for a new promotion, an entire lot of 800 orders will contain the same error. More commonly, errors will occur at some average percentage. Either way, order-entry clerks end up sending the faulty forms back to the sales office for rework, probably the next day (see Exhibit 9–1A). Meanwhile, time has passed and sales people are busy with other orders. They are no longer clear about the details of yesterday's orders and the likely root causes of yesterday's order processing errors.

If salespeople processed and forwarded orders in lots of 20 instead of 800 (Exhibit 9–1B), maximum damage would be 20, which could be sent back while the trail of causes is still warm.

Best of all would be for a sales associate to hand the order directly to an order-entry clerk (Exhibit 9–1C). They become a team, intolerant of errors on order forms. Large defective lots are no longer possible. When an error occurs, it is usually discovered right away while the cause is still obvious. The team finds ways to permanently eliminate the cause of the errors, steadily driving down the rate of defective order forms.

Principle 13:   Decrease cycle interval and lot size.

Inspection costs merit similar scrutiny. Inspectors facing large lots have the big job of sorting out the bad ones. However, some companies avoid large lots by adopting just-in-time techniques. They avoid large *bad* lots by implementing strict process controls to prevent defects rather than merely detecting defects. The tie-in between inspection costs and lot-size quantities is clear, and the conclusion is that even inspectors may be treated as a carrying cost.

Last is a perverse carrying cost. When inventories are at their highest, inventory handling is usually the slowest. Heavy transaction and stock-picking workloads cause delays in materials offices and stockrooms. Stock record accuracy falls, and some items are hard to find or lost. Customer service deteriorates—the most serious kind of cost. The best

EXHIBIT 9–1
Effect of Lot Size on Rework/Scrap

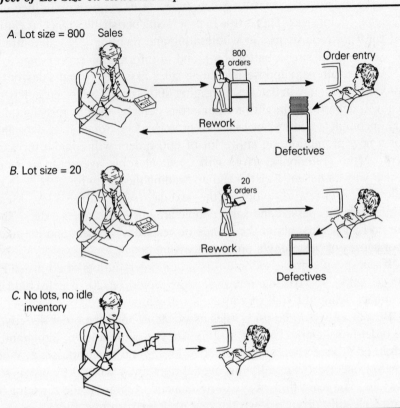

A. Lot size = 800   Sales

800 orders

Order entry

Rework

Defectives

B. Lot size = 20

20 orders

Rework

Defectives

C. No lots, no idle inventory

ways to avoid this cost are by keeping lot sizes small, move distances short, and supplier partnerships strong. Then, service materials and supplies flow cleanly and quickly to their destinations, thus helping to preserve and strengthen bonds to customers.

Uses of Carrying Cost

In some organizations inventories are such a dominant cost that virtually every investment proposal has an inventory effect. Therefore, it is important to use a realistic carrying cost when doing a financial analysis for a proposal.

Traditionally, carrying cost has been stated as an annual rate based on the item's value. Older books on inventory management suggested a rate of 25 percent as a good average. But that rate is based on the obvious carrying costs and possibly some of the semiobvious costs.

If all carrying costs are included, as they should be, what is the proper rate? No studies have answered that question definitively. However, Ernst & Young suggests a rate of at least 48 percent.[1] To see what 48 percent means, imagine a $100 chair sitting in a stockroom for a year. The owner would be paying another $48 for the chair in the form of the costs of carrying it.

The best-known financial analysis that uses carrying-cost rates is in calculating an economic order quantity or lot size, our next topic.

ORDER QUANTITY

Common sense is plentiful at Poge, Poge, Perry, and Wacker. In the mail room, Arvin follows the commonsense practice of accumulating two hours' worth of incoming mail and faxes (interdepartmental as well as external) before delivering them to the departments. In accounts receivable, Latoya generally spends mornings on problem accounts, then completes her work on new invoices and forwards them to another desk in the afternoon. Every other desk in every other office follows similarly sensible practices: Accumulating a reasonable pile of similar items to work on before attacking the pile, and waiting for a reasonable load before forwarding it to its next stop.

What the Poge employees don't see, however, are the consequences of their so-called reasonableness. Important letters and faxes arriving in the early afternoon may not reach the addressee until late in the day or the next morning, and then they may end up in a high in-basket pile. Moreover, invoices for completed work must pass from desk to desk and department to department before being mailed to clients who owe the firm money. New business also gets the same slow treatment, which sends some clients to the competition.

These inefficient business practices are common in law offices, banks, insurance companies, government agencies, hospitals, and manufacturing companies. The remedy is to cut the process lot sizes.

One way of thinking is that the customer's lot size should be the supplier's lot size: the *lot-for-lot* idea. It may be passed down through several stages of supply: "The customer bought four premium tires, so we pulled four from stores, and they ordered four from our distributor, who ordered four from the manufacturer." With no batching into larger lots, orders are frequent. While this might cause order processing costs to be high, inventories are low, and supplier activities closely match real demand.

Is there a way of weighing the extra order processing costs against the lower inventories? There is. The method is to find the economic order quality (EOQ), which is one of the oldest tools of management. Our purpose here, beside giving a brief example of how it works, is to show why EOQ tends to be at odds with synchroservice.

EOQ and TQM

While the EOQ concept is to find the economically correct lot size, TQM strives for continuous improvement. That means driving lot sizes down continuously. Benefits of smaller lots cut across departments and reach out to customers (and thus would not be apparent to an isolated inventory manager). They include:

1. Smaller lots get used up sooner; hence, defectives are caught earlier. This reduces scrap and rework and allows sources of problems to be quickly caught and corrected while the evidence of possible causes is still fresh.

2. With small lots, floor space to hold inventory can be cut and workstations can be positioned very close together. Then employees can see and talk to one another, learn one another's job (which improves staffing flexibility), and function as a team.

3. Small lots allow tasks to be closely linked in time. A problem at one workstation (or supplier firm) has a ripple effect; subsequent operations (or customer sites) are temporarily starved of inventory. Provider and user must treat the problem as a joint problem, and a team attack on such problems becomes natural and common.

4. Flow control is simplified, and costs of support staff, handling and storage devices, control systems, and so forth, are reduced.

5. Most important, customers are served more quickly and flexibly, which increases revenue and avoids the expenses of attracting new customers when present customers exit.

Smaller Trains at Conrail

In a strategic shift, Conrail is putting fast freight movement, a requirement of its just-in-time customers, ahead of productivity. The key change is keeping trains shorter. "Although longer trains saved on crew and locomotive costs, they resulted in freight sitting in yards and missing connections."

Source: Daniel Machalaba, "Highballing Along: New Conrail Resembles a Growth Company," *The Wall Street Journal,* November 20, 1992.

The smaller the lot size, the greater the benefits. The limit? An ideal lot size of one. Two key steps in making small lots feasible are reduction of setup costs and order processing costs (via EDI and supplier–customer partnerships).

In our earlier example, at Poge, Arvin delivered mail every two hours. How far could Arvin reasonably cut that lot size? Could he cut it to 15 minutes' worth, reducing the nonvalue-adding delivery delay and raising customer responsiveness eightfold? It depends partly on the distance, and partly on the mode of transport. A 15-minute delivery interval would make sense if all the offices were together on one floor of an office building. If the offices are geographically dispersed, maybe it's time to bring them together. It might make sense to form office cells with complete teams in the same room, thus avoiding the mail room for all internal transfers.

> ***Principle 6:*** Organize focused cells.

Using the EOQ

Despite its limitations, the EOQ is used a good deal, but sometimes carelessly. We'll consider its use and possible misuse in a bookstore— Example 9–1. The store uses a common formula:

$$Q = \sqrt{\frac{2DO}{IC}}$$

where

D = Demand (per year)

O = Order processing cost (per order)

I = Item cost (per unit)

C = Carrying cost (per year)—expressed as a decimal proportion of item cost

EXAMPLE 9–1 Economic Order Quantity—Bookstore

B. K. White, manager of Suburban Books, is thinking of purchasing best-selling titles in economic order quantities. White has assembled the following data:

Inventory on hand (books):	
Estimated average last year	8,000
Estimated average cost per book	$10
Average inventory value	$80,000
Annual holding cost:	
Rental: Building and fixtures	$7,000
Estimated shrinkage losses	700
Insurance	300
Total	$8,000
Annual capital cost:	
Capital invested (tied up in books)	$80,000
Interest rate	15%
Total	$12,000
Annual carrying cost (annual holding cost + annual capital cost):	
$8,000 + $12,000	$20,000
Carrying cost rate, I (annual carrying cost ÷ inventory value):	
$20,000/$80,000	0.25
Purchase order processing cost, O:	
Estimate for preparation and invoice handling	$4 per order

Now White has the cost data needed to calculate EOQs. He selects his biggest seller as the first book to be ordered by EOQ—*Gone with the Wind,* which is enjoying a burst of renewed popularity in the store. The paperback recently sold at a rate of 80 copies per month and wholesales for $5 per copy. Thus, for the EOQ equation:

C = $5 per unit

D = 80 units/month × 12 months/year

  = 960 units/year

Then

$$EOQ = \sqrt{\frac{2DO}{IC}} = \sqrt{\frac{2(960)(4)}{0.25(5)}} = 78 \text{ copies/order}$$

The EOQ, 78 copies, is about one month's supply (78 copies/order ÷ 80 copies/month = 0.98 month's/order); it is also $390 worth ($5/copy × 78 copies/order = $390 per order).

White's assistant, M. B. Ainsworth, cannot resist pointing out to her boss a fallacy in this EOQ of 78 copies. She puts it this way: "Mr. White, I'm not so sure that *Gone with the Wind* is the right book to order by EOQ. The EOQ is based on last month's demand of 80. But demand might be 120 next month and 150 the month after. Also, the average carrying cost rate, *I*, was based mostly on larger hardcover books, which cost more to store. Maybe we should use EOQ only on our stable sellers in hardcover. How about Webster's *New Collegiate Dictionary*?"

When we see inventory on a shelf, some of it is there because of ordering in lot quantities. The rest of it is there for protection against uncertainty. That quantity is called safety stock.

SAFETY STOCK

Safety stock is like the spare tire in your auto or your homeowner's insurance policy. You hope you don't need it, but you don't dare operate without it. Safety stock is expensive, however, and needs careful management.

Retailers and wholesalers are very safety-stock conscious. For example, as Peters and Waterman told us, Frito-Lay's corporate culture centers on a 99.5 percent service level, which means that a store shelf will be empty of a Frito product only 5 times out of 1,000.[2] To achieve that, Frito must gather data on the variability (standard deviation) of demand for the product in that store. The standard deviation, plus replenishment lead time, go into a formula that computes the safety stock. (The statistical safety stock formula is widely available in inventory management books.)

Blind use of the safety stock formula, however, is poor practice. Safety stock should usually depend on more than just demand variability and lead time. Other factors are:

Cost. Higher cost items should have low safety stocks. For example, a hospital should not keep many high-cost prosthetic devices (artificial limbs) on hand. Its safety stock of low-cost tongue depressors, however, might be a year's worth.

Space. If the item is very bulky (e.g., pillows), the safety stock should be small, and vice versa.

Consequences of a stockout. Sometimes a wide variety of options, such as substitute items, are available in the event of a stockout; this cuts safety stock needs.

Obsolescence. High-tech items, such as heart valves, become obsolete quickly; thus, keep safety stocks small.

Uncertainty. For new items, demand and replenishment lead times are not very predictable; so keep larger safety stocks.

In practice, a user (or its supplier) could adopt a two-step safety-stock procedure. First, a computer routine computes and lists statistical safety stocks for large numbers of inventory items. Next, buyers review the listings and adjust safety stocks to account for the above five additional factors.

At a hospital, for example, computer listings might recommend a large safety stock of a certain rare blood type, chiefly because variability of demand is high. The buyer, reviewing the computer's recommendation, rates consequences of a stockout as high, which supports keeping a high safety stock. On the other hand, the buyer knows obsolescence for the blood is high, and in an emergency blood can be flown in; these two factors suggest low safety stocks. The final decision is to keep a minimum safety stock.

REPLENISHMENT

The common way of replenishing stocks is to reorder when they reach some low level, referred to as the reorder point. The idea is probably as old as humanity—maybe older, since some animals, such as squirrels, also replenish low stocks. The low-stock point should be just enough to get through the normal replenishment period, plus safety stock to allow for uncertainties.

Low-stock-point systems range from simple eyeball to computerized. The eyeball method is simply noticing when stock gets down to some easy-to-see low point, then entering the item on a replenish list. A single person in charge of stock will make the method work well. With more people in the stockroom, however, it is too easy to become lax. In busy times, someone will draw an item down to its low point, and think, "I'll record it later." It doesn't happen. The result later is a stockout, and then the blame shifting begins.

Laxness and failing to do things right the first time leads to excesses as well. One is double ordering: "Did I remember to record that item on the order sheet? Guess not." Another is not having definite locations for everything, which results in stocking the same item in more than one location.

Problems like this are naturals for the TQM treatment: Improvement teams attack root causes, plot results on wall charts, and attack again. One chart should show declining stockout frequency. Another, plotting inventory reductions, shows overall improvement in stock management. Charting the improvements is essential. The improvement that isn't measured doesn't stick.

Some problems in inventory management can benefit from information technology. There is no point in putting in bar-code scanners where simple visual stock management will do. At outer organizational boundaries, however, scanning is effective both for reducing errors and for cutting out nonvalue-adding administrative steps. Besides scanning, a software technology called material requirements planning (MRP) is sometimes useful. MRP is a way of improving the timing of material ordering and receipt.

TIMING: MRP AND JIT

Material requirements planning uses computer power to directly relate inventory needs to "parent" demands. In services, most parent (customer) demands are unknown until late in the game. Therefore, companies usually just keep common materials and supplies on hand, and special-order any items needed for a special service. Where services are specific and by appointment or reservation, however, MRP can work. The computer calculates material quantities and timing. It aims to ensure that the items arrive close to the time of the appointment.

MRP Applications

This method can plan the ordering of some (not all) of the supplies needed for scheduled surgeries, chartered tours, freight hauling, and catered dining. Example 9–2 illustrates the method for a caterer.

EXAMPLE 9–2 MRP for a Caterer

Imagine you are a caterer and have a schedule of parties to cater every night for the next two weeks. Your policy is zero inventories (except for incidentals like seasonings). To plan for zero, you consult menus for every

EXHIBIT 9–2
Planned Order Release Determination—Salami

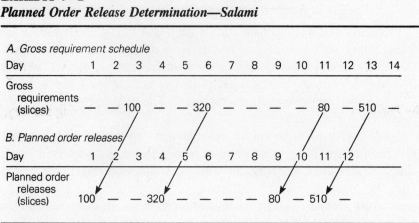

A. *Gross requirement schedule*

Day	1	2	3	4	5	6	7	8	9	10	11	12	13	14
Gross requirements (slices)	—	—	100	—	—	320	—	—	—	—	80	—	510	—

B. *Planned order releases*

Day	1	2	3	4	5	6	7	8	9	10	11	12
Planned order releases (slices)	100	—	—	320	—	—	—	—	80	—	510	—

food dish to be provided for each catering order in the next two weeks. Menu quantities times number of servings equals gross requirements. Let us say that gross requirements for salami are as shown in part A of Exhibit 9–2. Salami is required in the quantities shown on days 3, 6, 11, and 13.

You normally order salami from a deli two days ahead of time (purchase lead time for salami is two days). Therefore, you plan to release salami orders as shown in part B. Each planned order release is two days in advance of the gross requirement shown in part A.

The schedule of planned order releases is correctly timed and in the exact quantities needed. It is a material requirements plan for one of the components that goes into the foods to be catered. It is a plan for zero inventory, and is achieved if the deli delivers the salami orders in the planned two days. If deliveries come a day early, inventory builds. Also, if an order of salami arrives on time but a customer cancels the catering order, residual (leftover) inventory builds. Such supply and demand uncertainties create some inventory when MRP is used, but MRP cuts inventory considerably from what it is when the producer (caterer) *plans* to keep components in stock.

Thus far, MRP has seen only scattered uses in services (but is widely used in manufacturing). For example, under the ownership of American Airlines, Sky Chef, the airline's caterer, used a modified version of MRP. When Sky Chef became independent of American and began catering for other airlines, it reverted to less-precise methods. (MRP may have been easier to use with only one customer.)

Just in Time

MRP and just in time (JIT) are not equivalent. JIT is more often associated with simpler noncomputer-based methods. These include queue limitation, quick setup, creation of customer- or service-focused cells, and "hand-to-hand" (or desk-to-desk) processing. JIT's main purpose is to closely synchronize and quicken a sequence of operations leading to the final customer. Since that often slashes inventories all along the way, JIT is sometimes thought of as an inventory system.

In the pre-JIT era, closed, controlled stockrooms and computerized planning were favored for improved inventory performance. Discipline and accuracy went up, but responsibility moved one more layer away from frontline operations. Instead of frontline users owning their own stocks, inventory controllers (layer one) did, or computers (layer two) did. A mature JIT system is unlikely to have closed stockrooms. Instead, the far smaller stocks are back on the front lines, clearly marked off and queue limited. Computers still usually track purchases, final issues, and balances of purchased items on hand. (The value of inventory balances is a ledger item, legally required.) They need not monitor the quick flow of stocks from process to process.

Principle 8:   Reduce variation before automation.

MEASURING INVENTORY PERFORMANCE

Regardless of the inventory system, we need ways of measuring performance. Among the many in use, the following are good ones:

- *Stock record accuracy.* In simple form this is just the percentage of items whose stock records are accurate. The store or warehouse finds out when it does an inventory count. Good stockrooms today have 99–100 percent accuracy, whereas not long ago 90 percent was good.

- *Fill rate.* This is the percentage of stocked items on hand when a customer wants one. Its opposite is the stockout rate. Joseph Patton, a consultant, says that his clients typically achieve over 98 percent fill rates from their main stock point (usually the national distribution center).[3]

- *Pipeline efficiency.* In the age of quick response programs, we need new measures of flow control through the whole pipeline. This includes suppliers, freight carriers, distributors, and final users (e.g., stores, hospitals, schools, the Red Cross). These QRP partners should pay attention to elapsed time from the supplier's order to point of use at the retailer. Separate measures include, for carriers, time from receipt of the *advance shipping notice* (one QRP device) to store receipt of the goods; and for end users, time from receipt to availability in frontline services.

- *Annual inventory turnover.* This is the ratio of annual purchase cost to average inventory value. (A variation, usable in retailing, uses annual sales instead of annual purchases.) It reflects how many times the average inventory is sold (or used) per year. If annual purchases in a hospital ward are $500,000 and average inventory is $400,000, turnover is:

$$\frac{\$500,000}{\$400,000}, \text{ or } 1.25$$

This would be terrible, but typical of hospitals in the United States before the new era of belt-tightening. The very high cost of medical devices makes them an easy target for TQM teams. Turnovers of 5 or 10 should be attainable within a few years. In comparison, grocery store chains achieve turnovers of around 16 or more (higher if specializing in produce).

This completes Part III, on planning for service demand, which sets the stage for action—taken up in Part IV.

IV

TRANSLATING SERVICE DEMANDS INTO OUTCOMES

Planned orders generate activity, which results in service outcomes. The *kind* of activity depends on kind of service. One distinct kind is service *jobs,* which are high in variety and low in volume; we treat this topic in Chapter 10. Another is *projects*—complex efforts—taken up in Chapter 11.

Chapter Ten

Scheduling and Control of Service Jobs

Services: Job, Project, and Continuous Mode

Job Scheduling

Throughput-Time Elements

Work in Process

Backward and Forward Scheduling

Resource Scheduling

Gantt Charts

Expediting

Priorities

Monitoring for Control

 Much of life's work consists of small service jobs: Make six copies, flowchart a process, restring a tennis racket, complete a sale, repair three broken fence boards, or visit a client. In each case, the next job is different. It may take more or less time and consume more or fewer resources. Scheduling in this high-variety environment is difficult, control is elusive. Yet the difficulties must be overcome, or costs soar and customers defect.

The challenge is to tame the variety. Or overpower it with scheduling and control procedures and technology. Taming the variety, the path of least resistance, is preferred. However, clever scheduling and control devices still have their place. Before discussing these options, we need to note main differences between the job mode and other modes of service delivery.

EXHIBIT 10–1
Service Modes and Output Characteristics

		Service Output Characteristics	
		Unique	**Common**
Service Mode	**Project**	Architecture System development Remodeling Repairs Letter writing Restaurants Retail sales Schools Fast foods Payroll Insurance claims Security guard Patient monitoring	
	Job		
	Continuous		

SERVICES: JOB, PROJECT, AND CONTINUOUS MODE

Most human services and back-office support consist of a succession of service *jobs*. Some services, however, are delivered in the continuous mode. *Continuous services* consist of doing the same thing over long periods of time (e.g., a security guard or a heart-monitoring machine hooked to a cardiac patient). A third mode is the service *project*: a large, multitask undertaking that stretches out over weeks, months, or years. Projects are the most difficult to plan, schedule, and control. Continuous services are the least difficult. Jobs are in the middle.

Exhibit 10–1 shows the three service modes along with examples ranging from unique to common. The common, continuously delivered services (e.g., processing insurance claims and patient monitoring) are usually scheduled and controlled in a highly streamlined fashion. We start by standardizing the process so that its scheduling is routine and predictable. High levels of training and maintenance ensure high-quality service, shorter throughput times, low costs per unit or per time increment, and few surprises. Wouldn't it be nice if all service demands could be processed so easily? In view of the simplicity of managing continuous service activities, we need not say much more about it. Instead, we may treat this mode as an ideal. That is, in taming the variety for service jobs (in this chapter) and projects (next chapter), we look for ways to streamline so that scheduling and control may be more like those of continuous services.

The streamlining approach relies heavily on simplifying, sorting, and eliminating non-value-adding steps. The effect is to reduce the number of schedule-disrupting variables. This approach is taken up in various ways in most of the previous chapters, noted as follows:

- Get focused: Strategically limit the variety of businesses per organizational unit (Chapter 1).

- Reduce, simplify, and standardize designs for the line of services (Chapter 3).

- Control processes at the source, rather than discovering mishaps downstream (Chapter 4).

- Stay tuned to the pulse of the market via comprehensive demand forecasting (Chapter 5).

- Employ a cross-functional master planning team to plan capacity and master schedules so that demand and supply are a reasonably close fit (Chapter 6).

- Adopt quick-response and just-in-time flow controls to remove sources of non-value-adding delay and stay close to the actual demand changes (Chapter 7).

- Adopt simple queue limitation flow controls (Chapter 7), thereby avoiding flow-control transactions.

- Cut to a few good supplier–partners (Chapter 8), thus shrinking purchasing complications.

- Cut job, lot, and batch sizes so that materials are ordered or produced based on current demand, thus avoiding problems of having too many of the wrong items and being out of the right ones (Chapter 9).

The remaining chapter discussion, on the basics of scheduling, includes further points on how to simplify and streamline in the job mode.

Streamlined Patient Transfers: Hours to Minutes

The process of admitting patients to Northwest Hospital's Transitional Care Unit (TCU) in Seattle was cumbersome. It took 6 to 12 hours just to get the necessary approvals when a physician referred a patient to the TCU. Then the patient's chart had to be reviewed, which was delayed until the next day. Thus, it took at least 24 hours and often 48 hours for the patient finally to be moved to the TCU.

"Five people evaluated each patient" because, explained Gayle Ward, assistant director of nursing, "there were two different philosophies" for admission. One centered on control of patients and payments, the other on smooth management of evolving patient care. Because of the cumbersome admissions procedure, some physicians had become reluctant to refer patients; the TCU's beds were underutilized, and the unit had become a financial problem for the hospital.

Thus, the TCU admission process was ripe for improvement when TCU's total quality management training program began in July of 1992. In conjunction with training in the quality sciences by an outside consultant, a project team was formed composed of Becky Larson from care management; Matt Quaterman, admissions coordinator; Rebecca Pelroy, from TCU billing; Pat Ford, utilization review coordinator; and the acute care case managers, Jo Croot and Gayle Ward. The team developed a process flow diagram for the admissions process and then "streamlined it by eliminating complexity and rework. The staff didn't think [the new process] would work."

Jo said, "Give me one week. . . . That first day I had about 40 calls and messages with questions about the process. I kept saying, 'Stick to the diagram.' We started turning referrals around from six hours to less than one hour and filling beds as soon as they became empty."

Within two weeks, the new process of relying on the judgment of the case managers, rather than on the several review stages, was working. It reduced the admissions workload by eight hours a day for Jo and her staff. Delays for hand-carrying paperwork were also eliminated. "We do almost everything by phone [and let the] paperwork catch up." Admissions that once took as long as two days were cut to 20 minutes. "Physicians are happier with the service, beds fill quicker, there are more admissions from outside the hospital, and the evening shift is also admitting patients."

The streamlined procedure has exposed underlying stumbling blocks, according to Jo Croot. After implementation, however, Jo had continued to

---

Streamlined Patient Transfers—(continued)

feel frustrated by the number of referrals that were refused admission. "I tracked down the reasons why and made a bar chart." Her chart, tracking 51 such refusals, showed the following:

- 1 patient was admitted instead to the rehabilitation unit.
- 1 was sent instead to an outside gero-psychiatric unit.
- 2 had no insurance.
- 2 had died.
- 25 had been discharged directly to their homes.
- 20 been placed in some other nursing home, hospital, or other facility.

The study confirmed that "these 51 referrals were appropriately screened and placed elsewhere by our case managers." Thus, by her bar chart, Jo had developed the evidence that the new admissions process was not only quick but also producing correct (high-quality) referral decisions.

JOB SCHEDULING

In common usage the word *schedule* usually means a completion time or date and perhaps also a start time. A schedule may also state the quantity (e.g., number of passengers the taxi driver is to pick up, number of paychecks payroll must print tonight).

Scheduling a service requires answers to three questions:

1. When can the job be completed? (Based on standard times.)
2. When should the job be completed? (Based on date of customer need.)
3. When will the job be completed? (Based on realities in operating work centers.)

It simplifies things if all three questions have the same answer. For example, suppose a patient is undergoing a complete physical examination. An early step is withdrawing specimens of various body fluids. The physician may want the results of laboratory analysis of a certain specimen to be ready at the end of the exam, say, 30 minutes later; that answers question two (when should it be completed?). Perhaps the standard time, adjusted for efficiency and utilization, is also 30 minutes; that answers question one (when can it be done?). Suppose the lab has no higher-priority jobs that would interfere with this lab test; then the job can be expected to be completed in 30 minutes, which answers question three (when will it be done?). Since all three questions have the same answer, it is clear that the lab test should be scheduled to start upon withdrawal of the body fluids and be completed 30 minutes later.

Actually, it is not very likely that a lab can complete its testing as soon as the physician desires the results. In a lab queues of job orders form and jostle for priority. Some may spend long hours in queue awaiting their turn.

Throughput-Time Elements

In job operations, throughput or response time to provide a service usually contains much more delay time than actual work; that is, a client or document spends far more time waiting or idle than being processed. The elements of throughput time for a given service are as follows, roughly in descending order of significance:

1. Queue time.
2. Service time.
3. Setup/get-ready time.
4. Wait time (wait for instructions, transportation, supplies, etc.)
5. Inspection time.
6. Move time.
7. Other.

Queue time (the first element) often accounts for 90 percent or more of total throughput time. This is typical for customers buying tickets or paying tolls or for documents processed in offices. Other delays (items three through seven in the above list) take up part of the remaining 10 percent, which leaves service time (value-adding operations) with a very small percentage of total lead time.

Service time may be precisely measured using standard time techniques (see Chapter 12). Total throughput time, however, is hard to pin down. Accurate estimates, and therefore accurate schedules and promises to customers, are likely only when service centers are uncongested; only then can the typical job sail through without long and variable queue times at each service center. One of the scheduler's jobs is to keep things uncongested, that is, without too much work in process.

Work in Process

The work-in-process problem is attacked directly with quick-response techniques. The benefits of keeping service channels unclogged include the following:

1. *Service.* Low congestion means less queue time and quicker response to customers; also, with less queue time there is less uncertainty in the schedule and customers may be given better status information.
2. *Forecasts.* We know that forecasts are more accurate for shorter periods into the future, that is, for the shorter throughput times that result from smaller amounts of work in process.
3. *Flow control workforce.* Less congestion means less need for control by expediters and dispatchers.
4. *Customers are happy when they don't have to wait in long lines.* They get angry and may take their business elsewhere if lines get too long.

      Principle 11:   Cut wait time and inventory.

Despite the advantages of low work in process, it can also make managers nervous, fearful that service centers will run out of work. Each job in the work stream usually will require different operation times at each service center it visits. This causes work to pile up and overload some centers and, potentially, underload others. As the job mix changes, and it often changes quickly, the pattern of over- and underloading changes. The scheduler is under pressure to overload on the average in order to hold down the number of underloaded service centers.

Backward and Forward Scheduling

For services offered on demand, the usual customer need date is ASAP—as soon as possible. The service is performed immediately or is scheduled forward on the soonest possible date.

For services provided by appointment, *backward scheduling* may be used. An example is deliveries of checks and deposit slips from a small bank to a larger bank's computer service center. The service center may require delivery by 9 PM each day. If so, each delivery stop is backward scheduled; that is, the scheduler successively subtracts move and operation times from 9 PM. The resulting schedule might appear as shown in the accompanying diagram.

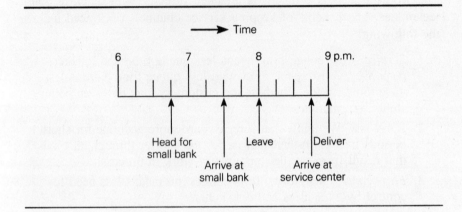

Backward and *forward scheduling* may be used in tandem. A scheduler might be asked to estimate the earliest date on which a job can be completed, which calls for forward scheduling. The date of need could be beyond the calculated earliest completion date; backward scheduling might then be used to determine the scheduled start date.

Retailers and wholesalers also use both forward and backward scheduling. Generally, inventories that are replenished by reorder point are forward scheduled. Goods needed for a special event (e.g., a wedding or New Year's Eve) may be backward scheduled from the date of the net requirement.

RESOURCE SCHEDULING

Usually when a client schedules an appointment, at the same time the service center reserves (schedules) the necessary resources. But how much is necessary? Will an appointment for tax advice tie up the tax advisor for 45 minutes or an hour and a half? In this case, it may not matter much. If several tax advisors are in the office, arriving clients—with appointments—just go to the available advisor. Staff flexibility makes resource scheduling easy.

Too often, however, staff skills are overly specialized. One hospital counted 598 separate job classifications, many filled by just one person! In such cases, every procedure that takes longer than expected, as well as every situation in which the skilled person is unavailable, ripples, disrupting schedules for other services. The point is that cross-training (with few job classifications) is necessary for effective scheduling—as well as for other reasons that have been noted in earlier chapters.

Principle: 7   Cross-train for mastery of multiple skills.

Reservations apply as well to physical resources: a table at a restaurant, a seat on an airplane, time on a personal computer at school, or rental of a bulldozer. These are limited or costly resources. As demands on them rise and fall, they alternate between being oversubscribed and underused. There is no way to schedule around those problems, but capacity policies mentioned in Chapter 6 can lessen their impact. One policy is offering incentives to induce customers to choose off-peak periods. Another, for transportation companies, is the shuttle system: When enough travelers or freight are present, add another flight or bus.

Shuttle systems may keep physical resources busier, but they raise havoc in scheduling staff. Retailers and other businesses that rely heavily on irregular part-time people are similar. Every employee on the rolls has personal preferences and shifting availability. Juggling those human concerns against changing staffing needs can be a full-time job. It helps if the staffing pool is experienced, cross-trained, and sufficiently large.

Scheduling aids include computer spreadsheets and customized software. More often, schedulers just enter the schedule manually on a calendar-based display. Many services rely on a form of display called the Gantt chart (named after Henry Gantt, one of the pioneers of scientific management).

Gantt Charts

Gantt charts have time on one scale and the resource or service to be scheduled on the other. Exhibit 10–2 shows three examples—for a machine, space, and people. Part A is a Gantt schedule for a business computer. Scheduled blocks of time are for running the payroll, accounts receivable, and inventory. Empty time blocks are available for other scheduled or unscheduled uses of the computer.

EXHIBIT 10–2
Common Forms of Gantt Charts

A. Schedule for a computer

Scheduled jobs	M	T	W	T	F	S	S	M	T	W	T	F	S	S	M	T	W	T
Payroll			■							■							■	
Accounts receivable				■							■							■
Inventory					■								■					

B. Schedule for classrooms

Classroom schedule	(Monday)			Hour				
	6	7	8	9	10	11	12	1
CBA 100				MGM 331	ACCT 101			MGM
CBA 101		ECON 205			ECON 400		FIN 394	

C. Schedule for labor

		Dentist's appointments
Mon.	8:00	Mrs. Harrison
	8:30	↓
	9:00	J. Peters
	9:30	Steve Smith
	10:00	
	10:30	
	11:00	↓

Part B shows a Gantt schedule for reserving classrooms. Schedule blocks indicate start and stop times, as well as the service (course of instruction) scheduled. Part C shows a schedule of patients for a single dentist. For a dental clinic, add columns for each dentist or dental hygienist.

There are endless variations on these three charts. The most common variation lists employee names on one axis and their schedules on the other.

EXHIBIT 10–3
Gantt Control Chart—Renovation Work

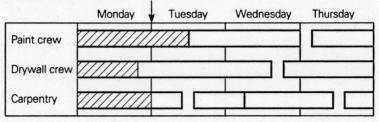

A. Schedule at first of week

B. Progress after one day

C. Progress after two days

Sometimes a Gantt chart is used for both scheduling and schedule control. This is especially the case in maintenance services. Examples are renovation, major maintenance, and extensive overhauls; nonmaintenance examples in which Gantt control charts might be used include computer systems analysis and programming projects, as well as computer program maintenance.

Exhibit 10–3 shows a Gantt control chart for renovation work. An arrow at the top of each chart identifies the current day. Part A is an initial schedule for three crews.

Part B shows progress made after one day. The shading indicates amount of work done, which probably is estimated by the crew chief, in percent of completion. Two thirds of the first paint job was scheduled for Monday, but the paint crew got the whole job done that day. While the paint crew is one half-day ahead of schedule, drywall is one quarter-day behind. Carpentry did Monday's scheduled work on Monday and is on schedule.

Part C for Tuesday shows painting falling behind, drywall on schedule, and carpentry ahead.

So that they are easy to adjust, schedule boards often use Velcro or magnetic strips, pegs, plastic inserts, and the like, to block out schedules and to show progress. Such boards are common in construction offices, project managers' headquarters, maintenance departments, and retail stores and restaurants.

Expediting

When a job is late or a key customer is getting impatient, our usual reaction is to *expedite:* do whatever is necessary to push the job through, and never mind the chaos and interruptions that might ensue. In almost any line of work, unexpected hot jobs and processing obstacles make expediting necessary at least once in a while.

In the complex case of dozens, or hundreds, of service jobs in process at any given time, the job mixture will generally include many nonurgent jobs along with a few hot ones. The scheduler's tendency (and the firm's policy) is to overload the schedule for each service center, let the less-urgent jobs or customers wait, and push the hot jobs through via some form of expediting. In formal systems, sometimes people called expediters may physically move jobs along, mustering whatever resources are necessary and pushing aside any less-important work.

It's easy to see how this system works in the case of an emergency patient at a clinic or hospital. Medical staffers simply make a judgment as to criticality and process more-critical patients before others who had earlier positions in the queues.

A disruptive form of expediting halts a job already in process. For example, work might be interrupted in payroll to process a special paycheck; in accounts payable, for meeting tight discount terms on a very large purchase; in sales, for processing a big sales order; or in guided tours, for guiding a group of VIPs.

Expediting has always been considered, at best, a necessary evil, and superior alternatives have emerged. Time-based competition drives services toward speedy processing every time, not just for hot jobs. Queue limitation practices plus high levels of readiness and quick setup pave the way. Still, some customers and jobs deserve special treatment. The best way to handle them is by priority in the scheduling and dispatching phase rather than later in the form of expediting.

PRIORITIES

At retail, the usual priority system is simply first come, first served. Customers are homogeneous; that is, one is not more important than another. First come, first served runs itself. The retailer need not pay a dispatcher to pick and choose among customers.

Are wholesalers and back offices blessed with such simplicity? Yes, but only if orders can be processed quickly enough, with no queuing or other delays at each service center. If wholesale orders can be filled in, say, a day or less, the company probably will elect just to process orders as they come in; an exception might be an urgent order, which can receive high-priority treatment, such as hand carrying.

Some wholesalers, offices, labs, and so forth, are striving for delay-free processing, but are still far from it. If it takes many days or weeks to process an order, the orders may need to be sorted by priority. Factors to consider in setting priorities for jobs include:

1. Customer importance.
2. Service urgency.
3. Service profitability.
4. Impact on capacity utilization.

For example, customer orders for items in the US Department of Defense supply system are scheduled to be filled based on a priority composed of two factors. One is urgency. The other, called the force activity designator, is the customer's importance. A combat unit deployed in a combat zone is a most important customer. If the unit orders bullets, the order will probably receive a high-urgency factor. The combination of customer importance and urgency yields an overall priority number calculated by computer, probably priority one in this case. The supply system has procedures for very fast delivery (say, 24 hours) for priority one requisitions; orders with very low priority call for delivery to take a certain number of days, weeks, or months. Note that priority decisions are simplified here because profitability is not a factor; neither is capacity utilization (though it affects the supply system's delivery performance).

In commercial businesses, profitability as a priority factor seems to make sense, at least when business is brisk. But few service businesses have reliable information on unit profitability for their various services. An activity-based costing audit can provide the data. Then schedulers or dispatchers can give higher profit business priority treatment, when appropriate.

The fourth factor, capacity utilization, gets plenty of attention. The person booking dinner reservations, medical appointments, and so on, tries to steer you away from days that are already nearly full and toward days that are mostly empty. Actually, in some cases, this factor probably gets too much attention. The plumber or gas company service technician who cannot come to your house at a time convenient to you (or can't even give you a time) lacks a customer focus. They are fixated on utilizing their capacity. Of course, that policy is an attempt to hold down their costs, which it may do in the current budget cycle. In the longer term, however, such a myopic, one-factor priority system often increases costs, since the real problem—inflexibility of capacity—goes untended. A good priority system gives appropriate weight to each of the four factors.

MONITORING FOR CONTROL

Most scheduling and priority systems include controls. The idea is to monitor progress and trigger corrective actions when schedules are not being met. Earlier controls relied on filling out forms and tabulating reports. Servers could get bogged down (or buried under) the scheduling, progress, and reporting paperwork.

As services themselves become computerized and bar-coded, however, it becomes easy to do the same for control. The paperless office, warehouse, or selling floor beckons. We return, however, to the point of the chapter: Simplify to avoid the need for a transaction, paperless or not. Cross-functional service teams co-located and queue limited allow for

---

CONTRAST

High-Variety Service Jobs

Conventional	*Contemporary*
Disruptive processing.	Smooth out the disruptions.
Long setups.	Improve readiness; cut setup times.
Specialized skills/equipment.	Group skills and equipment by type of service/customer.
Long travel/transport distances.	Co-locate resources for one-stop service.
Overtime and undertime for narrowly skilled employees.	Cross-train associates, who move to where the work is.
Complex scheduling and control.	Simplify, speed up, and visually control.

---

simple, visual controls. Work may flow forward, with errors noted and fixed, at about the same speed as bar-coded progress data can be assimilated into reports fed to remote bosses. High-tech controls are necessary in some sensitive kinds of services, but are overkill in many others.

Chapter Eleven

Managing Service Projects

 Human resources director: "Maybe someday everybody in this place will spend all of their time working in project teams."

Operations manager: "It's getting that way, all right. Half my associates are working for one of the project managers these days. And the rest are on improvement projects."

Marketing director: "Yes, when I started here, we sold the same things year after year. We hardly ever talked to people in other departments, much less joined project teams to launch new services or to team up on improvement projects."

The above exchange might be taking place, for example, at a bank, an airline, or a ticket-selling firm. It's basis is modern phenomena: the collapsing of product/service life cycles, awareness of the strategic value of time-based competition, and the total quality management mandate for continuous improvement. Each service introduction is a unique event—a project. Most continuous improvement endeavors (except small, simple improvement jobs) also are projects.

PROJECT MANAGEMENT: TEAMWORK AND ORGANIZATION

The complex, unique nature of projects presents special management difficulties. Still, some companies have been able to cut their project completion times by half and more. This permits pumping out many more projects in a given time period.

High-Performance Teamwork

Part of the formula for souped-up project management is to achieve high-performance teamwork. Specifically, synchroservice calls for project teams to be multifunctional; they must, for urgent projects, work simultaneously rather than serially; and they must employ data-based quality improvement methods continually.

Project teams may include suppliers, customers, quality specialists, equipment and materials people, frontline supervisors and associates, and others. Including these people greatly improves the quality of project outcomes, especially if they collect data on mishaps and hold team meetings to improve processes and prevent the mishaps from happening again, in this or future projects. Improved project quality is reflected by less project rework and scrap, in addition to speeding up project completion.

Principle 1:   Team up with next and final customer.

The diverse members of the project team may split their time and allegiance between the project and their functional unit. For example, an accountant may handle accounts receivable most of the time, but help the project team with cost estimating, as needed. Associates in operations may attend some project meetings to look for operational weaknesses of the proposed design, but spend most of their working hours on the front lines.

Project Organization Structures

Amount of time that people spend on projects versus their functional departments is partly determined by positioning in the organization.

EXHIBIT 11–1
Project Management Organization Structures

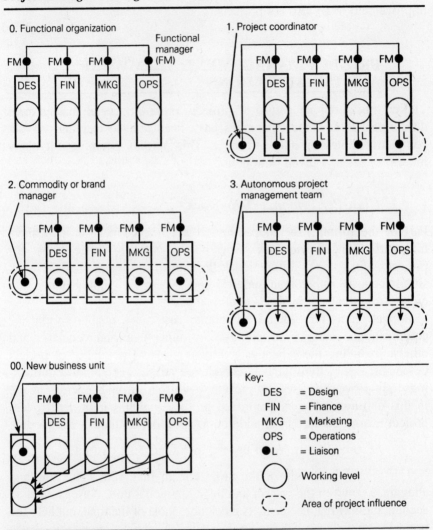

0. Functional organization

1. Project coordinator

2. Commodity or brand manager

3. Autonomous project management team

00. New business unit

Functional manager (FM)

Key:
DES = Design
FIN = Finance
MKG = Marketing
OPS = Operations
●L = Liaison
○ Working level
⌐ ⌐ Area of project influence

Source: Adapted from Steven C. Wheelwright and Kim B. Clark, *Revolutionizing Product Development: Quantum Leaps in Speed, Efficiency, and Quality* (New York: The Free Press, 1992), p. 191 (HF5415.153.W44).

Three degrees of project organization are shown in Exhibit 11–1, numbered 1 through 3, they are flanked by two nonproject forms, numbered 0 and 00. The five forms are explained below.

0. *Pure functional organization.* In this structure there is no project activity; everyone in every functional department is engaged in ongoing operations. In some slow-to-change organizations, such as a government agency out of the public eye or a monopolistic business in a remote area, this lack of projects (other than occasional renovation and remodeling) may persist for years.

1. *Project coordinator.* This is the weakest approach to project management; a coordinator has a short-term assignment but no project budget or staff. The project coordinator's limited activities revolve around arranging meetings, working out schedules, and expediting. The effective coordinator tries to achieve teamwork by working closely with liaison people in the functional organization, where the real power rests.

2. *Commodity or brand manager.* This second project form involves a career-track manager, sometimes with a small staff and limited budgetary authority. Responsibility is for an evolving commodity or service family (e.g., commercial accounts), brand (e.g., Yellow Pages), or succession of small renovation projects. To be effective, the project team must develop and work closely with a cohesive processing team of associates from the functional base, where most of the work is performed.

3. *Autonomous project management team.* Here the project manager has money to hire a full team out of the functional base (or outside the firm) to perform the work itself in its own space with its own equipment and other resources. The project manager is usually a high-level person who may even outrank the functional managers. Newer versions of this form of project management have been called tiger or bandit teams because of their aggressive, focused approach and disregard for practices standard in the rest of the firm. After completion of the project, the team disbands or its members join new project teams.

00. *New business unit.* Occasionally a super project is established as (or grows into) a separate division or business unit. In effect, it becomes a minicompany. As such, it may devolve into an ordinary functional organization, with no special project emphasis.

The three project management types in Exhibit 11–1 are general categories, not an exhaustive list. There are other ways to organize, staff, and fund projects, and many companies devise their own variations.

Any form of project management can greatly benefit from high-performance teamwork. However, a weak project structure can make that teamwork more difficult. A very strong project structure, such as the autonomous form, might seem to be synonymous with a high degree of teamwork. Not so. That form has long been common in defense and aerospace; nevertheless, in most cases most of the work was divided up by functional specialty and processed slowly one stage at a time instead of simultaneously using cohesive teams. The influence of total quality management may be instrumental in correcting this weakness.

Project teams organized in any of the project management forms in Exhibit 11–1 may look outside the firm for team members. Outside teams could include fully staffed supplier or customer projects; for best results, the inside project group would want to establish cross-memberships with the outside project teams.

An excellent example of a company that gets maximum service from outside project teams is McDonald's Corporation. Out of a long string of McDonald's products that met its requirements for quality, speed, efficiency, production in a squeezed space, popularity, and profit, only one, the Quarter Pounder, was developed by an inside project team. All the rest were developed by franchised restaurant owners (the customers of McDonald's Corp.) and hard-charging, innovative suppliers.

One of McDonald's successes, Chicken McNuggets, was launched in 1980. The basic nuggets idea emerged after an inside project team had spent 10 years working toward a chicken product. But the nuggets still had to be developed. Bud Sweeney, an account executive at Gorton's (the frozen fish company) came to the rescue. On loan from Gorton's, Sweeney organized and led a chicken SWAT team (like a tiger team), which found help from several sources. Gorton's provided the unique tempura coating. McDonald's product development and quality assurance people handled specifications and test marketing. A chef on loan from a Chicago hotel came up with four dips. Keystone Foods, a frozen beef patty supplier, developed production lines to debone chicken and equipment to cut it into random-looking chunks. And Tyson Foods, a chicken processor, developed a special new breed of bird, called Mr. McDonald, that was almost twice the weight of an ordinary fryer, which made deboning easier.[1]

Information Sharing

Members of the project team can do little without information. However, sharing information goes against the grain of most people in Western cultures. The common individualistic attitude is, "My expertise, my

---

CONTRAST

Ownership of Information

Private Property	*Team Ownership*
Task-related information retained by the holder of the position in the holder's personal space. Experience and training belong to the individual.	Task-related information, experience, and training belong to the team and the company and should reside in files easily accessible by all team members.

---

experience, and my information is my strength, and I'll keep it for myself."

While no one wants to snuff out the Western spirit of individualism, which is a healthful source of innovation, neither do we want team members to withhold information from other team members. Information is power, and project teams with wide access to information, including each other's, are powerful and effective.

But what is the mechanism for pulling knowledge out of people's heads, personal files, desk drawers, and other hiding places? Can the Far East, where the culture is group oriented instead of individualistic, provide answers? Perhaps so. Jeffrey Funk details systematic procedures for information sharing at Mitsubishi Electric Company in Japan, based upon his two-year assignment working as a project engineer at that company.[2] Every scrap of information gleaned from visits to libraries, customers, trade shows, conferences, committee meetings, and so forth, is required to be written up and inserted into common files, fully cross-referenced. Newly hired engineers at Mitsubishi spend a good deal of their orientation period getting to know the filing system and the rules for its use.

Principle 3:   Gain unified purpose via shared information.

Once such a system is established, it is easy for its users to identify anyone who fails to feed it. Peer pressure can shape behaviors for the common good.

At Mitsubishi, the information generally went into common file cabinets. The concept applies equally well to computer files. Patterson describes a project team at three geographically dispersed Hewlett-Packard sites: Waldbronn, Germany; Avondale, Pennsylvania; and Palo Alto, California. Each group was working on different parts of an operating system software project:

> The Palo Alto group agreed to maintain the current version of the total operating system and make it remotely accessible to the other sites through a WAN [wide-area network]. The next version ... would then ... be made available for remote access. Within minutes both the Avondale and Waldbronn teams would have the current system running at their sites, and development could continue with all teams once again synchronized. This development effort progressed well and resulted in a successful product.
>
> In contrast, an earlier effort, before the age of WANs, attempted ... the same thing through shipment of magnetic tapes. Shipment delays and time lost passing through customs hampered engineering efforts immensely. Engineers in the three sites were only rarely working with the same version of the operating system. Often as not, recently designed code would prove to be incompatible with operating system updates that had been two weeks or more in transit.[3]

The information sharing referred to so far is mainly what is used to create project outcomes: raw and semifinished information transformed by the project team into completed software, product designs, process specifications, architectural plans, and so forth. Besides this *operating information,* the project group must manage project *planning and control information,* our next topic.

PROJECT REPRESENTATION

The size and complexity of projects translate into a sizable project management task. Tailor-made for the job are two nearly identical planning and control tools: program evaluation and review technique (PERT) and critical path method (CPM). Both represent the project by a type of flowchart called a network chart or, commonly, a PERT chart. (PERT terminology is more widely used, except in the architectural/construction industry, which spawned CPM.)

A well made PERT chart reflects project complexity with enough detail to permit focused management of interlaced project activities. We'll consider a four-stage PERT planning method: building blocks, PERT sequencing, time estimating and critical path, and scheduling.

EXHIBIT 11–2
Building Blocks and Activities

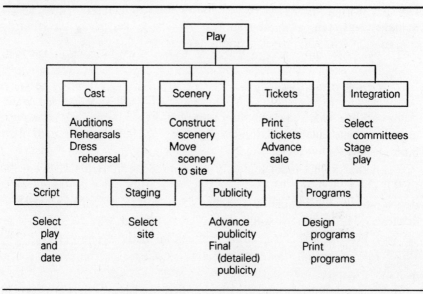

Say, for example, that a school is planning a play. Even a small play requires a variety of activities, several occurring at the same time by different groups. It could be mass confusion without a good project plan, which might include all four stages.

Building Blocks

Natural building blocks for the play are shown in Exhibit 11–2. (In PERT lingo, this is known as a work breakdown structure.) Script, cast, staging, scenery, publicity, tickets, and programs could each be assigned to a separate manager or subcommittee for focused management. (To keep the example simple, we've left out costumes, which would entail fitting, etc.) The last building block, integration, captures the work of a master committee or project manager, who coordinates the subcommittees. As much as possible, each building block should be an outcome that has value.

The *wrong* approach would be to break the project into hiring, purchasing, directing, acting, and selling. These are functions, not value-adding building blocks. Under functional management, it is too easy for one functional manager to blame another for delays and rework. Focused management puts responsibility for real outcomes on a single manager and team, and their success will be based partly on securing cooperation from diverse functional experts and managers.

PERT Sequencing

Each building block encompasses one or more activities, which experienced experts identify. Exhibit 11–2 lists 15 activities beneath their building blocks.

Next, the project team logically sequences the activities to form the PERT chart. Exhibit 11–3 illustrates. The 13 circles, called events, denote starts and completions of the 15 activities. Event numbering is arbitrary. The numbers simply offer a shorthand way to identify an activity. For example, "select committees" is activity number 1–2. The PERT rule is that all predecessor activities must be completed before a successor activity may start.

Activities 3–4, 6–9, and 9–10, signified by dashed lines, are dummy activities. They do not represent a task or consume time but have other purposes. Activity 9–10's purpose is logical: "Advance sale" of tickets, 10–12, should not start until all predecessor activities—"select committees," "select play and date," "select site," "auditions," "advance publicity," and "print tickets"—are completed. "Final publicity" (which includes names of cast members), requires completion of all of the same activities, except for "print tickets." The dummy activity going from 9 to 10 fulfills this logic; that is, it permits "final publicity" to take place independently of "print tickets."

Dummies 3–4 and 6–9 serve no such logical purpose. They just provide unique numbers for parallel activities. That is, "select play and date" is separate from but occurs in parallel with "select site." They would have the same event numbers, 2–4, if it weren't for insertion of dummy activity 3–4. Similarly, dummy 6–9 permits "auditions" and "advance publicity" to have different numbers. If the PERT data are computerized, the unique activity numbers become even more important—to avoid error messages pointing out redundancies.

At this point, PERT planning may stop, and often does. The PERT chart provides a plan that tells each project participant when to be ready

EXHIBIT 11–3
PERT Chart

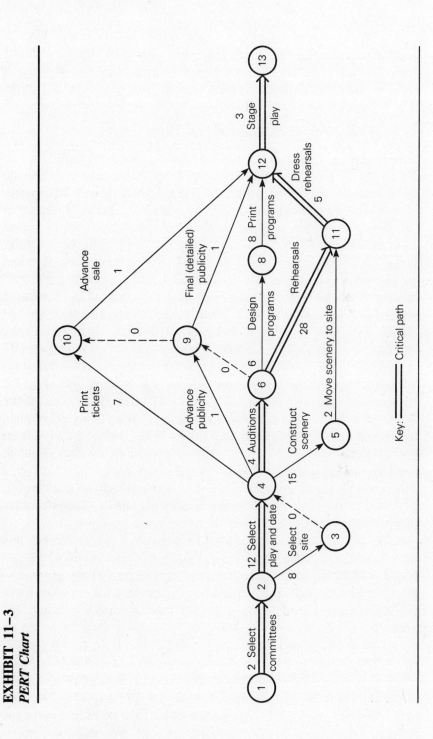

Key: ═══ Critical path

for their activities. This sequencing is usually the most important part of project planning. When project urgency is high, however, it is often useful to carry PERT planning to the next stage.

Time Estimating and Critical Path

Project managers may want to predict how long the total project or any part of it will take. For this they need experienced people to provide estimated completion times for each project activity. The PERT chart in Exhibit 11–3 includes their estimates for our play. Time estimates are in consecutive days (not working days), since play rehearsals are often seven days a week. The plan is for "rehearsals" to take 28 days, or four weeks. Then "dress rehearsals" (with real scenery) take five days and staging the play takes three. Three of the activities—"advance publicity," "final publicity," and "advance sale"—get an artificially low time estimate of one day. Their actual duration need not be carefully estimated and managed. The activities will simply fill whatever time is available. All other activities require a certain minimum completion time, carefully estimated.

The best estimate of completion time for the entire project is on the most time-consuming path through the PERT chart. This is called the critical path. To get it, we just add the activity times along every path. The critical path turns out to be 1–2–4–6–11–12–13, at 54 days. Next most critical—1–2–4–5–11–12–13—is much less, 39 days. Thus, to avoid project delays, the project managers may focus on critical path activities and not worry much about noncritical activities. However, delays are just one concern. Ensuring quality may be the greater concern for most of the play activities.

As the project plan is executed, actual activities may take more or less than the estimated times; then critical paths may change. If so, project managers shift their sights toward the new critical paths. This approach to managing project time may be sufficient. Alternately, the activities times may be converted to calendar dates for more precise scheduling and control.

Scheduling

If the play is to be presented on October 26, 27, and 28, 1994, then back-scheduling will yield scheduled dates for each preceding event and activity. Dress rehearsals would have to start five days earlier, on

---

"Continue to March"

Years ago one of the authors served as a consultant on a project management team for antiballistic missile (ABM) systems in the northern United States. Another project team had developed the ABM itself, this one was concerned only with preparing the sites. It took a few weeks for the project team to meet with all the experts to create the work breakdown structure (building blocks) and the PERT chart, which had about 500 activities in it.

Next step was to go back to the same experts and pry time estimates out of them—no easy task, since nobody wants to be pinned down that way. Data entry clerks entered the PERT chart and time data into a standard PERT computer package. The computer printed a critical path report.

Our project planning work was essentially done. Our small team of planners—two consultants and a master sergeant who served as military liaison—was congratulating itself in a bar that evening while examining the critical path report. The critical path wound through many activities that were definitely time-critical (urgent). The site had to be purchased, land cleared, a silo hole excavated and poured, and so forth, or the ABM could not be installed. However, the critical path also included a few not-so-urgent activities, such as preparing manuals for operation and maintenance of the site.

That raised questions. One of us asked the master sergeant—who had years of experience on similarly complex projects—"What would happen if the ABM arrived for installation, and the manuals were *not* completed?"

The sergeant furrowed his brow, drew on his beer, and finally said, "Continue to march, I guess." At that point it was clear to us. We had a phony critical path. None of the many books we were familiar with on PERT/CPM ever made the point that some project activities might be nonurgent—though still necessary for a quality project. And if a critical path includes such noncritical activities, it really isn't the critical path.

We were happy to have discovered a hidden truth about PERT. But it was clear that we had a bit more work to do. One solution would be to put artificially small time estimates on the nonurgent activities, so that they would not be on the critical path. Then those activities would be managed qualitatively, rather than based on time.

October 21; regular rehearsals would start 28 days before that, on September 23. Continued back-scheduling yields September 5 as the date for event number 1, when "select committees" should begin.

Noncritical activities have extra time allowance in their schedules. "Select site," activity 2–3, for example, may start on September 7. Its start could be delayed to as late as September 11, however, since its time estimate is four days less than the parallel activity, "select play and date." Activity 2–3, then, is said to have four days of slack, which offers flexibility in scheduling and more room to accommodate delays. (When a project gets behind, which is common, critical path activities will have negative slack.)

Often the scheduling process is reversed. Event number one gets a starting date, and adding times forward through the PERT chart yields dates for each successive event. The date for the final event may be unacceptable—too late. If so, certain nice-to-have activities may need to be chopped from the plan.

CONTINUOUS IMPROVEMENT IN PROJECTS

The high complexity and uncertainty inherent in project work is good reason for stressing continuous improvement in project management. Part of the problem is chronic project lateness.

Network Simulation and the Always-Late Syndrome

Calculating critical paths is methodical and easily performed on a computer. Unfortunately, the method treats each path independently of all others. It fails to allow for time variation, which affects all event completion times and the total project duration. It is easy to prove by Monte Carlo simulation that the deterministic critical path time under-states the likely project duration.[4] Exhibit 11–4 illustrates.

The exhibit presents the simplest possible project: two activities occurring at the same time. (A single activity is a job; multiple activities going on simultaneously are a key distinguishing feature of a project.) In part A, both paths are critical at five days; thus, it is a five-day project. In part B, the mean or expected task time on each path is still five days. Yet, as the table shows, the simulated mean project duration is 8 percent greater, at 5.4 days. In the table, we simulate the variability (four, five, and six days) by considering all time combinations and allowing equal chances for each time value on each path. For each combination the higher path time is the project duration, which pushes the expected (mean) project duration up to 5.4 days.

EXHIBIT 11–4
Effects of Variable Activity Times on Project Duration

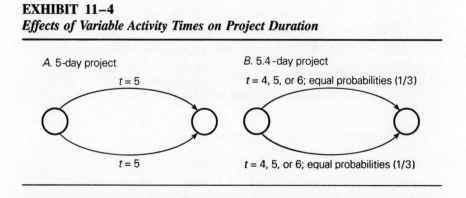

A. 5-day project

$t = 5$

$t = 5$

B. 5.4-day project

$t = 4, 5,$ or 6; equal probabilities (1/3)

$t = 4, 5,$ or 6; equal probabilities (1/3)

Possible Time Combinations

	Top Path	Bottom Path	Project Duration	
1	4	4	4	
2	4	5	5	
3	5	4	5	
4	5	5	5	
5	4	6	6	Mean = 49/9 = 5.4 days
6	5	6	6	
7	6	6	6	
8	6	5	6	
9	6	4	6	

With more variability, the expected project duration increases further. For example, if the path time is 3, 4, 5, 6, or 7, each equally probable, expected duration by simulation is 5.8 days, or 16 percent greater than the critical path time. If more paths are added, expected project duration also goes up. As a general rule, then, the fatter the PERT chart and the more variable the activity times, the more the project duration is in excess of the simple critical path time. This provides a mathematical explanation of why projects tend to be late.

Even though the critical path understates reality, it is widely used for the following reasons:

1. Path addition is cheaper to use and simpler to understand than Monte Carlo simulation.

2. Activity time estimates are rough anyway, and there are diminishing returns in more rigorous analysis of rough data.
3. It is difficult to know what to do with simulated network data. How should it change project management? For the 5.8 day simulation, if we add 16 percent to each activity, a new simulation pushes the simulated time out still further. No help.

Combating Project Complexity

We have just proved that projects are likely to be late. Still, the project management staff can work toward reducing the lateness by controlling its causes. Basically, the causes have to do with unnecessary project complexity and uncertainty. The *unnecessary* category includes having the wrong size and type of project management team, and lack of information sharing (common files), topics discussed earlier in the chapter. Related factors are high turnover of team members, poor communication, task unfamiliarity, and too many changes.

Project teams typically disband when the project ends. Team members scatter to the four winds. Some join new teams with new members and others return to a functional home, such as the mortgage loan department or human resources. Each time a new project forms, it takes weeks or months for team members to become well enough acquainted to be able to work well together. Through at least the early project phases, communication is poor, even when the team is multifunctional and working concurrently. Since the skills of each team member are not fully known, members get placed in the wrong assignment, and later are moved one or more times in an effort to get a better matchup of needs and skills. Instability hampers effectiveness.

To avoid these common problems, some firms are keeping team members somewhat intact from one project to the next. For example, Florida-based Harris Corp. does this in its government systems division. The division has established four project teams, each for a different series of its high-tech electronic products. Each team has a project manager, a project specialist, a material planner, a buyer, and others. The project manager and project specialist have complementary skills, one usually being an electrical engineer and the other a mechanical engineer. As one government contract winds down, the team gets started on the next contract.

Principle 11:   Cut start-up time.

Two other key means of controlling causes of lateness are drawn from other chapters:

- *Total quality management.* Effective project management includes collection of data on mishaps, followed by improvement projects to develop solutions to prevent those mishaps on following projects. Every team member should be involved. Continuous improvement seems to be late in gaining a foothold in project management, even though project work is badly in need of it to combat uncertainty and lateness. A probable reason, ironically, is that since projects are usually late, team members resist taking time to collect data and concern themselves with future projects, another project team's problem. When project teams stay somewhat intact from project to project, they have more incentive to improve the process.

  Principle 10:   Eliminate error and process variation.

- *Design-for-service-operations (DFSO) guidelines* (from Chapter 3). These guidelines call for using standard, already proven designs. This reduces not only complexity but also project uncertainty. That is, with standard designs, project time estimates will have lower margins of error, which would make a simulated project completion time closer to the critical path time.

We've examined the transformation process itself for both service jobs and projects. But there's another factor affecting the transformation: the right human and physical resources—the subject of Part V.

V

SERVICE RESOURCES: MEASUREMENT, MANAGEMENT, AND IMPROVEMENT

Synchroservice requires correctly placed, well-maintained, ready-to-go resources. In fact, management of service resources, the subject of Part V, is as important as management of the services themselves.

Chapter 12 looks at traditional and customer-focused ways of measuring productivity, especially of the human resource. Chapter 13 shifts over to physical resources: how to properly locate, lay out, and maintain service facilities for high quality and continuous improvement.

Finally, Chapter 14 puts *you* into the synchroservice equation: What is your role in an increasingly team-based, customer-centered world of work?

Chapter Twelve

Productivity, Pay, and Recognition
The Human Side of Quality

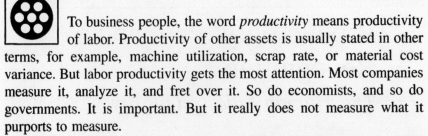 To business people, the word *productivity* means productivity of labor. Productivity of other assets is usually stated in other terms, for example, machine utilization, scrap rate, or material cost variance. But labor productivity gets the most attention. Most companies measure it, analyze it, and fret over it. So do economists, and so do governments. It is important. But it really does not measure what it purports to measure.

If labor productivity is low, that does not necessarily mean the labor resource is performing poorly. More likely, the management system is deficient. The system is failing to provide high quality and timely information, equipment, materials, training, designs, technical support, strategic guidance, and proper motivational climate. The quality and productivity of the labor resource depend on many factors. A few of these are topics in this chapter, but most have to do with resources and processes discussed in each of the other chapters.

Thus, this chapter's scope is necessarily narrow. We'll look at common productivity concepts and measures, along with strengths, deficiencies, and evolving changes. Companies track productivity in output units, cost (money) units, and time units; they try to improve productivity through time, quality, method, and delay analysis, plus feedback on each of the measures. These productivity and motivational factors—output, cost, time, quality, method, delay, and feedback—are the main topics of the chapter.

BOTTOM LINE FOR SERVICE OPERATIONS

As stellar guard of the Chicago Bulls, Michael Jordan scored over 30 points a game and dished out plenty of assists, too. He was productive, per number of minutes played and, probably, per dollar that he was paid: a quality asset, a bottom-line player. Sports fans judge a basketball player's productivity according to these kinds of output units (points and assists) but are savvy enough also to weigh input units such as game minutes and salary. The National Basketball Association might prefer to judge the productivity of an "Air Jordan" in number of fans per game who come to see him and his team; the Bulls filled arenas all around the league.

Whether you consider the din of shouting fans, humming office equipment, or babbling customers, the bottom line for service operations is usually output units compared with input units. The measures are used for performance appraisal, recognition, reward, and motivation for continual improvement. Therefore, getting the units right is important to every department, team, and associate.

Output–Input Measures

Cost and time-standards analysts have usually been in charge. One of their output–input measures is actual expenditures against budget. Others are actual cost against standard cost and actual time against standard time. Cost-based measures subdivide into expense or cost codes, sometimes many of them (electric power, gas, supplies, regular time, overtime, etc.). Exceeding the budget or standard cost suggests laxity, inadequate effort, or service breakdowns and returns. Frontline associates and supervisors get most of the blame.

The system is, in part, unsound and incorrectly used. For one thing, a budget is not a goal. It is like a demand forecast or the center line on a process control chart. Monitor it lightly. If it goes out of control limits, intensively investigate the cause and effect. If the effect is good (e.g., plunging customer complaints), seek to make the causes permanent (e.g., more-than-budgeted spending on new-employee training). If bad, do the opposite.

Other changes make weaknesses of the conventional system stand out. One is the realization that quality, not just output, is a key to competitive advantage. Another is the wholesale reorganization of resources (reengineering) that has been taking place in many businesses: away from fragmented and toward service focused or customer focused. This paves the way to simpler, more meaningful measures of performance. A third is the blurring of job responsibilities: Frontliners are assuming first responsibility for quality, good workplace organization, upkeep of equipment, data collection and diagnosis, problem solving, and, sometimes, interviewing and training new employees. Formerly, those activities were treated as professional, supervisory, and overhead.

Data Collection

Still another disadvantage of conventional productivity systems is the extensive data required to feed them. For example, some systems require data on when an associate starts and completes work on each different job or client. Others require expenses to be assigned to minute budgetary codes. To collect all that data, some companies have been persuaded to install data-entry terminals all over the operating area—not for value-adding services but just to monitor performance.

An alternative outlook favors lumping together all labor costs, not tracking labor job by job, and not separating direct labor from other payroll costs. As frontline associates team up with experts and managers, dividing lines blur, and so do the old labor cost categories.

Simple, Effective Measures

While productivity measurement has often become cumbersome, costly, and ineffective, there are plenty of examples of simple, useful ones:

• *Retailers.* A widely used measure is sales per square foot. Stu Leonard's food stores and Circuit City electronic stores rate exceptionally high on this scale. Under this measure, store managers and sales associates become more attuned to customer needs—for example, for quality, quick service, and attentiveness—because these factors bring in business. On the other hand, if stores are rated on sales per salesperson, managers might tend to cut staff, resulting in declining service and, finally, less business.

• *Accounting, legal, and consultancy firms.* A common measure is billable hours (an hour of time billable to the client) per professional associate. This measure, again, reflects ability to attract customers. Moreover, it gives managers and professionals room to be real service managers, that is, to weigh the value of different types of staffing, equipment, training, thoroughness, after-sale service, and so forth.

To summarize, these examples illustrate measures that are more effective, complete, and simple:

• *Effective.* The measures are directed toward business activity, customers, and the services themselves. Less effective are measures of resource activity instead of business activity, and functions rather than service and customer allegiance.

• *Complete.* The aim is to include not just frontline labor but all operations and operating costs.

• *Simple.* Complex data collection, person by person, job by job, function by function, is out; using already available data is in.

Employees are likely to be supportive of measures that are truly customer oriented, with simple-to-determine accuracy.

CONTROLLING CAUSES OF COST

If companies abandon detailed cost measurements and substitute overall measures, aren't there some risks? Won't it be all too easy for shirkers to escape detection, for poor performance to be hidden?

The answer to these questions is a multifaceted system of eliminating the *causes* of cost, poor quality, delays, and other wastes. A key element of cause reduction consists of teams of associates solving problems and displaying what they are doing and the results visually on large wall charts. The visual measurement data fall into three categories:

> ***Principle 16:***   Cut reporting; control causes.

1. *Service, component, or customer specific.* Rework, returns, claims, scrap, mishaps, nonconformities, on-time completions, response time, flow distance, space, and idle inventory.

2. *Process specific.* Process setup and get-ready time, response ratios, check sheets, and control charts.

3. *Activities, recognition, rewards, celebration.* Present improvement projects, present training programs, completed projects, completed training, number of suggestions, appreciation letters from customers, awards won, plaques, photos of recognition ceremonies, and so forth.

Visual Controls

This system is visual, located where the work is performed, usually owned by operating people, and up to date. Controlling causes in this way is, in the words of H. Thomas Johnson, "unlike the distant, often distorted financial echoes of those causes that appear in traditional cost and performance reports."[1] The full system of visual measures empha-

---

On the Wall

- "I can, literally, look at a wall and see what's going on in my department," says Jim Talbot, supervisor, Florida Power and Light, first non-Japanese winner (in 1989) of a Deming Quality Prize.
- At US Healthcare facilities, electronic signboards in waiting rooms flash service excellence scores (claim-processing speed, etc.) for all to see.

sizes all of the factors listed in Chapter 1 (Exhibit 1–1) as "customer requirements," namely, quality, flexibility, service, cost, response time, and variability.

The improvement charts have several purposes. If there really is progress, the people involved can take pride in the visible display of improvements. Further, improvement trends silently call for more of the same, a motivational benefit. Finally, a good assortment of wall charts can be an excellent tool for communication among operations, support people, management, and visiting customers or suppliers. The charts may even help draw timid managers and others out of their offices to the source of problems. While it is not natural for a manager to carry a computer report to the floor to use in discussing problems, performance charts in the workplace are a natural focal point for discussion.

Principle 14:   Record data at the workplace.

In the cause–control system, cost ceases to be used for controlling productivity. The on-the-spot visual signboard system controls the causes, and productivity improvement (as well as improvement in quality, response time, etc.) follows.

That does not mean that costs are no longer measured; they are. Regulatory agencies require data such as the value of inventories and statements of profit and loss, but those reports require only a fraction of the data needed for a full-blown budget-and-cost system. The overall cost data needed for periodic profit and loss accounting (high-level scorekeeping) will, of course, prove the value of the cause controls.

Improving the Old System

Existence of a visual cause–control system is becoming a requisite for winning a prestigious quality prize. Still, many companies are looking for ways to salvage some of their traditional productivity measures by correcting some of their weaknesses.

One weakness, the fixation on productivity of frontline labor, is reduced when associates assume responsibility for quality, data collection, and other duties usually handled by large staffs of overhead people. More of the factors included in the productivity measures thus come under the control of frontliners, and the size of the overhead group and its cost shrink.

Another weakness, the focus on counting *anything* as output, even customer-rejected output, is greatly reduced when teams are successful in slashing response times; this ties servers more closely in time to real customer demands. Related to this is the movement of people and equipment into service-focused groupings, which makes any measure of productivity more likely to consider only what the customer is paying for.

Despite these improvements, the old productivity measures retain the weaknesses of being periodic, delayed, staff directed, and not cause oriented.

Cost of Services

Insurance Agent A: "How can the company be making money on these individual policies? Those clients are a pain to sell to, and a headache when they've got a claim."

Agent B: "Who cares, as long as you get your commission?"

This scenario repeats itself in nearly all large businesses, where costs are not easily tied to the actual service or customer. While frontline people—managers and cost accountants, too—have long asked these kinds of questions, only recently has the truth emerged. And the truth often is that the low-volume specials (individual insurance policies, perhaps) are not profitable. They are not priced high enough to make money, because they are not assigned their fair share of company costs. By company costs we mean, especially, overhead costs, which sometimes dwarf direct-service costs. High-volume "commodity" items (e.g., group insurance policies), on the other hand, usually receive far more than their share of overhead cost. As a result, they are often overpriced or inaccurately judged to be financial losers.

By now, hundreds of articles and many books have noted this systematic bias in company costing systems. Consider the following scenarios for a catering business:

An improvement team of buyers, cooks, helpers, and drivers has come up with several productivity improvement ideas for high-volume catering customers (e.g., an airline), but at the same time a management group decides to abandon the high-volume business because the biased cost system falsely shows it to be losing money.

Low-volume catering (weddings, etc.) actually is the money-losing business segment, but aided by biased costing, it looks profitable (in fact, the sales manager for that segment has received a hefty pay hike). No one has had an incentive to improve it, service quality is barely adequate, and before long this segment is losing customers and—now, clearly—money.

Costs are important, as well, for a few other common service management activities, including evaluating process, method, and equipment alternatives, and making make-or-buy and sourcing decisions.

Activity-based costing (ABC) directly addresses the bias in overhead cost allocation. ABC methods attempt to assign overhead costs to a service only where there is actual overhead activity related to that service. Briefly, in the ABC method a team, consisting of an accountant and representatives of an overhead activity such as scheduling or maintenance, forms to search for simple activity cost drivers. For example, operating overhead costs could be allocated to a service based on a single driver, throughput time. The reasoning is that if a service item (e.g., a loan application) is in process for five days, it probably actually receives five days of overhead cost; if another service item zips through in just one day, it is scarcely seen or handled by overhead people and therefore should receive proportionately less overhead cost—in this case, only one-fifth as much.

Since its development in 1986, activity-based costing has spread quickly. An important application is in sales: What is the real cost of selling to a new customer versus a long-standing one? And what is the real cost of serving small accounts as compared with large ones? With accurate information, the company may make several decisions that amount to reengineering itself. For example, it may split into two companies within the company. One provides sales and service to large accounts at lower unit prices; the other specializes in small accounts, perhaps pricing higher than the market but offering attractive service extras.

The same accuracy-enhanced cost data could also be used for correcting the inaccuracies in cost-based productivity reporting. Some believe, however, that the cost system has outlived its usefulness. A number of other measures are available and are more effective and less costly to administer, so the reasoning goes. In the remainder of the chapter, we present some of these other performance measures and motivators, starting with a few that date back to the beginnings of scientific management.

PRODUCTIVITY AND SCIENTIFIC MANAGEMENT

The first organized approach to improving the productivity of labor arose in the United States at the turn of the century from the work of the pioneers of scientific management. Prominent among them were Frederick W. Taylor, Frank and Lillian Gilbreth, and others, including Harrington Emerson, who specialized in office processes. Their approach was to standardize the labor element of operations: standard methods and standard times. Nonstandard labor practices were simply too expensive and wasteful.

CONTRAST
A Fair Day's ...

Nineteenth Century: A Fair Day's Grog*
Company A: "All hands drunk; Jacob Ventling hunting; molders all agree to quit work and went to the beach. Peter Cox very drunk and gone to bed."

Company B: "Men worked no more than two or three hours a day; spent the remainder in the beer saloon playing pinochle."

Twentieth Century: A Fair Day's Work
Standard methods and standard times provide a basis for uniform measurement of human performance and, therefore, control of it.

Twenty-First Century: A Fair Day's Improvement
Broad array of tools of data collection, analysis, problem solving, measurement, customer focus, teamwork, reward, and recognition make continuous improvement a normal part of everyone's job.

*Source: Shoshana Zuboff, *In the Age of the Smart Machine*, New York: Basic Books, 1988, p. 32.

Impact of Scientific Management

Methods and time standards programs had their beginnings in manufacturing. Beginning in the 1940s, however, they found their way into hospitals, food service, hotels, transportation, and other services. So carefully industrially engineered is the McDonald's hamburger that Theodore Levitt calls it "the technocratic hamburger."[2] By the early 1980s, the industrial engineering department at United Parcel Service (UPS) had grown to 3,000 people and "had so perfected manual package handling that UPS had the industry's lowest costs."[3] In many service businesses, it has been hard to compete without good methods design and labor standards.

Scientific management is not without its critics, however. Labor unions often have resisted time standards. Some believe that under work measurement a person is treated like a microcomputer memory chip. At the first sign of performance deterioration, the chip is discarded and replaced; it's just not cost-effective to attempt to repair or recycle it. Often the ultimate plan is to replace the entire memory system, and even the computer itself, with faster memory and more powerful equipment.

Taylorism: Boon or Bane?

Many business executives, consultants, and writers have blasted Taylorism. The basis for the criticism is Frederick W. Taylor's advocacy of specialist-managers.

The fairness of charging Taylor, who died in 1915, with today's sins of excessive specialization throughout business and government is uncertain. But there is no question about Taylor's central role in the development of methods study and time standards. The methods techniques have been absorbed into modern-day total quality management and continuous improvement, and thus are highly esteemed. Time standards have been misused and reviled, but nevertheless they have a valued role in time-based competition.

Process Improvement and Productivity

Modern improvement tools, presented in Chapter 4, are a mixture of old and new: process flowcharting from the Taylor/Gilbreth era, plus several newer tools that originated in connection with quality improvement (see the 11 tools for process improvement, Exhibit 4–1). Here we take a second look, from a productivity angle.

Systematic productivity improvement, as developed by Taylor, the Gilbreths, and other pioneers of scientific management, involved *methods study,* with *flowcharting* at the core. Methods study always has been aimed at improving not only productivity but also safety and ease of performing the work. Making the work easier to do safely increasingly gets into issues of human physiology, stress, and bodily limitations, and has spawned a subfield of process improvement called *ergonomics.*

Of particular concern are cumulative stress disorders, such as the carpal tunnel syndrome, affecting some people who spend long hours at computer terminals. "A single case of carpal tunnel syndrome, a painful condition involving compression of the wrist's median nerve, costs up to $30,000. . . . Eliminating this type of ergonomics problem sometimes requires less than $1,000."[4]

Methods study takes place at the job level and at the process level and employs standard flowcharting methods. Job-level methods study pertains to the productivity (and ergonomic conditions) of direct labor, but not overall productivity, including typically out-of-control overhead costs. Improvement teams may use process-level analysis in directly attacking the high overhead costs and wastes, along with some direct-labor wastes.

Flowcharts do not readily reveal *how much* productivity improvement is achieved. If it is really important to know, a cost analyst could be called in to estimate and compare the costs of the old and new processes. Industrial engineers, who've used process flowcharts for decades, have rarely found it necessary to translate improvements into before and after costs. It is clear that productivity improves with the elimination of non-value-adding steps, which are visually portrayed by flowcharting symbols: arrow (transport), upside down triangle (storage), big D (delay), and square (inspection). (Some accountants advocate activity-based costing analysis of non-value-adding activities, as revealed by process flowcharts. Worthy idea? Or costing overkill?)

Though it may be unnecessary to determine degree of productivity gain for each improvement project, what about determining it for a whole organizational unit? That is our next topic.

BUSY AND PRODUCTIVE RESOURCES

Walk into a drugstore when it is moderately busy, and what do you see? A clerk in the cameras and film department flitting back and forth taking care of three customers; one cashier up front ringing up a customer's purchases, and another cashier trying hard not to look idle and bored; customers bumping into each other in the cold remedies aisle while most other aisles are empty. The cameras and film clerk is busy, and working very efficiently as well. One cashier is busy, the other idle. The space around cold remedies is highly utilized, whereas most of the rest of the store isn't even justifying the power to keep the lights on.

We have identified some common, noncost ways of evaluating the productivity of various resources. Terms like *efficiency, busyness* and *idleness,* and *utilization* can be used loosely; they also have precise meanings and can be measured numerically. Examples follow, first for equipment and other nonhuman resources; then for people.

Equipment Utilization

A general formula for *utilization* of labor or equipment is:

$$\text{Utilization rate} = \frac{\text{Time in use}}{\text{Time available}}$$

Equipment utilization reports, expressed as a percentage, are common in larger companies. For some equipment, 40 hours (one shift operation) is used as available hours per week. Sometimes two or more shifts are the basis. Data for the reports sometimes can be collected automatically by timers in the vehicle, data terminal, or other equipment.

The report has at least three purposes. First, it serves as a check on how well site or company personnel plan in advance for the right capacity. Second, trends in utilization suggest when more capacity will be needed so that equipment can be ordered in advance. Third, a report showing decreasing utilization suggests the need for sales promotions aimed at generating more work for the unutilized capacity.

With today's mood of questioning virtually everything in service management, the equipment utilization report has come under fire. Why? Because the reports can cover up certain faults and result in treating symptoms, not causes. The following are potential weaknesses in equipment utilization reports or the way the reports are used:

- High utilization can be achieved by disposing of slow equipment and running all jobs on new, fast machines. But old, slow equipment can be valuable when considering moving equipment into cells or other focused zones within a building.

- Utilization may include bad time (e.g., a copier making blank or wrinkled copies) or get-ready and setup times. If the firm adds capacity when equipment is engaged in such ineffective activities, poor habits set in.
- Utilization reports can encourage dabbling in peripheral services to keep equipment busy; over time, the facility becomes unfocused.
- Utilization is usually measured in hours, when the real concern should be utilization of capital (return on investment).
- Finally, and perhaps most importantly, 100 percent utilization is not even desirable. For example, no computer center wants its mainframe to be 100 percent utilized because the effect would be long backlogs, interminable delays in getting jobs run, and anxious customers squabbling for priority.

Utilization of Space, Information, Materials, and Tools

Besides equipment utilization, some firms, especially larger ones, measure and report on space utilization. The reports express space in use as a percentage of total space, which may be broken down by type of space or type of use. Colleges and universities generally report based on several room-use categories, which in the United States are specified by the Department of Education.

Use of information resources can also be measured. Typically the measure is frequency of use rather than percentage of time in use. For example, an organization may archive records and files based on a certain standard of use or nonuse and dispose of them completely in the next phase of records/file control. (*Migration* is a common term for moving information from active storage to archives to disposal.)

Measures of materials utilization might include scrap, theft, deterioration, obsolescence, and misplacement, all of which hinder productive use of materials and supplies. Approximately the same utilization measures may be applied to tools.

Labor Utilization

For the labor resource, it is common to keep track of absences resulting from illness, jury duty, military duty, labor union activities, tardiness, and so forth. Each of these eats into productive time.

More specifically, the equipment utilization formula also works for the human resource. Assume, for example, that a five-person office group spends 2,000 minutes at work on an assortment of 38 jobs (such as letters and reports) in an 8-hour day, which for five people is 2,400 minutes ($8 \times 60 \times 5$). The utilization rate is

$$\text{Utilization} = \frac{\text{Time working}}{\text{Time available for work}} = \frac{2,000}{2,400} = 0.83, \text{ or } 83\%$$

And what about the other 400 minutes of the 2,400-minute day? We should not be too quick to label it idleness. The five office associates might use that time for worthwhile activities such as cross-training or teaming up on improvement projects—activities that quality-minded managers ought to encourage.

Work Sampling

The utilization formula is simple, but it requires data on time working. A *work-sampling* study yields data on percentage of time working, idle, or delayed. Further, the study team can subdivide idleness into categories, thereby showing process bottlenecks. Example 12–1 illustrates.

EXAMPLE 12–1 Work Sampling—Pathology Lab

Anna López, director of Midtown Pathological Labs is concerned. Costs are going up rapidly; the staff has plenty to do, yet is often idled by assorted problems. López decides to probe the sources of delay by conducting a one-week work-sampling study. Of special interest are lab equipment failures, supply shortages, delays waiting for instructions, excessive coffee breaks, and lab technicians absent from the work area. López prepares a work-sampling data sheet that includes those five categories of delay (plus an *other* category); she also works up a schedule for taking 100 sample observations (20 per day).

The schedule and completed form are shown in Exhibit 12–1. The results, the staff not working 35 percent of the time, confirm López's impression of serious delay problems. The breakdown into categories of delay yields insight as to causes.

The management system can be blamed for the first 18 percent of non-working time. Equipment failure (3 percent), supply shortages (6 percent), and wait for instructions (9 percent) are failures to provide technicians with resources for keeping busy.

EXHIBIT 12-1
Work-Sampling Data Sheets—Midtown Pathological Labs

	SCHEDULE OF OBSERVATION TIMES			
Mon.	Tues.	Wed.	Thurs.	Fri.

8:01
8:13
9:47
9:59
10:12
10:59
11:16
11:32

1:00
1:15
1:19
2:52
2:55
2:56
2:57
3:02
3:29
3:37
4:07
4:32

WORK-SAMPLING FORM		
Category of activity	Observations (tallies)	Percentages
Working	ЖИ ЖИ ЖИ ЖИ ЖИ ЖИ ЖИ ЖИ ЖИ ЖИ ЖИ ЖИ ЖИ ⑥⑤	65%
Not working:		
• Equipment failure	/// ③	3%
• Supplies shortage	ЖИ / ⑥	6%
• Wait for instructions	ЖИ //// ⑨	9%
• Coffee break	ЖИ ЖИ /// ⑬	13%
• Out of area	// ②	2%
• Other	// ②	2%
Total	100	100%

The 13 percent of delay for coffee breaks is an employee problem. Authorized coffee breaks are a 15-minute morning break and a 15-minute afternoon break. This amounts to 30 minutes or, in percent of an 8-hour day:

$$\frac{30 \text{ min.}}{8 \text{ hr.} \times 60 \text{ min./hr.}} = 0.0625, \approx 6\%$$

López may deal with the coffee-break abuses immediately. The data on resource shortages do not offer a solution, but they do tip off López on where to look.

Besides delay statistics, work sampling yields the complement, utilization rate. As we have seen, utilization (65 percent in the example) means busyness—hours busy divided by hours available. But most of us are very busy at times and not so busy at others. To avoid bias, the analyst doing work sampling must take care to do the study in a representative time period—representative of average conditions, if that is the goal, or representative of very busy conditions if peak periods are being examined.

Labor Efficiency

Human labor is a unique resource that is not merely utilized. Unlike the nonhuman kind (e.g., equipment and materials), the human resource has a will; it can choose to work at a normal pace or much faster or slower than that. We'll examine one of the uses of *standard time*—determining *labor efficiency*, which is done in one of two ways (**Standard time:** The time a person is expected to need to complete a task under normal conditions.):

1. Efficiency $= \dfrac{\text{Standard time per unit}}{\text{Actual time per unit}}$ or, simply, $\dfrac{\text{Standard time}}{\text{Actual time}}$

2. Efficiency $= \dfrac{\text{Actual units per time period}}{\text{Standard units per time period}}$ or, simply, $\dfrac{\text{Actual units}}{\text{Standard units}}$

Note that the two versions are mathematically equivalent; each is an inversion of the other.

We may illustrate the formulas by returning to our five-person office team, which turned out 38 jobs yesterday. Assume that 34 is the standard output per day (for five people). Then, by the second equation:

$$\text{Efficiency} = \frac{38 \text{ actual units/day}}{34 \text{ standard units/day}} = 1.12, \text{ or } 112\%$$

To use the first equation, the data must be converted to time per unit. Say that in their 2,400 minutes, the office staff actually spends 1,900 minutes at work on the 38 completed jobs. The other 500 minutes include coffee breaks, cleanup, improvement meetings, and time off for someone to visit a dentist. Then:

$$\text{Standard time} = \frac{1,900 \text{ minutes/day}}{34 \text{ standard units/day}} = 55.9 \text{ minutes/unit}$$

And

$$\text{Actual time} = \frac{1,900 \text{ minutes/day}}{38 \text{ actual units/day}} = 50.0 \text{ minutes/unit}$$

Then

$$\text{Efficiency} = \frac{55.9 \text{ minutes/unit}}{50.0 \text{ minutes/unit}} = 1.12, \text{ or } 112\%$$

In this example, the 38 jobs (letters, reports, etc.) are not uniform. Thus, the standard time of 55.9 minutes represents an average job, but of course some jobs could take all day and others just a few minutes. With such a nonuniform product, an efficiency measure still can be meaningful, but only if it covers a sufficiently long time period, in which the mix of complex and simple jobs would tend to even out. One day and 38 jobs are not enough for a fair efficiency reading. Monthly reporting would be more acceptable.

Efficiency and Time Standards for Nonuniform Operations: Book Cataloging

Most college libraries use computers to produce catalog cards. A cataloging aide with book in hand enters data about a new book at a terminal, and the data are transmitted to a central library cataloging service center. The center's computer database is searched to find (in the United States) a Library of Congress catalog number for the book. For the search to be successful, the cataloging aide must enter the right data. This can be difficult, for example, for foreign-language books, musical compositions, and government documents.

Managers at one college library set a monthly standard rate (historical) of 300 books per cataloging aide. Aides deeply resented the standard rate because some aides arrived early in the morning in order to fill their carts with easy books, which allowed them to easily exceed 300 books per month. Other aides who liked the challenge of the tough books actually looked worse when the monthly report came out. The solution: distribute books to cataloging aides at random each morning. That way, each receives about the same variety of types of book over a period of weeks.

Fairness becomes less of an issue when the output units are high in volume and uniform, or nearly so, such as stuffing envelopes in a mass political mailing. A fair efficiency rating could even be turned out daily (although it is hard to think of reasons for doing so that often).

Productivity Reporting in Perspective

Reports on resource productivity tend to proliferate and get out of hand, sometimes to the point where as much is spent on reporting as on paying for the resources. It is staff organizations, such as purchasing, human resources, and accounting, that generate resource reports. They are input oriented, and they exist only for serving line operations, which are output oriented and customer oriented. But preservation, growth, and power instincts can conflict with the mandate to provide only the resources necessary for use in serving customers. Those instincts tend to result in too much resource management and too many reports. When large organizations fall on hard times, regaining economic health may include cutting staff employees and many of their reports. The tens of thousands of jobs lost in the North American financial services industry in recent years serve as a reminder.

Thus far, we have considered cost and noncost approaches to productivity management. Next we more closely examine the time standard, a key source of data for these approaches.

TIME STANDARDS AND THEIR USES

Work is simply a form of exertion. But a unit of work (such as a job, task, or project) is defined more specifically, including the time taken to perform it.

Sometimes work time is estimated in advance. For example, in a two-person operation, if person B must wait for person A to finish a job, B will want an advance estimate of how long A's job will take. A and B as an improvement team may want to time their operations as part of a process improvement project. Others may want time estimates in order to judge whether A and B can handle the work or will need help (more staff). Still others may use these time estimates in preparing an estimate or bid. In addition, the existence of time estimates is likely to have motivational value—a target for A and B to shoot for.

To summarize, we have identified five purposes of time standards (time estimates): coordination and scheduling, process improvement, staffing, estimating and bidding, and motivation.

Coordination and Scheduling

The primary use of time standards is in coordination and scheduling. Actually, by definition, a schedule is a time standard, with proper

---

Time Standards for Staffing Attorney's Offices

In one effort to set time standards on lawyers' tasks, the sole purpose was to straighten out a staffing mess. The lawyers worked in 36 program offices of the US Department of the Interior, and it was hard to assign the proper number of lawyers to each office.

The department hired a consultant to help define work units and set standards. The basic work unit was a *matter* (not a case, because matters often did not result in cases). Secretaries kept records on the time lawyers spent on fifty-nine varieties of matter. The results were fairly consistent throughout the United States, and the average times served as historical (not highly refined) standards for use in staffing decisions. That is, in a given office each matter could be forecast (by trend projection, etc.) and multiplied by standard time to yield labor-hours, which converted into staff needs.

Professional work like that of a lawyer is not only variable but often seen as something of an art and resistant to standardization. The lawyers cooperated because the limited purpose—better staffing—was made clear. Probably there would have been no cooperation had the purpose been to judge efficiency or even to schedule lawyers' tasks.

Source: Part of the consultant's story is told in Marvin E. Mundel, *Motion and Time Study: Improving Productivity,* 5th ed. (Englewood Cliffs, NJ: Prentice-Hall, 1978), pp. 485–94 (T60.7.M86).

---

adjustments for efficiency and utilization. Where coordination demands are light, formal scheduling of work units may be unnecessary. But there is nearly always at least a vague time plan for starting and finishing an upcoming task. This plan is an implied time standard.

Analysis, Planning, and Motivation

Examples of the other uses of time standards include:

- *Analysis of alternative methods and equipment.* Analysts may use time standards in estimating amount of labor required for each alternative.
- *Staffing.* Staff (labor) needed is the product of units forecast times standard time per unit. Labor budgeting goes a step further. Labor budget equals staff needed times average wage.

Cracking the Electronic Whip

America's is a postindustrial service economy, runs the conventional wisdom, an economy wherein the product is information and work occurs in a clean, well-lighted place. It's the age of the telemarketer, the customer-service rep, and the flight reservationist—all of whom rely on computer technology to do their jobs. Abuse of workers in this new economy would seem unlikely, but it's here, with age-old cruelty. Twenty-six million employees nationwide, from telephone operators to elevator mechanics, have their work tracked electronically. For ten million of these men and women, computer-generated statistical evaluations are used to judge job performance and, it is held, to increase productivity. But the computer can't measure the physical and mental toll exacted by the stress of second-by-second surveillance.

Examples, from a supervisor's hand-written comments on a computer printout showing performance of one airline reservation agent:

- Agent is "reprimanded for taking 0.39 minutes" (about 23 seconds) "to complete her paperwork for each call."
- Agent's "percent utilization," 93.55 percent, is below this airline's 96.5 percent minimum standard. Agent must do better or will get a warning "or even unpaid suspension."
- Agent's UNM ("unmanned") time, "almost always time spent in the bathroom," adds up on the printout to 22 minutes—unacceptably high.
- Total number of calls handled, 79 for the day, is way below the airline's expectation of 150 to 200 calls a day. "Raw totals, and not customer needs, are what management is concerned with."

Source: Adapted from Sharon Danann, "Cracking the Electronic Whip," *Harper's Magazine*, August 1990, pp. 58–59.

- *Estimating and bidding.* The staff component of an estimate or bid is computed the same way as the staff budget. Accurate bidding is critical to profit and loss in project work. Estimates or bids are also important in services such as medicine, law, consultancy, and automotive repair.
- *Motivation.* Without a deadline, people tend to put things off. A time standard acts like a deadline, helping to keep people motivated to meet the standard. A weakness of a time standard as a motivator is that it may not seem like a real need to employees.

People are more likely to respond to a known, valid customer need date or quantity, which itself could be based on a time standard. The motivational value of a time standard also depends on whether people believe it is valid, which depends on the techniques used in developing the standard.

HUMANITY AND FAIRNESS ISSUES

Scientific management is a two-edged sword, one edge sharp and the other dull. The sharp edge raises productivity; the dull one leaves wounds and scars (see "Cracking the Electronic Whip").

Employers have long sought solutions to the human problems associated with the application of methods and time standards. The most promising approaches, past and present, lie in putting variety and meaning back into the task or job. Closely related is the need to make sure that the reward system will recognize task differences and the many ways in which employees can serve their employers and customers.

Tasks, Jobs, and Service to Customers

The design of work and work systems has evolved through three phases. First was scientific management, which focuses on the task itself. Next came job design, which aims at improving the job and therefore the life of a jobholder. Today's approach, emphasized throughout this book, is on service to the next and final customer and related feelings of satisfaction by the server. A review of the three phases follows.

Tasks. Division of labor, performed scientifically using methods-study techniques, yields a well-engineered task. Consider the task of scraping food leavings off a stainless steel tray into a garbage can. Is that task also a job? That is, can the firm define it as a job and hire someone to do just that task over and over? The answer is yes. Such narrow tasks are sometimes treated as a whole job.

Jobs. If all jobs were developed like the plate-scraping one, wouldn't work life be intolerable? A collection of concepts called job design attempts to avoid such a fate for working people.

Best known among the job design ideas are job enlargement and job enrichment. Job enlargement dates back to the 1950s, when Thomas Watson, founder of IBM, promoted the effort out of his strong belief in providing people with meaningful work. Job enlargement means expanding the number of tasks included in a person's job, for example, cooking, serving, and scraping plates; it offers horizontal variety. Job enrichment, a later development with roots at Texas Instruments and AT&T, expands on the job enlargement idea. Enlargement means more tasks; enrichment means more meaningful, satisfying, and fulfilling tasks or responsibilities. For example, an enriched job may entail use of mental and interpersonal skills—scraping plates and teaming up with others to select new dishes, scrapers, and dishwashing equipment.

The liberating effects of enlargement/enrichment are not necessarily in conflict with the restrictions of prescribed methods and time standards. In fact, one could argue that without standards, an enlarged/enriched job might be poorly defined, exposing the employee to frustration and criticism. Existence of job standards offers a guidepath for avoiding problems, thereby offering more freedom for the associate to work on process improvements, which translate into still better job standards.

Customers, Internal and External

Enlargement and enrichment, as originally conceived, were oriented to the individual, not to the team and not to the next or final customer. The following will correct this deficiency:

- Ensure that enlargement is directed toward mastery of the jobs of fellow team members, that is, cross-training.

  Principle 7:   Cross-train for mastery of multiple skills.

- Ensure that enrichment is customer-oriented. Specifically, this calls for associates to acquire the data collection, analysis, problem-solving, and teamwork skills and responsibilities required in total quality management.

An obstacle in the way of learning more skills is the job classification system, or work rules. (When management blames the union, it's for rigid work rules. But, in the name of division of labor, *management* created work rules/job classifications.) Skill-based pay fits with the new requirement for associates to master multiple skills. It is often palatable to the employee, union or nonunion, because the concern has shifted somewhat from job security to work-life security; each new skill mastered becomes another line on the employee's résumé, should a résumé be needed some time.

Pay and Other Motivators

The concept of skill-based pay emerged in connection with TQM and JIT: TQM calls for all employees to get involved in data collection, analysis, and improvement; assume process ownership; and take first responsibility for quality. Both TQM and just-in-time require that associates become cross-trained, able to move to where the work is, and fix things that go wrong on the spot; otherwise, there will be delays, and work will not get done just in time.

Principle 15:   Frontline teams: first line of attack on problems.

If associates assume all these new skills and duties, shouldn't they be paid more? Of course. It's only fair (though some companies cannot immediately afford it). This concept of fair pay (pay for skills) does not easily replace other fair-pay ideas, however. Exhibit 12–2 lists six popular views on fair pay, skill-based pay being the sixth.

Fair pay.   One concept of fair pay is that everyone should be paid the same; minimum-wage laws are a means of bringing that about. Pay by time worked is a second fair-pay concept, and a popular one. Pay by job content also seems fair, especially in large organizations where unequal pay for the same work would be a visible problem; evaluating job content has been a major function in larger human resource departments. A fourth concept of fair is pay based on output against standards, often called incentive pay. A pure incentive is simply a piece rate; for example, a store coupon counter's piece rate might be $1 per hundred. But laws (such as the United States wage-and-hour laws) require that piece-rate earnings not fall below the minimum wage, based on hours worked.

Another popular system is measured daywork, which is only nominally an incentive-pay system. In measured daywork, standard output serves as a target that trainers and supervisors help the employee attain. The employee who cannot attain it is moved to another position or advised to seek work elsewhere.

Reward and recognition.   Pay, of course, is not the only effective motivator; it may not even be the strongest. To complete our discussion of productivity, we must note the impact of low-cost and no-cost rewards, recognition, celebration, and personal pride.

EXHIBIT 12-2
Concepts of Fair Pay

What Is Fair Pay?	Who Subscribes to This?
1. Everyone paid the same. Rationale: We are all created equal; we are all products of our environments and partners in society. Means: High minimum wage applied equally to all.	Organized labor Socialists
2. Pay by the hour (or week, month, year). Rationale: Though we are products of our environment, society's work must be done, and work is most easily measured in time units. Means: Have employees punch time clocks, and reprimand them for tardiness.	Supervisors (easy to figure out pay) Organized labor (employees like to "put in their time"—or their time and a half)
3. Pay according to job content. Rationale: It is not the person who should be paid but the position; "heavy" positions should be paid heavily, "light" positions lightly. Means: Job evaluation, using job ranking/classification, point plan, factor comparison.	Personnel managers (requires a large pay-and-classification staff) Bureaucrats (seems rational and impersonal; fits concept of rank or hierarchy)
4. Pay according to output. Rationale: Though we are products of our environment, society's work must be done, and work should be measured in output (not merely time on the job). Output efficiency is based on a count of actual units produced as compared to a standard. Means: Piecework, incentive pay, gain-sharing.	Industrial engineers Economists
5. Pay according to supply and demand. Rationale: Society's messiest jobs must be done too, and more pay for less desirable jobs is necessary to attract employees. Means: Let the labor market function (or list jobs needing to be done, and set pay according to willingness to do each job—The *Walden II* method)	Some economists (e.g., those advocating below-minimum wages for teenagers) B. F. Skinner (see his book *Walden II*)
6. Pay for skills. Rationale: Pay system should encourage learning so employees can take "ownership" of their processes, and can quickly fix problems. Means: Extra pay for passing tests of mastery of more skills and knowledge.	A growing number of some of the best-known companies.

- *Suggestions.* Companies that win Baldrige or Deming quality awards generally have very high rates of employee suggestions. Until recently one suggestion per employee per year would have been impressive among Western companies. Now, a growing number of Western companies are in double digits. At least one, Milliken & Co., 1989 Baldrige award winner, has achieved the suggestion-rate level of top Japanese firms (52 per person in 1992 at Milliken), and Milliken showers praise and recognition upon everyone who contributes. While most firms pay something for even small suggestions, others bestow only praise and recognition, which has similar effects.

- *Personal, team, and group awards.* Companies are devising numerous awards to help sustain continuous improvement momentum: Friday afternoon pizza parties, cookouts, and keggers; a day off, with the supervisor filling in; a next-to-the-door parking place; T-shirts, mugs, and plaques; theater or sports event tickets; dinner for two at a fancy restaurant; all-expense-paid trip to Hawaii; and trips for the whole team to a fine hotel to present its improvement at the annual management conference. While standard reinforcement theory does not distinguish particularly between private and public praise, today's leading companies tend toward a strong preference for making it public: wall charts, ceremonies, company and public news media, and so forth.

- *Meet the customer and supplier.* Superior companies, especially in North America, are sending their frontline employees to visit customers and suppliers, who are sometimes out of town or even out of the country. Reorganization into cells has the effect of putting individuals into continuous contact with their next-process customer and prior-process supplier. Whether in the next state or at the next desk, being in contact with one's customer or supplier may offer the chance for genuine satisfaction; being denied this opportunity tends to reduce the possibilities for feeling real pride.

When the individual feels fairly paid, is justly praised in a public manner, and can personally see the impact of good work on the customer's face, the productivity loop is effectively complete.

Chapter Thirteen

Service Facility Management

 As the last century ended, daring individuals accomplished spectacular feats of travel, circling the globe in less than 70 days, making real the fiction of Jules Verne's 1872 classic, *Around the World in 80 Days.* As this century ends, the ordinary citizen could make the trip in less than 70 hours. Rather than guessing what lies another century ahead, we will simply note that it takes little time to move people or things from one spot on the globe to another. Communications advances are equally impressive. Satellites, microwave links, fiber-optic cables, and so on, make nearly immediate voice and facsimile transmission a global reality, as the box illustrates.

Is This Dublin or Montego Bay?

If you are a New Yorker who needs to get some program assistance from Quarterdeck Office Systems, the California-based software company, your early morning call will be answered in (where else?) Dublin, Ireland. Or if you plan on flying from Winnipeg to Salt Lake City, the toll-free number you call to make your reservation might be handled by an operator in Montego Bay, Jamaica. Telecommunications advances coupled with aggressive efforts by some nations to boost their educational systems have "put wings on everything from insurance work to engineering and computer programming."

Satellite dishes connect the United States to 3,500 Jamaicans in office parks, where they make airline reservations and process tickets, handle calls to toll-free numbers, and do data entry. Also, over 25,000 documents a day (such as credit card applications) are scanned in the United States and then transmitted to Jamaica for processing.

Beginning at 4:00 AM, New York time, long before Californians are at work, calls to Quarterdeck are routed to Dublin, where Quarterdeck has its second phone-answering operation. At the same location, scores of multilingual employees handle inquiries from all over Europe. That would have been impossible until a few years ago when the Irish government spent billions to upgrade the country's phone system. The aim was to provide infrastructure needed to turn the island into a telecommunications service center.

Source: Brian O'Reilly, "Your New Global Work Force," *Fortune*, December 14, 1992, pp. 52–66.

As technology causes the globe to shrink, potential sites for service facilities expand, making location decisions more complicated. In this chapter we consider ways of reducing the complexity in finding the right location. Once the site is picked, the concern shifts to making it efficient—through good facility layout and continuing high-level maintenance. These chapter topics—facility location, layout, and maintenance—are essential elements of competitiveness and must not be treated as afterthoughts.

LOCATION

Any official of a city that has gained or lost a major business or government facility will be able to point out the economic impact on the community. Location is far-reaching because where the jobs go, the money goes. Payrolls, along with the jobs and tax revenues generated as payrolls are spent, separate the haves among cities, states, and nations, from the have-nots. Communities recognize this and keep increasing what they are willing to spend to attract businesses and jobs.

Besides communications advances, other factors in concert are causing service firms to move or expand geographically as never before.

- Trade pacts and unilateral actions are breaking barriers that once restricted country-to-country movements of banks, insurance companies, retailers, transportation companies, consultants, and other service firms.
- Travel and communications media have produced better-informed consumers. People who have been resigned to long waiting lines, surly servers, and inefficiency eagerly welcome McDonald's, IKEA, MasterCard, and Federal Express.
- Many of the world's top-quality service companies have saturated markets in their own regions or countries; remote markets beckon.

The narrower issue is *where* to locate. Sometimes, there are no choices. It has to be your kitchen (or basement or garage). Usually, however, a business has a boggling number of location choices. Some sort of systematic rating and weighting scheme is needed.

Rating Alternative Locations

Expansion Management magazine gives an example of a three-step ranking and weighting method used by one company in planning a new facility—which we'll assume is a new design center.[1] In the first step the location team selected 14 location factors. The team used a matrix to rate the importance of each against each of the other thirteen factors. The top six factors and their weighting points were:

33 points: Availability of higher education.

31 points: Labor cost.

31 points: Stable and experienced labor pool.

26 points: Other technology-related companies in the same area.

23 points: Availability of sites.

20 points: High quality of life/reasonable cost of living.

The following factors received lower point totals: availability of or nearness to air transportation, freight lines, suppliers, highways, and customers; utility/tax costs; and favorable business/community relationships. State aid, the 14th factor, got zero points.

In the second step, the team used a 1-to-10 scale for rating 7 possible locations against each of the remaining 13 factors (no longer including state aid). In the third step, the team multiplied the ranking points for the 13 factors times the 1-to-10 ratings. Final results, displayed in another matrix, summed up points for each of the seven sites. The highest point total indicated the best site.

The main value of this kind of analysis is not to *make* the decision. The location team and the final decision makers use the analysis as a way to remove clearly poor location choices from further consideration. Top choices will usually require more penetrating study. Also, intangibles, such as the whim of a CEO, could change the decision, or politics could intervene. In any case, systematic analysis is valuable because it reduces a lot of data to a few numbers, which can be used to influence the final decision. As we see next, however, gamesmanship also can figure into location strategies.

Preemptive Strategy

If you are a bridge player, you know that a preemptive bid is a very high opening bid made when one has few points. The purpose is to raise the stakes enough to discourage competitors from making their own bids, even though they may have more points. A similar strategy occurs in locating businesses or adding production capacity. A grocery chain, hotel, or pizza franchise may decide to open its next facility in a sparsely populated location in the hope of discouraging competitors. Sometimes just an announcement (which itself can be a bluff) of an intent to add capacity somewhere may convince a competitor not to do likewise because overcapacity, with resulting lower profit expectations, might result. The practice is called a preemptive strategy in business just as it is in the game of bridge.

Regardless of location, or even of the strategy used to make location decisions, deployment continues by looking inside facilities, at facility layout.

LAYOUT

At precisely 12 noon, the entire insurance staff—nearly 500 clerks, technicians, and managers—piled their personal belongings on office chairs and said good-bye to fellow employees. Pushing the chairs along crowded corridors, crisscrossing and colliding at intersections, all 500 made their way to newly assigned work areas.[2]

That's the sound of moving day at Aid Association for Lutherans (AAL), an insurance company. But this moving day was different. Departments and sections weren't just changing offices; the organization structure itself was on the chopping block. The 500 employees were shaken out into 15 focused teams in two tiers. The top tier is five groups, each serving insurance agents in a different region. Within each group are three bottom-tier teams of 20 to 30 people, one team for new policies, one for claims, and one for services.

Note: Physical layout of facilities in a building entails decisions about organization of associates who use the facilities. In the broad sense, then, we are talking about organization of resources, not merely layout of facilities in space.

Layout Types

There are four basic types of facilities layout:

1. *Process layout.* Also known as the functional layout, the process layout groups like facilities or functions together: human resource people in the HR department, marketers in the marketing department, and so forth. The process layout tends to emerge as small organizations grow, and functional groups appear (e.g., bookkeeping and accounting, sales and advertising, packing and shipping). Putting people with like functions together may create a climate for mutual support and learning. However, the process layout has a substantial disadvantage; it puts distance between provider and customer.

2. *Product layout.* In the product layout, facilities are arranged along the flow of goods or services. The customer (next process) is adjacent to, or very near, the provider. Cafeterias or order processing lines are examples. The major disadvantage to product layouts is with how they usually are managed. If associates along a flow line are allowed to do only one small job day in and day out, they can hardly be expected to grasp the overall operation. Their worth is diminished, boredom sets in, and morale drops. With cross-training and flexible product-flow cells, however, those problems can be eliminated.

3. *Cellular layout.* In the cellular layout, the idea is to arrange work stations and employees into cells that process families of services that follow similar flow paths. Cells perform better with the addition of a number of subconcepts: services deliberately designed to have as many common features as possible, high-use tools and data located within the cell, cross-trained servers, and the cellular layout itself. A cellular layout is similar to a product layout, although most people think of product layouts (flow lines) as handling only one or just a few products instead of a family.

Principles 6 and 9: Organize resources by item families. Assign equipment to focused cells.

Cells are a natural result when customer-oriented companies break apart functional departments and process layouts—the re-engineering idea. Human resource specialists, accountants, and other functionaries (along with their desks, file cabinets, computers, etc.) may join cells that provide a family of services. For the Bank of Boston, such a service family is its securities processing business, as the box explains.

4. *Fixed-position layout.* In the fixed-position layout, it is the item to be served whose position is fixed, and resources (people, equipment, materials, etc.) must come to it. Construction is a good example. Other examples are patients in hospital beds, or an actor being dressed, made up, and coached before the performance.

Mixed layouts—two or more layout types in a single facility—are common, if not the norm. An example is a restaurant that sets up a buffet brunch line on Sundays. The main service is to transform a hungry patron into a fed one. The patron has the choice of going through the buffet line or sitting down and ordering from the menu. The two types of patrons are processed through two types of facilities layout. The buffet customer goes

Moving Facilities for Moving Money

"Garbage—or something like it—was what the Bank of Boston found when it looked at its securities processing business . . . , which handles stock transfers, dividends and interest payments, pension plan administration, and related tasks—about 25 million transactions a year. It had six separate operations, each with its own mainframe, scattered over 11 locations. Work for one customer could shuffle through several systems—one for dividends, another for stock sales, a third for bond interest—costing time, labor, and money at each point.

"[Working with a consulting firm,] the bank put everyone in securities processing at one location with two computer systems and set up the work around its core process, moving money. Computer cables run across the ceiling like track lighting, allowing the bank to change the layout overnight. The idea was to mimic a just-in-time, flexible factory. Says senior vice president John Towers: 'We created a utility that could service all the product lines.' Productivity soared: After 2½ years, with 17% fewer employees, the division does 80% more securities-processing business."

Source: Adapted from Thomas A. Stewart, "US Productivity: First but Fading," *Fortune,* October, 1992, pp. 54–56.

through a product or cellular layout (hard to narrow it down to one or the other). It is a flow line. The menu customer receives service in a fixed layout: Menu, waiter, food, drinks, and check come to the fixed position.

Exhibit 13–1 is a sketch of such a restaurant, identifying the product layout and fixed layout. The restaurant also includes a process layout in the kitchen. There foods, not patrons, are the products being transformed. Process areas include grill, salads, range, desserts, ovens, freezer, and pantry. Arrows show the jumbled flow patterns.

Compared with a single-layout facility, a mixed-layout facility is more difficult to plan, more costly to equip, and more troublesome to maintain. But it may be easier to keep busy because it offers a wider variety of services to a larger pool of potential customers.

U-Shaped

The main feature of both flow lines and cells is the close proximity of workstations, speeding up flow and reducing in-process queuing.

EXHIBIT 13-1
Mixed Layout in a Restaurant

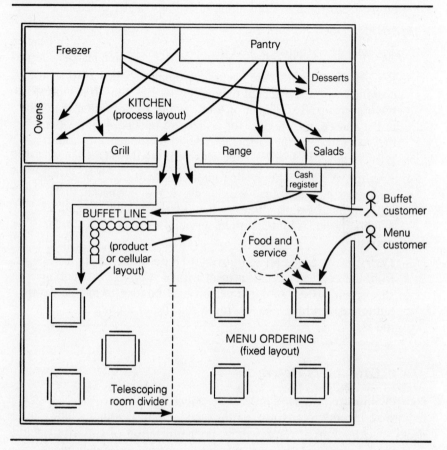

Another feature is layout of stations into a U shape. At least five advantages for cells or lines may result from U-shaped layout.

1. *Staff flexibility and balance.* The U shape allows one associate to tend several workstations, adjacent or across the U, since walking distance is short. Also, more options for balancing work among personnel exist; as demand increases, labor may be added until every station in the cell is tended by an associate.

2. *Teamwork.* Getting all staff into a cluster enhances teamwork and joint problem solving. Slowdowns or stoppages quickly ripple through the cell, and cell members form a natural team that must

collectively solve the problems and get the process going again. Natural teams can hardly form, much less work effectively, if employees are strung out along long lines or dispersed and separated by walls.

Principle 1: Team up with the customer—the next process.

3. *Rework.* When a mistake occurs, a common policy is to send the customer to the complaint department or the item to a separate rework group. But a tenet of total quality management is quality at the source, which calls for correcting mistakes right where they occurred. In the U-shaped layout, the distance to return a mistake is short, making it easier to follow the TQM tenet.

4. *Passage.* A long, straight line interferes with travel of servers, customers, and supplies. We object when supermarket aisles are too long, and people protest when a freeway cuts through a neighborhood. A long, straight service line may be a similar imposition.

5. *Distribution.* Since all stations in a U are immediately accessible from the center, it is easier to distribute supplies, instruction sheets, and so on. A single person may be able to handle distribution tasks while also tending a starting or ending station in the U.

Layout and Re-Layout

New facilities require new layouts. Existing facilities get out of date and require re-layout. Symptoms of the need for re-layout include bottlenecks, backtracking, overcrowding, poor utilization of capacity (including space), poor housekeeping, missed due dates, too much queue time, and a high or growing ratio of total throughput time to actual work content.

Some service businesses undergo frequent re-layout. Office employees may begin to "wonder where my desk will be on Monday morning." The desk may be across town in newly rented office space. Physical obstacles are few; most offices can move overnight if telephone hookups can be arranged. With few physical problems, office re-layout commonly focuses on people and work climate, as the accompanying box illustrates.

Perhaps people and work climate should be central concerns in all layout and re-layout work. We will see this in the next sections when we undertake a detailed layout-planning example.

Re-Layout: Employee-Centered Style

When Woodsmith, a Des Moines–based publisher of catalogs for do-it-yourself carpenters, recently redesigned its offices, CEO Donald Peshke chose to forgo the use of outside contractors and instead asked each of the 35-person staff to do his or her own area. Peshke's goal was not so much to save money as to save time.

Outside installers would have required over a week to break down the office's movable wall panels and modular furniture and transform the office. With a Friday evening kickoff pizza party, the Woodsmith staff launched the weekend stint, and by Monday morning had the walls redone, furniture installed, and equipment relocated.

With help from a local Herman Miller dealer, each employee had designed a layout for his or her work area, deciding where to locate work surfaces and position computers, file cabinets, and other equipment. Peshke explained: "Our approach was to get them involved in the design so they'd understand what couldn't be done. They accept limitations a lot better that way, instead of the boss saying, 'This is what you're going to live with, like it or not.' " But the best part of the whole experience, according to Peshke, "turned out to be the comraderie it developed."

Source: Robert A. Mamis, "Employees as Contractors," *Inc.,* November 1992, p. 53.

Layout Planning Steps

In a complex layout situation, hundreds of jobs may be in progress at any given time. Both job and project work may be included, with work and resources moving to work centers via many routings.

When routes are so diverse, how work areas are arranged in a building makes a difference. Dominant flow patterns are there among the apparent jumble of routings, and layout analysis helps to find those patterns.

One layout principle is to arrange work areas in the order of dominant flow. A goal is to get work or resources into, through, and out of each service center in minimum time at reasonable cost. The less time spent in the flow pattern, the less chance of collecting labor and overhead charges and the faster the immediate and final customers are served.

Other factors besides flows may be important. If so, the nonflow factors (e.g., teamwork) may be combined with flow data. The combined data will suggest how close work areas should be to one another, and a rough

EXHIBIT 13–2
Layout Planning—Steps and Possible Tools

Steps	Possible Tools
1. Analyze work (customer) and resource flows.	Flow diagram From-to chart
2. Identify and include nonflow factors, where significant.	Activity-relationship (REL) chart Combined REL chart
3. Assess data and arrange work areas.	Activity arrangement diagram
4. Determine space arrangement plan.	Space relationship diagram
5. Fit space arrangement into available space.	Floor plan Detailed layout models

layout can be developed. The next step is to determine the space requirements for a rough layout. The last step in layout planning is to fit the rough layout into the available space, that is, the proposed or existing building. Several layout plans can be developed for managers to choose from.

The layout planning steps just described are listed in Exhibit 13–2, along with planning aids usable in each step.

Layout Planning Example

Example 13–1 demonstrates the layout planning steps. The method and some of the tools were developed by R. R. Muther, who calls the approach systematic layout planning (SLP).[3] SLP is widely respected for its practicality. Though developed in an earlier era, SLP works well in support of a modern, customer-oriented approach to layout.

EXAMPLE 13–1 Layout Planning—Globe County Offices

Citizens' main contact with Globe County offices is in registering and licensing vehicles. Many people complain because the three county offices involved have not consolidated their services. On busy days there are waiting lines at all three offices. Many vehicle owners must visit all three, and it is common for a citizen to find out, after shuffling forward for awhile, that it is the wrong line.

The elected officials who run the three offices have decided to consolidate. Mr. Ross, a consultant, has been hired to conduct layout analysis using SLP.

Ross's analysis reveals that 12 activities are to be located in the available space, as follows:

Activity	Space Requirements (square feet)
1. County assessor's office:	
a. Management.	600
b. Motor vehicle—counter.*	300
c. Motor vehicle—clerical.	240
d. Assessors.	960
2. County clerk's office:	
e. Management.	840
f. Recording and filing—counter.	240
g. Recording and filing—clerical.	960
h. Motor vehicle—counter-clerical.*	960
3. County treasurer's office:	
i. Management.	420
j. Motor vehicle—counter-clerical.*	1,600
4. Support areas:	
k. Mail and copier.*	240
l. Conference room.	160
Total	7,520

*Significant flows.
Source: This is adapted from a real case. Thanks go to Ross Greathouse of Greathouse-Flanders Associates, Lincoln, Nebraska, for providing original case data.

We see that four of the activities have significant flows: three service counters, plus the office copier. The space requirements are based on careful measurement of desks, files, and so forth, plus use of widely available industry space standards (e.g., 300 square feet per auto in a parking lot).

Flow analysis. For those four activities, Ross gathers flow data, which he enters on a from-to chart (which resembles the distance chart found on many road maps). The from-to chart shows number of trips from one activity to another. This includes patron trips from office to office and employee trips from, say, office to copier and back. It also shows backtracking trips when patrons find themselves in the wrong office.

Ross codes totals from the from-to chart *A, E, I, O,* or *U.* Those letters are standard SLP symbols for flow volume, and they stand for *A*bnormally high flow, *E*specially high flow, *I*mportant flow, *O*rdinary flow, and *U*nimportant flow.

EXHIBIT 13–3
Combined Activity Relationship (REL) Chart—County Offices

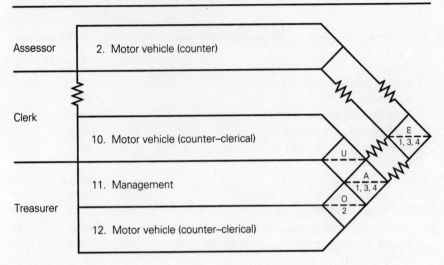

	Code	Reason
	1	Work flow
	2	Supervision
Reasons	3	Employees sharing (between departments)
behind the	4	Share counter
"closeness"	5	Personal communication
value	6	
	7	
	8	
	9	

Source of REL chart form: Richard Muther and Associates, Kansas City, Missouri. Used with permission.

Nonflow factors. Next, Ross lists nonflow factors, such as the need for employees to be near their supervisor, and rates them using the same five vowel designators. He combines flow and nonflow factors on an activity relationship (REL) chart, a segment of which is shown in Exhibit 13–3.

EXHIBIT 13-4
Activity Arrangement Diagram—County Offices

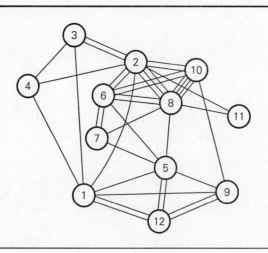

The REL chart is easy to interpret. The single A in the chart indicates that it is absolutely necessary for customer service people in the clerk and treasurer offices to be close together. Reasons are "work flow" (1), "employee sharing (between departments)" (3), and "share counter" (4). The same reasons apply to the E, for especially important, in the box connecting customer service counter people in the treasurer and assessor offices.

Activity arrangement. Now Ross converts the combined REL chart to an activity arrangement diagram, which shows the arrangement of all activities but without indicating requirements for space, utilities, halls, and so on (see Exhibit 13-4). In this diagram, number of lines between activities stands for flow volume: Four lines corresponds to an A rating on the REL chart, three lines stands for an E rating, and so forth. Distances between circles are set according to desired degree of closeness, as much as possible. Activities 2, 6, 8, and 10, at the core, are all service-counter activities, which earlier ratings showed should be placed close together.

Space arrangement. Ross's next-to-last chart includes the space data. The result is a diagram that is in the generally rectangular shape of the space into which the activities must fit; activity blocks are sized according to space needed. The space relationship diagram (not shown) may be regarded as a rough layout.

Layout into available space. Finally, Ross is ready to draw some final layouts, complete with walls, halls, aisles, and other needed elements.

EXHIBIT 13–5
New Layout and Motor Vehicle Licensing Counter

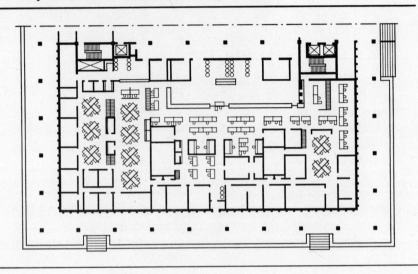

Exhibit 13–5 shows what Ross might have developed. It is an actual layout of the county office renovation that is the basis for this example. The main feature of that layout is a shared counter. The layout was developed by an architectural firm (though the systematic layout planning process, as presented here, was not fully used) and approved and implemented by newly elected Lancaster County officials in Lincoln, Nebraska.

The Globe County Offices example is fairly simple. In large, complex layouts, analysis within each activity area could include the full SLP treatment, that is, all the SLP steps. In later steps, various two- and three-dimensional models (manual or computer graphic) can be manipulated to produce workable layout options. In the Globe County example, we also glossed over all the trial and error usually involved in the diagramming.

Open Layouts

One of the special influences on office layout is the open-office concept. It eliminates many floor-to-ceiling walls and deemphasizes functional compartmentalization of people. One key advantage is that the open office is more customer-friendly, especially in establishments that are trying to promote customer service. By opening up to customers, providers remove some of the mystery or secrecy from their operations. Banks are good examples, as the box illustrates.

Layout: Making Banks Look Like Stores

"Come see Chicago's newest architectural wonder," the advertisement proclaimed. The "wonder" is actually one of Citibank's new branches, unobtrusively placed on the ground floor of the USG Building in Chicago's Loop. Why all the fuss over a new branch bank? Layout.

When financial panics were more common, people were reluctant to let someone else guard their money. To win confidence, banks had to convey a trustworthy, solid image; massive stone and steel buildings with imposing granite counters and bars separating tellers from the public helped create the impression of security in customer's minds. Today, with banking an accepted way of life, security is largely a given, and bankers want their names associated with a new concept: service.

Increasingly, banks are being laid out like stores, though they resemble convenience stores more than top-of-the-line retailers. In the Citibank facility, for example, an employee in the "greeter station" directs customers to nearby areas for tellers, loan counselors, or investment sales personnel. The space is open, bars are gone, and signs promoting the bank's line of products and services are prominent.

The store concept is spreading throughout the banking industry. "We are a retailer of financial services," says Chuck Shoemaker, a senior vice president at First Chicago Corp. "I tell our employees we're no different from Marshall Field's, except they're selling shirts and ties and we're selling checking accounts and investment products."

Source: Blair Kamin, "Edifice Exits: Banks Assume Retail Look," *Chicago Tribune*, Section 3, p. 1, November 12, 1992.

Other advantages of open layouts are that they foster better employee communications and provide flexibility for easy re-layout. Modular office furniture and movable, partial-height partitions aid in achieving these goals.

Open offices in Japan, where the concept is deeply ingrained, often are truly wide open. North Americans, in contrast, have emphasized maintaining a degree of privacy and cutting noise. Interior designers use wall carpeting, sound-absorbent panels, acoustical screens, fabric-wrapped desktop risers, and free-standing padded partitions. Office landscaping (use of plants) is also commonplace. In fact, plants are so prominent in the offices of Mars (candy bars) in Veghel, Holland, that people there call it the office garden concept.

With the facility properly located and its resources laid out for high-quality service delivery, what remains is upkeep. Synchroservice requires not just fixing what breaks but preventing facility breakdowns that lead to service failures.

TOTAL PREVENTIVE MAINTENANCE

Perhaps the classic image of a preventive maintenance (PM) reminder is the TV-commercial automobile mechanic who warns us to change our oil and oil filter regularly. By so doing, the ad implies, we will prevent engine damage and thus avoid costly repairs. A real mechanic would support the preventive benefits of regular oil changes, but would also remind us that we will need to replace tires and other worn parts and perhaps even to overhaul key components like the transmission if we wish to avoid breakdowns. Thus, the mechanic has summarized the three goals of total preventive maintenance (TPM):

- Regular preventive maintenance, including rigorous housekeeping.
- Periodic replacement or overhauls.
- Intolerance for breakdowns.

The philosophy of TPM is that by giving up a little, we gain a lot: a resource that remains in a high state of readiness.

Quality through Readiness

A work environment that is ready for use when needed prevents many problems. Consider how often customers wait for a service provider to find the proper form, or a pen, pencil, stapler, or other tool. Inability to find a needed resource due to a cluttered or poorly organized workplace is an obvious sign of poor upkeep. So too are scattered piles of repair parts and their identifying forms, broken fixtures, dirty equipment or work areas, and sloppy personal appearances. More subtly, overflowing in-baskets and disorganized files (even if hidden in cabinets, desks, or on computer disks) reflect poor maintenance too. Unavailable or improperly trained human resources can also be delay-causing culprits. In short, if it impedes timely and responsive high-quality customer service, it is a target for better maintenance.

Maintenance Success Indicators

The payoff from a sound investment in maintenance (training as well as money) is often not immediately obvious; results might show up much later or appear elsewhere in the organization. Successful TPM results in faster and more dependable throughput times, higher productivity, improved quality of outputs, lower scheduling and control costs, increased health and safety, and lower operating costs (see Exhibit 13–6). These general-level payoffs stem from the efforts of people across the organization. The centerpiece of this effort is frontline ownership.

Operators, Teams, and Functions

The phrase *employee ownership* refers to the associates' believing that equipment condition is their responsibility and that maintenance, engineering, and outside service representatives are backups. This parallels the shift in responsibility for quality from quality professionals to frontline associates. TPM and TQM are cut from the same cloth. As earlier chapters have noted, in the service- or customer-focused organization, associates not only perform value-adding transformations, but they are also cross-trained to perform some of their own operations support. Maintenance specialists and other experts are often assigned to the group to provide on-the-spot training and technical support.

Principle 7: Cross-train for mastery of multiple skills.

The case for employee-centered maintenance is multifaceted. Frontline associates learn their equipment better, gain fuller control over their own processes, and take greater pride in their workplace when they assume cleanup tasks and responsibility for minor repairs. This cuts repair time since there is less waiting around for someone from maintenance to come and change a bulb, for instance. Furthermore, the trend towards multiple, smaller, more mobile equipment and furnishings makes frontline associates less dependent on maintenance; they can perform much of the relocation and installation themselves.

EXHIBIT 13-6
The Total Preventive Maintenance Payoff—General Indicators

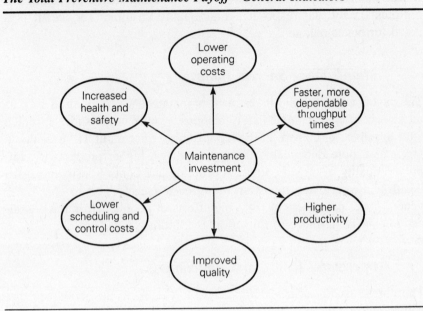

Principle 9:   Look for flexible, movable equipment.

In addition, the involved employee is more likely to develop ideas for fail-safing, which is a superior form of failure prevention. Finally, workforce scheduling is easier because maintenance can often be performed at times when scheduled work has been completed early; this is true, at least under JIT, which calls for associates to perform maintenance and other improvements rather than overproducing.

The backup role, however, is still important. While well-trained operators become the first line of defense against breakdowns, special expertise is needed to handle nonroutine trouble or direct maintenance-related training and other projects. That expertise might come from a central maintenance department or, especially in more recent years, from cross-functional teams dispersed throughout the organization.

Shifting primary maintenance responsibility to frontline associates doesn't put the maintenance department out of business; in fact, its responsibilities can become more focused and better defined. In addition to providing training and auditing of the TPM program, the maintenance department typically has plantwide responsibilities for buildings and grounds, utilities, environmental control, health and safety, facility design and improvement, and overall facility economics.

CONTRAST

Maintenance Responsibilities

Traditional	Employee Ownership/TPM
• Maintenance is a functional support activity; employees rely on specialists in the central maintenance department for custodial services and preventive and repair maintenance.	• Frontline associates have first responsibility for maintenance in their workplaces. • Specialists from a maintenance department or on cross-functional teams have backup responsibility to handle difficult or unusual problems.

Dedicated Maintenance

Operationally, each additional increment of PM tends to shift reliability upward. Without PM, reliability deteriorates and failure becomes increasingly likely. A few companies are renowned for their intolerance of failures; Walt Disney Company is an example. Disney World in Florida has become a popular destination not only for vacationers but also for benchmarking teams wanting to study Disney's breakdown-intolerant maintenance program.

Another company famed for its maintenance is United Parcel Service, which keeps most of its over-the-road and delivery vehicles operating and looking as good as new for 20 years or more. A feature of the UPS program is dedicated mechanics and dedicated drivers. A driver operates the same vehicle every day, and a mechanic maintains the same group of vehicles. Many military aircraft maintenance programs also use dedicated operator/mechanic programs; often, the names of both the pilot and the maintenance crew chief are painted on the aircraft. Both individuals proudly claim ownership and are responsible for the performance of the aircraft.

At UPS, mechanics work at night on delivery vehicles driven mostly during the day, but drivers and mechanics stay closely in touch. Drivers complete a posttrip vehicle inspection report every day, noting any problems. The mechanic goes to work on those problems that evening, and records completed work on the form. The driver uses the form in conducting a pretrip inspection every morning. Thank-yous and other personal comments between driver and mechanic are common. Similar interactions and documentation between pilots and maintenance crew chiefs have long been standard in military and (in some cases) commercial aircraft maintenance programs.

Principle 6:   Organize resources into focused family groupings.

The interdependency of driver, vehicle, and mechanic keeps responsibilities focused and avoids blaming. In the more typical situation of changing mechanics and drivers, any of the individuals can become lax, fail to keep good records, and leave problems for the next person or shift.

Maintenance Records

Clearly, a vital aspect of aircraft and UPS vehicle maintenance programs is thorough recordkeeping. Everything that happens to a vehicle or plane is recorded, every problem and every maintenance action. A complete history of engine, chassis, and all other major components is available.

Complete records permit computer calculation of failure rates, necessary for determining prefailure replacement schedules; mean times to repair, useful in scheduling maintenance people's time; and component reliabilities, which designers use to improve next-generation components.

As an added service to regular customers, some garages maintain computerized records of automobile maintenance. Customers are freed from some recordkeeping worry, but the garage also benefits: Mechanics know when to call and suggest appointments, what parts are likely to need replacement, and what, if any, warranty time remains. Like aircraft and UPS vehicles, well-designed and well-maintained automobiles can have long operating lifetimes, and an automobile's value is enhanced if it is accompanied by a thorough set of maintenance records.

Chapter 14

What's Next for You and for Synchroservice?

 The first 13 chapters have focused on a few closely integrated new and evolving goals:

- Total quality.
- Data-based continuous improvement.
- Customer- and service-focused organization and measurement.
- Cross-functional teams.
- Streamlined, seamless flow of people, information, and service delivery.
- Flexibility.
- Simplicity.

PEOPLE, TEAMS, JOBS, AND CAREERS

These elements of synchroservice do not describe a profession or function. Rather they unify the efforts of all the diverse professions, functions, jobs, and people who are part of the extended service organization.

Getting all that diversity aligned is a tall order. The effort needs direction from the top. Those who set strategy have the power to send clear signals that service management is in the midst of a period of rapid change. When senior executives do not exhibit this kind of leadership, however, that does not excuse inaction by others. Each of us can—and must—push for change in our own spheres of influence.

Key changes have to do with broadened skill levels and teamwork. It is, or will be, important for your own career to expand your skills and learn to function in a team environment:

- *Cross-functional teams.* In nearly every chapter, we have noted the importance of cross-functional teams for solving problems and improving processes. Most teams should involve both professionals and frontline associates. Regardless of your profession, your membership on such teams will expand your own effectiveness and enhance your career.

- *Career-broadening training and assignments.* Regardless of where your career path begins, you need experience elsewhere. It is partly up to you to break out of your specialty and broaden yourself. If you're lucky, your employer will help. Knighton Optical, a Utah-based chain of retail optical shops with its own optical laboratories, has cross-trained accountants who can fit glasses for customers. In addition, Knighton has trained retail clerks to grind lenses and finish glasses in the labs. Hyatt Hotels is launching cross-training experimentally at its facility in Schaumburg, Illinois.[1] Home Depot even has its board members involved: Each director must anonymously visit 10 Home Depot stores every quarter. They chat with customers and employees, check for quality of service and store appearance, evaluate employee training, and then reveal their identities to store associates.[2]

Employees who broaden their skills improve their work life security. Employers and customers gain even more. Director visits to a Home Depot store help unite associates behind common values extending from the very top to the front lines, and they support Home Depot's open corporate culture. Common values and culture show up to customers as consistency of service.

More directly, broadly skilled employees are flexible. Flexibility breeds responsiveness, reducing the time customers must wait while providers get the right mix of human resources together. In addition, as Edward Lawler puts it, a "broad perspective helps employees to be innovative in improving operations. Thus, they become more effective in a quality circle, or any other problem-solving group."[3] Thus, for example, a buyer with receiving or stockroom experience will not only be a better buyer but also be better able to work with receiving and stockroom associates on work-flow improvement projects. Similarly, a staff professional who has taken orders from customers in an order-entry position will be more inclined to look outward, toward customers and overall business success, instead of inward.

Principle 7: Cross-train for mastery of multiple skills.

Lawler makes the related point that since high-performance organizations have been flattening their organization structures, they need to create "new career tracks that do not depend on upward mobility" and that provide "a new 'nonlinear' way for people to grow and to succeed in their careers."[4]

The large baby-boom population exerts pressures in the same direction: many associates seeking few vertical advancement openings. Since the boomers will remain in the labor force for another two decades, employers will not soon escape the need for policy changes such as horizontal promotions.

Other human resource trends (besides population cycles and employee cross-training) will surely cause further changes in service management. We will examine some of these forces and speculate on their effects in the remainder of this chapter.

CHANGE

Change in service management has been so extensive that many concepts treated in this book were unknown before the 1980s. The future is unpredictable, and the present, which contains the roots of future directions, is hard to assess. Even so, we can suggest at least a few desirable changes, such as those that improve people's work lives, the environment, and standards of living. We would also like to see the benefits of today's best service practices spreading from leading service organizations to the rest, and we would like to see people in minimum-wage jobs and economically depressed countries helped by these practices as well.

When leading service providers caught TQM fever in the latter years of the 1980s, common assumptions had to be laid to rest:

1. We had believed that many services, such as health care, sales, and teaching, were resistant to productivity improvement, and we had failed to realize how much rework, waste, delay, returns, and customer dissatisfaction is typically embedded in these services. We now realize that room for improvement is a Grand Canyon.
2. We also realize that most of the concepts and techniques of continuous improvement are effective across the entire service sector.

However, the pace of improvement is mixed. Service organizations in highly competitive businesses are under pressure to change quickly; more insulated organizations may be able to avoid this necessity for the time being. The following are examples of service businesses that are more competitively exposed.

Retailing. The opening of Toys 'R' Us stores in Japan sent shock waves through Japan's creaky distribution system. Japanese laws have been changed to accommodate high-volume, low-price retailers because consumers demanded it; many mom-and-pop toy shops are being put out of business. Wal-Mart has been doing the same thing in North America, forcing smaller retailers into niches or out of business.

Toys 'R' Us and Wal-Mart are two very successful chain retailers. (Examples could also be cited from specialty goods and general merchandise.) Central in their success formulas is partnering up with suppliers and freight carriers to minimize total inventories while still keeping the shelves stocked. These just-in-time partnerships eliminate intermediate warehousing and slash ordering and shipping transactions. In addition, project teams with members drawn from the retailer, freight carrier, producer, and even the producer's supplier are at work solving all sorts of intercompany problems.

Principle 13:   Operate at the customer's rate of use.

The cover of *Business Week* for December 21, 1992, featured Wal-Mart, Toys 'R' Us, Home Depot, and Circuit City, along with the cover-story title: "Clout!" These retailers are using their power and influence in transforming the supply chain and "revolutionizing the way consumer products are bought and sold" (cover). However, Sears, Roebuck & Co., along with Hudson Bay stores in Canada and Marks and Spencer in the United Kingdom, had equal clout in the pre-Wal-Mart era. They were famous for using it, too, for driving a hard bargain on price. But in that era, concepts such as JIT, supplier partnership, and cross-functional problem-solving teams were not taught and were largely unknown.

Today, these ideas are common knowledge. They have become part of the mainstream of business studies and are finding their way into textbooks in government, education, and other fields as well. Retailers achieve competitive advantage by using these techniques, and when a retailer has a blind spot, a knowledgeable supplier may take its just-in-time proposal to the retailer, pointing out ways to jointly cut costs and improve service. Milliken & Company's textile managers have taken such proposals not only to their customers in the apparel and upholstered furniture business and transport companies, but all the way to clothing and furniture retailers.

Principle 6:   Organize chains of customers.

Many high-performance retail–supplier partnerships are partially founded on TQM concepts, but the situation is a bit different in information services.

Information services.   Increasingly, companies are farming out computer software development and heavy-duty data-entry jobs to information service companies in India. Grocery chains fly sacks of merchandise coupons to Caribbean islands for counting. Designers scattered around the globe jointly develop new products for Texas Instruments and the Gap. Omaha has become a center for telephone services such as airline reservations and credit checking. Satellite communications, E-mail, global area networks, computer-aided design, air freight, and other technologies make these arrangements possible. Thus, the lowering of trade barriers that is occurring around the world is in some ways incidental; data and information already move from country to country without customs inspections.

So far, these out-sourcing arrangements do not appear to be based on total quality or continuous improvement. Just-in-time is not managed in; it simply seems to be a part of the technology. Management wants to harness special skills (e.g., pattern makers in Hong Kong or a neutral English accent for telephone answerers in Omaha), or to find useful skills at a very low wage (e.g., computer programmers in India).

Although any firm can use communications technology to out-source information services, it seems inevitable that firms will have to do more than just chase low wages or special skills to be competitive. Superior companies will gain an edge by employing TQM methods to improve quality and flexibility, eliminate waste, and continuously improve.

Public services. Denied the option of global out-sourcing, public agencies have even more reason to implement total quality management. TQM is now a dominant subject of employee training in public services. Results include, for example, substantial error reductions in the US Internal Revenue Service, many times faster repair of city vehicles in Madison, Wisconsin, and elimination of chronic misplacement of X-rays in the San Diego Naval Hospital system.

Doubters may say that TQM in government is just a fad and that the government's customer is not clearly enough defined for customer-focused TQM to be effective. However, a more significant factor is that government has fewer ways to measure success than profit-making firms have. This can be frustrating to dedicated public servants, who may see TQM as a way to finally make a noticeable impact. Moreover, concepts that greatly improve an agency's ability to provide quick, accurate response and increase productivity may help make government service more personally fulfilling.

Many other service organizations have only a weak or nonexistent interest in TQM. Their turn will come, either prodded by a competitor or fed by awareness of the advantages. Awareness may be the most likely path. It is increasingly difficult to remain in the dark. Quality councils have sprung up in many cities and regions, and quality-related awards are publicized in the popular press. Most of the 1,600-odd community colleges and technical schools in the United States and Canada offer subsidized instruction in statistical process control. Moreover, books and articles on quality and continuous improvement flood the market.

At one time, a popular service, a hard-to-copy technology, or superior marketing could make up for weak service management. Moreover, weak management usually did not have life-and-death consequence to a service organization. That is beginning to change. Synchroservice—blending superior frontline operations, design, marketing, accounting, supplier relations, human resource management, and business strategy—will become the essential of success.

Thus, we may be approaching an age in which the majority will improve their service management dramatically. Those that don't will probably fail rather swiftly, and strong companies will acquire their valuable assets cheaply. The wave of business mergers and acquisitions in the 1970s and early 1980s was driven mostly by financial objectives, but the new wave will be aimed at creating success through synchroservice.

QUALITY OF WORK LIFE AND THE ENVIRONMENT

Personal fulfillment can be a powerful motivator, at least for those whose basic personal needs are taken care of. But what about people working at the minimum wage, in a clerical, fast-food, data-entry, janitorial, or general labor capacity? Their employers may deliberately encourage high turnover to reduce the pressure to grant pay raises. They may also offer mainly part-time work to avoid paying benefits, and call in extra part-timers to avoid paying overtime. Job-holders in these businesses may fall below the poverty line; be unable to pay for proper medical care, housing, and food; and have many unmet physiological and security needs.

Improvement Scenario

Nevertheless, there may be a role for TQM in these businesses. Here is a possible scenario:

- Burgers, Inc., launches a "world-class services" program via a two-day training course for every employee, including office support and managerial associates.
- Baseline performance measures, such as customer wait time, food and packaging waste, store cleanliness index, inventories, and invoice processing time, are plotted on large charts.

  Principle 14: Record quality, process, and problem data at the workplace.

- Project teams, both spontaneous and assigned, are formed to improve performance, which they record on the wall charts. The teams capture and deal with root causes, then plot new points on the charts.
- Team members who are enthusiastic leaders, communicators, or innovators stand out. Supervisors and store managers don't want to lose these employees, so they are given more hours, benefits, and pay raises.

- The overall level of competence and motivation of the workforce rises, and increasing numbers of associates rise up through the ranks to become supervisors, store managers, and executives. Other employees move on to other careers but with impressive problem-solving credentials.
- Better pay brings some of these standout associates up out of poverty, so that their physiological needs can be met. Burgers, Inc., values their continued employment, which meets their security needs. These associates are better fixed to pursue higher-level needs. Later on in life, some of these people may be at the level of high personal fulfillment, but meanwhile, they see learning, innovation, and continuous process improvement as a path out of poverty and a way to improve their credentials and résumés.
- Burgers, Inc., enjoys a reputation for the best quality and service in its industry at competitive prices. Though it offers pay raises, benefits, and security, the improvement teams drive out costly wastes so that its costs are no higher than those of its less-capable competitors.

The same scenario could help uplift people in underdeveloped countries from poverty and no-hope existence. We cannot cite any low-wage service companies that have adopted these measures sufficiently to show their merits. We think such measures make eminently good sense, but it remains to be seen if this approach will come into wide use.

Environmental and Labor Protection

Improvement teams will devote some of their time to job and environmental health and safety. They will do so in their own self-interest and because insurance policies and governmental regulations may require certain levels of protection. Environmental activists also press the issue and sometimes prove that strong safety and environmental policies pay.

Principle 7:   Continually invest in improved health, safety, and security.

International trade pacts also appear to be moving companies in this direction. For example, political leaders in the United States threaten trade restrictions unless Mexico upgrades and enforces antipollution and employment standards. The European Community is at least as firm about incorporating tough environmental and labor standards into its internal and external trade pacts. The United Nations also regularly debates these issues. Although international environmental and labor standards are being developed, implementation must occur at a much lower level. Frontline and cross-functional process improvement teams seem to be the natural instrument for implementation.

CURRENTS AND COUNTERCURRENTS

Globalism affects service management in many ways, but especially in the phenomenal growth of market size as trade barriers fall. A Big Mac now is available almost everywhere, a potential market of over 5 billion people. But a few years ago, McDonald's was excluded from most of the Soviet bloc, China, and India. The company's business strategy is simple: Expand, hold up quality standards, and form supplier partnerships of all kinds.

Bank of America, Metropolitan Life, and other service businesses may follow similar strategies. The vast world market offers relief from the limited strategy of just fighting Burger King, Citibank, and Prudential for local market share.

But there is a countercurrent: While the big get bigger in new and massive markets, opportunities are growing for custom suppliers of speciality services in those same mass markets. Unfortunately, however, while the Burger Kings and Citibanks of the world have always offered fairly good quality and high efficiency, most specialty companies have been woeful performers by today's standards. Customers may wait interminably and have little input or feedback; when the service is finally delivered, it's often wrong and needs to be redone. This description could apply to a tailor, a doctor, a lawyer, or a city agency.

We have included ways to improve low-volume specialty services in almost every chapter, in part, because specialty operations are so complex and nonroutine. Design for service operations guidelines (Chapter 3), queue limitation (Chapter 7), supplier partnerships (Chapter 8), and total preventive maintenance and cells (Chapter 13) are just some of the concepts important to improving specialty services.

FIRST TO KNOW

In studying service management, we have been exposed to several major evolutions in strategy. In the early 1980s quality consciousness began to sink in, and *quality as competitive advantage* became the dominant new strategy. A few years later, the focus was on *time-based competition,* then *globalization,* and lately, *flexibility.*

These ideas were developed as an integrated whole in certain pioneering books of the late 1970s and early 1980s, and they gained extra prominence after being blessed in prestigious business periodicals such as the *Harvard Business Review.* Moreover, each of these strategies tends to move like an avalanche through the adopting service business. People wonder, Is there more? If so, what's next?

We don't know. Rather than trying to guess, we would rather make this point: What's important is being the first to know and, therefore, having the first chance to implement and gain the advantage. It seems likely that the first to know will be organizations having strong benchmarking and competitive analysis, supplier and customer partnerships, a global presence, extensive continuous training, ethnic variety, and highly involved employees skilled at getting things done right the first time. In your own career, taking charge of building these first-to-know capabilities can be your best protection.

Notes

Chapter 1

[1]This phrase is attributed to the late Kaoru Ishikawa, a Japanese authority on quality.

[2]Kenichi Ohmae, *The Mind of the Strategist: Business Planning for Competitive Advantage* (New York: Penguin Books, 1983), chap. 8 (HD31.0485).

[3]Cited in Bruce D Henderson, "The Origin of Strategy," *Harvard Business Review,* November–December 1989, pp. 139–43.

[4]William H Davidow and Bro Uttal, "Service Companies: Focus or Falter," *Harvard Business Review,* July–August 1989, pp. 77–85.

[5]Andrew E Serwer, "America's 100 Fastest Growers," *Fortune,* August 9, 1993, pp. 40–56.

[6]Ibid.

[7]Karen Bemowski, "Three Electronics Firms Win 1991 Baldrige Award," *Quality Progress,* November 1991, pp. 39–41.

[8]M Scott Myers, *Every Employee a Manager,* 3rd ed. (San Diego: University Associates, Inc., 1991).

Chapter 2

[1]Leonard L Berry, Valerie A Zeithaml, and A Parasuraman, "Quality Counts in Services, Too," *Business Horizons,* May–June 1985, pp. 44–52.

[2]America's discovery of Deming has been traced to Clare Crawford-Mason, a television producer. Working on a documentary on the decline of American industry in the 1970s, Crawford-Mason heard of Deming's work in Japan and pursued her journalistic instincts. See Mary Walton, *The Deming Management Method* (New York: Dodd, Mead, 1986), chap. 1 (HD38.W36).

[3]J M Juran, "The Quality Trilogy," *Quality Progress* 19, no. 8 (August 1986), pp. 19–24.

[4]Armand V Feigenbaum, *Total Quality Control,* 3rd ed. (New York: McGraw-Hill, 1983), p. 11 (TS156.F44).

[5]Philip B Crosby, *Quality Is Free: The Art of Making Quality Certain* (New York: McGraw-Hill, 1979), p. 146.

[6]Robert C Camp, *Benchmarking: The Search for Industry Best Practices That Lead to Superior Performance* (Milwaukee: ASQC Quality Press, 1989).

[7]Ronald E Yates, "Lawyers Not Exempt from Quality Crusade," *Chicago Tribune*, December 1, 1991.

[8]Harry V Roberts and Bernard F Sergesketter, *Quality Is Personal: A Foundation for Total Quality Management* (New York: The Free Press, 1993).

Chapter 3

[1]G Lynn Shostack, "Designing Services That Deliver," *Harvard Business Review*, January–February 1984, pp. 133–40.

[2]David E Bowen and Edward E Lawler III, "Total Quality-oriented Human Resources Management," *Academy of Management Executive*, Spring 1992, pp. 29–41.

[3]Bruce Nussbaum, "What Works for One Works for All," *Business Week*, April 20, 1992, pp. 112–13.

[4]For a critique of QFD, see Edward Knod and Ann Dietzel, "Quality Function Deployment: Potential Pitfalls," *P/OM Proceedings*, Midwest Business Administration Association, March 1992, pp. 33–40.

[5]Detailed matrices are discussed in Bob King, *Better Designs in Half the Time: Implementing QFD, Quality Function Deployment in America* (Methuen, MA: GOAL/QPC, 1987).

[6]Charles A Cox, "Keys to Success in Quality Function Deployment," *APICS—The Performance Advantage*, April 1992, pp. 25–28.

[7]Geoffrey Boothroyd and Peter Dewhurst, *Design for Assembly* (Wakefield, RI: Boothroyd Dewhurst, Inc., 1987).

[8]Susan Moffat, "Japan's New Personalized Production," *Fortune*, October 22, 1990, pp. 132–35.

[9]Joseph F McKenna, "From JIT, with Love," *Industry Week*, August 17, 1992, pp. 45–51.

[10]Michael Hammer, "Reengineering Work: Don't Automate, Obliterate," *Harvard Business Review*, July–August 1990, pp. 104–12.

[11]Robert M Pirsig, *Zen and the Art of Motorcycle Maintenance* (New York: William Morrow, 1974), p. 25.

[12]David F Noble, *Forces of Production: A Social History of Industrial Automation* (New York: Alfred A. Knopf, 1984), p. 25.

[13]*The Wall Street Journal*, March 3, 1992.

[14]Michael C O'Guin, "A New Approach to Capital Justification," *P&IM Review with APICS News*, November 1989, pp. 35–36, 42.

Chapter 4

[1]A V Feigenbaum, *Total Quality Control: Engineering and Management* (New York: McGraw-Hill, 1961).

[2]Lloyd Dobyns and Clare Crawford-Mason, *Quality or Else: The Revolution in World Business* (Boston: Houghton Mifflin, 1991), p. 139.

[3]*Statistical Quality Control Handbook,* 2nd ed. (Indianapolis: AT&T Technologies, 1956), p. 217.

[4]William M Burrus, " 'Immediate Savings' from Statistics-based Quality," *Quality Matters,* March 1993, pp. 7–8.

[5]This is an actual case, with data slightly modified: Cort Dondero, "SPC Hits the Road," *Quality Progress,* January 1991, pp. 43–44.

[6]Ibid.

Chapter 5

[1]Al Ries and Jack Trout, *Bottom-Up Marketing* (New York: McGraw-Hill, 1989), p. xii.

Chapter 6

[1]Adapted from W Earl Sasser, R Paul Olsen, and D Daryl Wychoff, *Management of Service Operations* (Boston: Allyn & Bacon, 1978), pp. 303–5 (HD9981.5.S27).

[2]Stephen Franklin, "Layoff Fever Spreads to Robust Firms," *Chicago Tribune,* September 12, 1993, Section 7, p. 1.

Chapter 7

[1]Jon Van, "Retail and Apparel Trades Tailor New Technology, Systems," *Chicago Tribune,* Monday, March 16, 1992.

Chapter 8

[1]Jeffrey G Miller, Arnoud DeMeyer, and Jinichiro Nakane, *Benchmarking Global Manufacturing* (Homewood, IL: Business One Irwin, 1992), p. 83 (HD 9720.5.M55).

[2]Michael Barrier, "Overcoming Adversity," *Nation's Business,* June 1991, pp. 25–29.

[3]Leonard L Berry and A Parasuraman, *Marketing Services: Competing Through Quality* (New York: The Free Press, 1991), p. 141.

[4]Yash P Gupta and Gia A Neel, "The Origin of EDI and Changes Associated with Its Implementation," *Industrial Engineering,* August 1992, pp. 25–29.

[5]Myron Magnet, "Meet the New Revolutionaries," *Fortune,* February 24, 1992, pp. 94–101.

[6]ABC analysis is another example of Pareto's observation concerning maldistribution. Here, most of the value lies in but a few of the inventory items.

[7] "In Failed Bid for UAL, Lawyers and Bankers Didn't Fail to Get Fees," *The Wall Street Journal*, November 30, 1989, p. A1.

Chapter 9

[1]*Total Quality: An Executive's Guide for the 1990s* (Homewood, IL: Dow Jones-Irwin, 1990), p. 185.

[2]Thomas J Peters and Robert H Waterman, *In Search of Excellence* (New York: Harper & Row, 1982), pp. 164–65.

[3]George Johnson, "Fill Rate Calculation and Records Retention," *APICS—The Performance Advantage*, June 1993, p. 21.

Chapter 11

[1]John F Love, *McDonald's: Behind the Arches* (Toronto: Bantam Books, 1986).

[2]Jeffrey L Funk, "Case Study: Managing the Organizational Complexity of Applying CIM to Semiconductor Manufacturing in the Mitsubishi Electric Corporation," *Manufacturing Review*, March 1991, pp. 5–17.

[3]Marvin L Patterson, *Accelerating Innovation: Improving the Process of Product Development* (New York: Van Nostrand Reinhold, 1993), pp 149–50 (TS176.P367).

[4]An explanation is given in A R Klingel, Jr., "Bias in PERT Project Completion Time Calculations for a Real Network," *Management Science* 13, no. 4 (December 1966), pp B-194–B-201.

Chapter 12

[1]H Thomas Johnson, "A Blueprint for World-Class Management Accounting," *Management Accounting*, June 1988, pp. 23–30.

[2]Theodore Levitt, "Production-Line Approach to Service," *Harvard Business Review*, September–October 1972, pp. 41–52.

[3]Peter Coy and Chuck Hawkins, "UPS: Up from the Stone Age," *Business Week*, June 15, 1992, p. 132.

[4]Paula M Noaker, "Ergonomics on Site," *Manufacturing Engineering*, June 1992, pp. 63–66.

Chapter 13

[1]Eugene Bauchner, "Making the Most of Your Company's Resources," *Expansion Management*, 1989 Directory, pp. 20–25.

[2]John Hoerr, "Work Teams Can Rev Up Paper-Pushers, Too," *Business Week*, November 28, 1988, pp. 64–72.

[3]R R Muther, *Systematic Layout Planning* (Boston: Cahners, 1973), pp. 3-1– 3-8 (TS178.M87).

Chapter 14

[1]Faye Rice, "Why Hotel Rates Won't Take Off—Yet," *Fortune,* October 4, 1993, pp. 124–28.

[2]Joann S Lublin, "Corporate Chiefs Polish Their Relations with Directors," *The Wall Street Journal,* October 15, 1993, pp. B1ff.

[3]Edward E Lawler III, "Pay the Person, Not the Job," *Industry Week,* December 7, 1992, pp. 19–24.

[4]Ibid.

Index

Other books of interest to you from Irwin Professional Publishing. . .

THE ISO 9000 ALMANAC

1994-95 Edition

Timeplace, Inc.

All the information you need to ensure ISO 9000 compliance and registration success! Includes time-saving ISO 9000 resources, such as consultants, 1994 seminars and events, books, videos, registrars, software, associations, and much more.
ISBN: 0-7863-0243-7

THE TQM ALMANAC

1994-95 Edition

Timeplace, Inc.

An all-encompassing guide to quality-related materials, resources, and information to help you start and maintain a successful TQM program. Includes an overview of the current trends in the quality improvement field, as well as a listing of TQM books, videos, software, consultants, seminars, conferences, and more.
ISBN: 0-7863-0242-9

WHY TQM FAILS AND WHAT TO DO ABOUT IT

Mark Graham Brown, Darcy E. Hitchcock, and Marsha L. Willard
Co-published with the Association for Quality and Participation

Discover the root causes for the collapse and failure of total quality and find practical advice for correcting and preventing them.
ISBN: 0-7863-0140-6

THE SERVICE/QUALITY SOLUTION

Using Service Management to Gain Competitive Advantage

David A. Collier
Co-published with ASQC Quality Press

Improve your service strategy and survive the pressures within today's marketplace with Collier's 16 tools for effective service/quality management.
ISBN: 1-55623-753-7

Available at bookstores and libraries everywhere.